"Dad!
I think the farmers
market is this way!"

Two Pans and a Pot

Two Pans and a Pot

First Printing: 2015

ISBN 978-0-692-37377-4

Barry Sayewitz

15 East 10th Street

New York City, NY 10003

www.twopansandapot.com

Ordering Information:

Special discounts are available on quantity purchases by corporations, associations, educators, and others. For details, contact the publisher at the above listed address.

U.S. trade bookstores and wholesalers:

Please contact Barry Sayewitz. Tel: 347.515.3786 or email bsayewitz@nyc.rr.com

Two Pans and a Pot

A cookbook about family, push-ups and fresh foods

BY BARRY SAYEWITZ

Special contributions:
Recipes: Chef Royal A. Sayewitz
Edited by: Mallory Murphy Viscardi and Asher Spruill
Recipe Editor: Dalila Nouvel
Indiegogo Editor: Bay Ewald
Photography consultants: Michelle Holden and Clark Slater
Photography: Barry Sayewitz
Book designers: Jacqueline Sanz and Gustavo González
Special thanks to the Union Square NYC farmers market
vendors and patrons.

PUBLISHED BY BARRY SAYEWITZ
2015 ©

Dedication

*This is for all the parents who are craving to cook
nutritious meals for their family but feel it's impossible.*

*This is for all the moms and dads whose lasagna came out lousy
and mashed potatoes tasted like mush.*

*This is for all the dads who teach their sons how to bake cookies
and their daughters how to sink a jump shot.*

*This is for all the dads who turn their heads in the
supermarket when a little squeaky voice calls out, "Dad."*

*This is for all the moms who froze their buns off cheering the team
on every Saturday morning.*

*This is for all the parents who have read "Green Eggs and Ham"
twice a night for a year
and then read it again, one more time.*

*This is for all the parents who have turned
ransacking the house to find their keys into an Olympic sport.*

*This is for all the parents who have to say, "No,"
when they really want to say, "Yes."*

*This is for all the children who are so busy with school, friends,
and activities, but all they really want sometimes
is a smile and a hug from mom and dad.*

Acknowledgements

Thanks to my loving and supportive Peaches. Your encouragement, tasters table nights, spiritual strength, and believing in me were instrumental in completing this book. To Peach, my deepest gratitude and heart felt thanks. Amy Cole you are my light.

Thanks to Royal Sayewitz, my son, my inspiration, and the author of the three-cooking-technique concept and most of the recipes in this book. Royal's passion for meaningful dialogue that connects families to food and to the earth was the whispering voice that inspired this culinary song. Thank you, boo boo, for being the curious individual you are. I love you.

And finally, I cannot express enough thanks to my Indiegogo.com crowdfunding supporters for their donations and encouragement. The completion of this project could not have been accomplished without their support.

Main supporters:
Amy Cole
Hara Schwartz
 & Chris Buck
Robert Sayewitz
Robert Slater
Stuart Sayewitz
Vanessa Gold

Supporters:
Alex Hong
Ann Dedman Neal
Barbara K. Cole
Benjamin Cohen
David Mechanic
 & Michelle Parker
Edna & Schmuel Kerhous
Ellen Weinberg
Eve R Bender
Gary Schoichet
Haviland Morris
Helen Contino
Isabella Malbin
Jackie Droesch Brown
Jay kantrowitz
Jeffrey James Frank
Joanne Honigman
Joseph Lovett
Joyce Raimondo
Julia Mulligan
Ken Lee

Supporters:
Kirsten Major
Kristin & Dean Sposato
 & family
Lisa & Todd Waszkelewicz
 & family
Markus Marty
Mary Joan Giansante
Melissa D Stewart
Michael J Borbone
Michelle Holden
Robert Brenner
Robert Silverstein
Sherry W Varian
Susan Lerner
Suzanne E Grinnan
Tenn Grant
Theresa Vitucci
Toni Navy
Tracey Berglund
Terri Heiman

Contents

Processed Foods
Account
for Roughly
70%
of our
Nation's
Calories

Introduction

A Foundation That Shapes Your Family's Wellbeing

You love your children and would do anything for them, so why not cook for them? As parents it's our obligation to give our kids a fighting chance to maintain good health throughout their lives. Feeding our children nutritionally sound food and promoting exercise is the way we equip them for health and wellbeing when they step out of the nest into this world.

At this moment the American food system is hurtling in the opposite direction. Kids are eating more processed foods than ever before. In the confusing world of food marketing, it's becoming harder and harder to determine which foods are actually nutritious. Childhood obesity rates are skyrocketing in the United States, and it's now known that childhood obesity puts nearly one third of America's children at early risk for Type 2 diabetes, high blood pressure, heart disease and even stroke.[1] These conditions have historically been associated with adults.

After decades of public blindness to this rising epidemic, obesity has finally received the exposure it deserves. Today parents and consumers are more invested than ever in where their food comes from, how it was processed, and what it contains. The proof is reflected in the article "2014 Hot Food Trends."[2] This report details more than just the passing culinary fad. Rather, it examines trends in the food and restaurant industries' responses to consumer demand. And parents' concerns over what they feed their children made the list.

2014 Top Hot Food Trends
- Locally sourced meat and seafood
- Locally grown produce
- Environmental sustainability
- Healthful kid meals
- Children's nutrition
- Gluten Free cuisines
- Non-wheat noodles

Despite all the nutritional information at our disposal, we remain confused about what constitutes healthy food and healthy eating. So many Americans are now seeking to eat healthier, yet the food industry's lack of transparency leaves us unsure about which information to trust. This is not an accident. Food manufacturers and industry lobbyists deliberately make misleading claims about ingredients and nutrition facts. Their marketing aims to create a buzz that drowns out the voices of truth, to spread claims that clutter the information landscape. This is because the truth would cause consumers to demand drastic changes.

Since the 20th century, vitamins and nutrients have progressively been bred out of most of the fruits and vegetables we eat.[3] Wild dandelion, once a springtime delicacy foraged by Native Americans, contains seven times more phytonutrients than modern day spinach, a food largely considered to be packed with nutrients. Corn from the Mayan era contained so many nutrients that today it would be an ultimate super food. Instead, selective breeding has depleted the nutrition in corn in favor of a sweeter taste for mass consumption.[4] The food industry does not seek to improve our health; it seeks to formulate products that will sell. Armed with the right information, parents can escape the nutrition-poor products that dominate the food market.

My ambition for the pages that follow is to help you transition yourself and your family out of the present epidemic as you learn to separate food fact from food fiction, to cook healthy meals, and to exercise properly.

But better knowledge about food isn't the only thing parents' need. Everybody knows the recipe for better health—eat right and exercise. And every busy parent knows that it's easier said than done. That's where this book comes in. My ambition for the pages that follow is to help you transition yourself and your family out of the present epidemic as you learn to separate food fact from food fiction, to cook healthy meals, and to exercise properly. Being conscious of nutritious food and exercise fundamentals is necessary to keep your family healthy and to restore health to our country's communities.

Once you've decided to get your family healthy, everyone will be amazed how quickly this decision begins to pay off. Even the smallest first steps can yield remarkable results.

What are some benefits of combining exercise and nutritious food? For children, an increased ability to concentrate, amplified physical strength, weight loss, improved agility, better sleep and more engaging interpersonal skills, just to name a few.[5] But the kids aren't the only ones who benefit from the whole family getting healthier. Research has shown that adults who get the recommended amounts of nutrients and exercise saw a thinner overall appearance with improved muscle tone, the ability to maintain a stable, healthy body weight, increased energy, and reduced risk for many chronic diseases. They also saw improved immunity and reduced stress.[6]

I hope that the information in *Two Pans and a Pot* will be accessible to everyone. Although organic foods and farmers markets are making their loud appearances in the media and in many kitchens, organic food remains a luxury that is neither affordable nor accessible to many Americans. I hope that the information I share in this book will teach you how to make smart food choices whether you purchase organic or traditional ingredients.

My Home Cooking Epiphany

I was on my own for the very first time as the single parent of a six-year-old boy. That night my mind began to race through countless thoughts concerning the day-to-day tasks I now found on my plate: school drop off and pick up, sporting events, play dates, homework, food shopping for breakfast, lunch and dinner. With all these concerns, I always came back to the same fundamental mantra: keep this little guy safe and healthy, physically and spiritually.

In my heart I knew the key to success in raising my son was to consistently keep his life structured and normal, both in school and at home. And so I participated in events at his school, shuttled my son and his friends to all the sporting events, befriended the other moms and dads, hosted sleepovers, and fed my son healthy meals.

As I cooked dinner the first official night as a single dad, thoughts about my own childhood began to bombard me. My favorite childhood memories revolved around the kitchen table, a place where my family and friends had remarkable conversations about life, cracked jokes, and ate the incredible meatballs my mom made.

Family meals made me feel safe and loved. I realized that cooking for your family goes far beyond the obvious notion of just feeding your family. The dinner table creates a continuous thread of woven memories that turn into family traditions.

I thought about the memories my son will have. The time I spent with him at the kitchen table when he was little would shape his future outlook on family life and relationships. As a single parent I had been relying on processed, takeout, microwaveable, or fast food options to get us through our busy days together. I began to question myself. Was I depriving my child of the same warm and wonderful memories I had growing up? Would his childhood food memories be of a pizza delivery guy, or of a clown who flipped burgers? I didn't want that for my son. I felt so guilty. I knew I had to do something about it.

Faced with the challenge of putting dinner on the table every night for my own child, I began to appreciate my mother's cooking. I decided that cooking and eating dinner together was a tradition I must maintain for us, no matter how difficult the circumstances might be. I had always loved cooking. Even when my wife had been a larger part of our family, I had been the one who did the majority of the family cooking.

Cooking made me feel grounded, and like I was in control. Food is our most basic life necessity, but it was also so much more than that for me in those early days as a single parent. I loved the creative outlet cooking provided and I loved knowing that the food I made at home was healthier for my son than restaurant food or takeout. I had always enjoyed cooking because often there were times it was the only thing that made sense to me after a long, hectic day.

Cooking gave me the opportunity to be a role model for my son. It helped me create a healthy environment with delicious meals made from simple, nutritious ingredients. I loved challenging myself to use everything in the fridge before anything spoiled.

We are all secret chefs. I challenge you to let go of any negative preconceived notions that you have about cooking meals from scratch and open yourself up to the thought that you, too, can come to enjoy and master the process of putting good food on the table. If you know how to eat, you can figure out how to cook. Think about it: how many times have you had a meal at a restaurant and found you had an opinion on the food you were served? Trust your own instincts. You know your children and your partner better than anyone else. Who better than you to make healthy meals you know your family will love?

We are all food critics. We know what tastes good to us. The art of cooking is taking a recipe and making the dish your own. A recipe is a roadmap to your family's food consciousness. Food wisdom begins at home.

Being a parent today is like training for a triathlon on a daily basis, which makes it easy to perceive cooking as either an additional task to accomplish at the end of a long day or as merely entertainment to watch on TV. But cooking for your family can be so much more than your least favorite chore of the day. The fact is, cooking is a core ingredient that feeds the household spirit and nourishes the family bond. Home cooking is a foundation that shapes your children's wellbeing and sense of security. If there's one thing I've learned as a single father, it's that cooking meals with my son made us feel like a family again.

Whether you are a single parent or not, I'm willing to bet your family's schedule is jam-packed. Cooking for your family may seem overwhelming and impossible, but don't worry. You are not in this alone. I will help streamline the process and introduce efficiencies so you can begin to prepare delicious, nutritious meals. You will quickly learn fundamental techniques that will empower you to handle any recipe.

There is nothing more satisfying in life than feeding the ones you love. Cooking can be both simple and gratifying. I'm here to prove it. You only need to master some basic techniques to create amazing meals for your family to enjoy.

Compelling Reasons to Cook For Your Family

There are many reasons you should cook for your family, but who would have thought that self-defense would be one of them? The undisputed fact is that the American diet is causing you and your family physical harm. It will continue to pose a threat to your health and well-being unless you fight back. We are truly poisoning ourselves. Severe health issues such as heart disease and diabetes that are on the rise today are largely preventable.

They're triggered by diets brimming with the unhealthy ingredients we'll discuss throughout this book. The information delivered by the media and government regarding healthy foods is often little more than a diluted flavor-of-the-month focused on what's trendy rather than on what's true. What we are not being told is a huge concern.

The Government and the Food Industry Have Misinformed Us

We all remember being taught about healthy eating when we were in school, and memorizing the suggestions provided by the Department of Agriculture's food pyramid. But in the past 20 years, the recommended diet prescribed by that pyramid has changed no fewer than three times. In fact, today it's no longer a pyramid at all-it's a plate. In 2005 the food pyramid was changed from the 1992 recommendations and was renamed MyPyramid. Six years later, in June 2011, the dietary recommendations for children was altered again and reconfigured visually into a plate icon, called MyPlate. [7]

It's encouraging to know that the Department of Agriculture is still refining its model and aiming to make good recommendations as the American food landscape continues to evolve. However, while MyPlate is definitely an improvement over the pyramid, it still has its flaws. For example, there is practically no mention of the importance of dietary fats, like the healthy monounsaturated fats in olive oil, fish, and nuts.

As humans it's our nature to feel compelled to protect our children from harm and threats. We live to keep them safe, secure, and healthy. Contrary to this instinct, we continue to knowingly feed ourselves foods that hold little nutritional value and contain harmful chemicals. Why would you want to feed your family a food-like substance that is designed to last for months on a shelf and not rot? The answer could be as simple as marketing.

We can only understand how we've come to this point by considering that the processed food industry has successfully positioned itself as an iconic hero over the last century. Foods now come with buzzwords right on the label: low-fat, free-range, organic, calcium-enriched. We'll take a closer look at the language later in the book. For now, suffice it to say that it takes tremendous effort to alter your perspective, to see through the subtle propaganda, and to recognize the truth of this contemporary food risk and the need to combat it.

Separating the facts from the fiction takes time, research and a lot of effort, something the large food corporations are betting you're not going to do while planning meals in between ballet recitals, little league games, and school plays. But the fact remains that uncovering the truth about what's in our food is not only an effort worth taking for the health of our children but also arguably necessary for our survival. Question and educate yourselves and your family. Enlighten friends and neighbors. Our future—and our children's future—depends on it.

And such efforts are not in vain. Besides keeping yourself healthy, it's possible you can help make a larger change. In a recent article titled "Chick-Fil-A Removing Artificial Dye, High Fructose Corn Syrup", released by the Associated Press in November, 2013, the fast food chain claims to be removing high-fructose corn syrup from its white buns and artificial dyes from its sauces and dressings. The changes are a result of blogger Vani Hari's 2011 post, "Chick-fil-A or Chemical Fil-a?" that revealed that the chain's signature sandwich contained nearly 100 ingredients, including peanut oil with TBHQ, a chemical made from butane. [8]

Today, more and more parents and families are developing food ingredient awareness, especially when it comes to packaged and fast foods. Parents and kids alike want to know a lot more about where their food comes from, how it's made, and what it contains. And food isn't the only thing consumers are starting to look at more closely. People are curious about the materials in a myriad of household products, from food storage containers to bathing suits.

Greater scrutiny has led more consumers to look for chemical- free foods for their families. There is a collective increase in desire to eat at home and cook using fresh ingredients. Companies are responding to consumer demand to know what is in packaged and fast foods, but the rate at which they're willing to transparently share this crucial information is too slow. Currently the FDA is moving forward to ban trans-fat and partially hydrogenated oils. In some cities restaurants are required to publicly post calorie counts of their foods and are required to be publicly posted on the restaurant premises.

Last year, PepsiCo, Inc. committed to removing a controversial ingredient found in Gatorade due to customer awareness and demand.

Once you decide to eliminate processed food from your family's diet, you discover how engulfed in the processed food culture we are. You begin to see how much

of our food is processed and how challenging it is to avoid. When you decide to take the plunge, don't tackle everything at once. Set yourself up for success and start with the basics:

Breaking Free from the Processed Food Culture

❶ *Hydrate properly.* Of all the beverage choices out there, what's calorie-free and essential to all living things on the planet? You guessed it! Plain old H_2O. Water makes up more than half of your body weight. Your body has lots of important jobs, and it needs water to perform many of them. Water aids your body in taking off weight because it suppresses your appetite and increases your metabolism. Health risks can be decreased by drinking water because it helps cleanse and rejuvenate the body. Foods are dissolved better and nutrients are distributed more efficiently to different parts of your body. Drinking water also helps regulate your body temperature and organs, which is essential when you and your kids are physically active.[9] And a little vanity never hurt anybody: bask in the radiant glow that staying hydrated gives your skin.

❷ *If you cannot pronounce an ingredient on the label, shelve it.* Disodium inosinate. Ethoxylated diglycerides. Azodicarbonamide. Any idea what these are? Food companies have labs where various flavors, preservatives, and other additives are developed to create products that taste good, have appealing textures, and last a long time on the shelf. In other words, foods are not grown but manufactured—and the dangers of these artificial additives are not yet fully known.

❸ Nix the soda, diet soda, and drinks with artificial sweeteners. We've become sugar-induced carbivores consuming fast food and junk. Make the switch to the good carbohydrates our bodies crave: fruits, vegetables, and whole grains. The human body is made of a protein substance, not a sugar substance.

❹ Buy fresh, cook fresh, eat fresh. When we make smart food choices for our children their muscles, organs, and bones receive the vitamins and minerals necessary to help nurture and sustain growth, strength, and endurance.

My Journey to Healthy Living

The first time I truly experienced the benefits of exercise and nutrition was when I became a single dad. When my ex-wife moved out, we decided that our son would live with me. As you can imagine, mentally I was all over the place. I was desperate to somehow shut my mind off, even for just a minute. I began to reflect about what had given me peace in years past. Exerting myself in the gym seemed like the best solution. It turns out it was.

At the same time, I decided to eliminate all processed foods from our house and start cooking from scratch using fresh ingredients only. I loved to cook, but there were many times when I was overwhelmed or exhausted, and it was easier and faster to simply order in, or microwave a frozen dinner, or make something uninspired. I found myself making "Dad's Famous Crispy Chicken" over and over again. One evening my son finally said, "Dad, I like your cooking, but maybe we could eat something besides chicken!" I was amused and a little caught off guard. But I resolved to go ahead and make the switch to cooking from scratch.

When I commenced this lifestyle change, I was experiencing high levels of stress. I was worried about my new family situation. I was worried about my son's well being. And, like so many parents, I was worried about money. It took me eight months to sleep soundly through the night. I was a new single dad suffering paralysis by analysis. However, after a few months of clean eating and exercise, I began to feel restored emotionally and physically. An interesting side effect occurred: not only did I lose weight on the new health program, but my confidence level and self-esteem also began to improve.

Feeling stronger and healthier encouraged me to dig deeper into the nutritional value of the foods my son and I were eating. I became extremely curious about the source of the food that I bought in supermarkets. I discovered the scientific health benefits of eliminating processed foods, salt, fine sugar and simple carbs. [10, 11]

I stopped dining out and ordering in. I began cooking like crazy using fresh ingredients and continued going to the gym three times a week. I used frozen, boxed, or canned food only on rare occasions.

Along with cooking fresh ingredients, exercise and physical activity is so important to childhood. When I was growing up in the 60's my friends and I had two educations; we had school and we had after school. We played in the schoolyard, on the block, or in someone's backyard. In my neighborhood we played until dark in mixed-age groups almost every day after school. We played all weekend from sun up until sun down. I hated that I always had to go home for dinner. Now, all these years later, I wouldn't trade those memories of family dinners for anything in the world! And I wanted to create memories like that with my son.

Humans are meant to move. [12] Babies love to rock their bodies, flail their arms and kick their feet. Toddlers love to run around, dance to music, climb, jump and roll around. Older kids enjoy organized and non-organized sports, playgrounds and rough and tumble activities too. This is all great fun, and a fundamental ingredient for growth from childhood and throughout adulthood.

I wrote *Two Pans and a Pot* both to chronicle my journey and to explain the benefits of feeding our children tasty, healthy dishes amid a confusing American food kingdom. Two Pans teaches us how to combine a healthy diet along with exercise and physical activity for our families. We can help our children build strong minds and bodies with the right food and activity regimens. *Two Pans and a Pot* breaks cooking down into mastering simple, basic cooking techniques while building efficiency, and nutritional awareness. You'll learn about flavor profiles, how to use herbs and spices, and shortcuts to cook dishes from around the world. I'll also touch on deceptive labeling practices, the specific nutritional benefits of ingredients, and the path food takes from the farm to your table.

The Path to Home Cooking

It may seem like your children want nothing more than to eat McDonald's, pizza or takeout, but contrary to what they tell you, your children are craving good ol' home cooking. My hope is that this book will help and inspire you to take good care of yourself and your family as you give endlessly to your children on this amazing journey of life.

Home cooking isn't new—for most of the past 10,000 years humans cooked every meal for themselves. Humans are the only animals on the planet with this ability. Fast forward to today, and a new transformational food phenomenon has occurred worldwide. We no longer cook for ourselves. Today food is manufactured for us in many different forms using artificial ingredients. In a mere 60 years the human race has managed to reverse the nutritional progress made over one thousand centuries.

This new food transformation is causing the opposite results that the invention of fire had on the human race. Instead of advancing the mind, body, and spirit that roasting awakened in our ancestors, manufactured food today is diminishing our health, raising obesity levels, and bankrupting the environment. Fire led us to cook, which advanced thinking, problem solving and creativity, resulting in better health and longer life expectancy. Those are things we need to remember and celebrate today. Home cooking is the only way to break the current processed food trend.

As a parent I understand with your busy schedules it is difficult to always feed your family and friends meals and snacks without using some sort of processed ingredient. There are minimally processed foods to use in a pinch like bagged greens and salad ingredients, cut vegetables and roasted nuts, although they tend to be more expensive for that convenience. Frozen fruits and vegetables, canned beans, and canned salmon and tuna are healthy alternatives, too. For frozen veggies I'm talking about cut veggies, not the packages soaked in sauces and cheese. Those are exactly the type of foods you want to avoid for your family. Pre-cooked rotisserie whole chickens are a true-life saver. Steam a head of broccoli; heat up left over rice—done! If you have access and the budget for organic rotisserie chicken go for it; it costs more but is well worth it.

Cooking can be simple too. Whether you are roasting, braising, or cooking pilaf, all you need are a few veggies, a protein, olive oil, salt, pepper, and an herb or spice to cook a delicious nutritious meal for your family. Change up a few ingredients and spices and change the ethnic flavor. Asian, Mediterranean, American Southern or Spanish flavors are easily in your command.

I spent years teaching my son about nutrition and exercise. I wanted to make sure he understood why it was so important to eat right and stay active. And then one day, after years of talking, hoping he was listening, he showed me that he was.

Straight out of high school my son, Royal, attended and graduated from the Culinary Institute of America. I was so proud. He quickly surpassed my cooking abilities and began teaching me. My son became the chef, and I became the student. A tweak here, a spice there, turn the heat up, turn the heat down—under the tutelage of my son, my true culinary education blossomed. Our dialogue was inspiring, his bravado smart, meaningful, honest, and in the spirit of socially conscious endeavors. Roy turned my novice home cooking experience into an educational bonding experience. The techniques, concepts and flavors defined within these pages are an outcome of his culinary education and experience. Royal has worked in many of New York City's top restaurants honing his skills and learning about different facets of our food system.

During his years on the line, Roy fell in love with locally grown ingredients and the sustainability movement. One summer, he decided to work on an organic farm and a farm-to-table restaurant in Nantucket, Massachusetts. His passion led him back to school, where he's studying environmental studies and sustainability. The recipes in this book are tried-and-true family favorites, along with new recipes Royal developed specifically to be simple, affordable and healthy.

A Letter from the Chef

As a culinarian, I pursued a profession born of a passion that has deep roots dating back to childhood. Intrigued by and devoted to the culinary industry and its many facets, I have spent countless hours perfecting my craft. However, outside of restaurant kitchens, I constantly found myself either in the kitchen of my own home, or the kitchens of family and friends, lacking the tools necessary to recreate the dishes and techniques so thoroughly entrenched in my culinary psyche. As I came to understand, in the setting of culinary school and restaurant kitchens, both outfitted with an abundance of uncommon tools, arduous approaches toward cooking are understood to be normal. It is in this disparity that home cooks become discouraged; and it makes sense. Home cooks are frequently confronted with recipes that haven't been adapted to normal kitchens, and often include an extensive list of ingredients and overcomplicated directions—neglecting the most critical and determinant factor of one's diet: time. This is where industrial food finds its market, providing cheap and quick answers to culinary defeat—this book envisions a society that does not have to resort to industrial expedience, but has full agency over what it consumes.

Many of the great dishes we cherish and savor are thought to be rare treats, accessible only through restaurants or hours of work. Consequently, many endure countless unsatisfying meals for the opportunity to celebrate at their favorite restaurant. This doesn't have to continue. Many perceive scratch cooking to be demanding. And let's be honest, some parts of scratch cooking are. But building flavor in a dish is a beautiful science, and an art, constantly evolving and currently in need of a revolution tailored to contemporary needs.

My father has dedicated incalculable time and energy to making fresh and healthy food more accessible. The wealth of knowledge he has amassed in this book offers a novel approach to uniting food, family and health. May the contents of this book function as your culinary compass.

Who Really Controls Your Food Purchases in the Supermarket?

Most parents I know will agree that grocery shopping with their children is a special kind of torture. Even the most patient parent among us is pushed to their last nerve as the kids beg and cry for product after product. But can we really blame the kids? Food packaging is not only designed to entice your children; it's also fortified with language to convince you to buy it as well.

The reality is that most food on the shelves today has been engineered for a long shelf life. Processed foods account for roughly 70 percent of our nation's calories.[13] Processed foods are an illusion, often appearing to be healthy when they are in fact the mechanism adding to the childhood obesity epidemic.[14] With confusing and vague claims like low-fat, low-carb, vitamin-fortified, no trans-fat, contains omega-3s, etc., listed right on the packaging, it's easy to become convinced that your food purchases are sound.

The Irresistible Trio: Salt, Sugar, and Fat

When we walk down the supermarket aisles with our kids we are confronted by the processed-food industry's irresistible trio of ingredients: salt, sugar and fat. They call that perfect combination of the three tastes "the bliss point," because that is the magic formula to conquer customers.[15]

The human body needs salt, but too much can be a problem. [16]

The body uses salt to carry electrical impulses to the muscles and nerves and to regulate blood pressure. Normally the body is pretty good at regulating salt levels. If there's too much salt, you become thirsty and drink fluids to flush it out. But there's only so much the body can do, and when it becomes overloaded with salt, it's impossible to flush all the excess away. Researchers looked at the health and diets

Research has proven that added sugars equate to empty calories containing no nutritional value. This puts both kids and adults at risk of obesity. Most dietary sugars are simple carbohydrates.

of more than 6,000 kids. They found that the ones with higher sodium intake were more likely to have high blood pressure, and that was particularly true for overweight children. [17]

What is added sugar, and why is it a problem?

Added sugar is used as an ingredient in processed foods, like breads, cakes, soft drinks, jams and ice cream, or is added to foods at the table. Examples of processed sugars include white sugar, brown sugar, raw sugar, corn syrup, high fructose corn syrup, malt syrup, maple syrup, pancake syrup, fructose sweetener, liquid fructose, honey, molasses, anhydrous dextrose, crystal dextrose, and dextrin.

Research has proven that added sugars equate to empty calories containing no nutritional value. This puts both kids and adults at risk of obesity. [18] Most dietary sugars are simple carbohydrates. As a rule, the more processed and refined the carbohydrate, the faster it breaks down in the digestive system, and the bigger the sugar rush it delivers. That's why refined flours, sugars and sugar syrups pose such a problem for our systems: our bodies simply aren't built to breakdown so much extra sugar. If the body does not immediately burn the excess sugar through physical exertion, that excess sugar turns into fat.

The body needs sugar, but fruit is a healthier source than processed foods with added sugar. Whether your kids are doing their homework or playing soccer, their bodies depend on ample supplies of calories to fuel them. Glucose —or blood sugar broken down from carbohydrates— is one of your body's most important fuels. Sugar is a naturally occurring carbohydrate. Good sugars are those found in fruits and some vegetables. The great thing about your kids getting the bulk of sugar from fruits is that it's almost impossible to overdo it.

Not all fats are bad fats.

In fact, our bodies need fat from our diet to function properly. Unsaturated fat is the kind of fat you want to make sure you eat. It helps us produce good cholesterol. Unsaturated fat helps keep arteries clear. It also reduces bad cholesterol, which is associated with heart problems. [18] Good fats are essential for proper nerve activity, vitamin absorption, immune system function and healthy cells. [19] There are two types of polyunsaturated fat: omega-3 and omega-6. These are also known as essential fatty acids. These good fats come from cold-water fish, plant oils such as olive oil, and nuts and seeds.

Trans-fat, on the other hand, you want to avoid. This kind of fat increases the production of bad cholesterol, can reduce good cholesterol, and can increase the risk of heart disease later in life. Sources of bad fat are many processed and packaged foods, fast foods, fried foods, and fatty cuts of meat, including skin-on cuts of chicken. For more detailed information about fats, don't miss the oil section of this book.

Where Does our Food Come From?

If You Ask Most Kids Where Their Food Comes From, They Will Probably Say, "From the Supermarket."

Where does our food come from? In this section we'll dig into many of the questions on your mind about the difference between organic, conventional, and locally grown foods, and what it all means to you and your family. Your food choices are serious considerations because when you feed your family, you are feeding our future.

The incredible growth of the organic food business in the United States and overseas has been nothing short of spectacular. While the popularity of organic food continues to increase, there is still confusion about what defines organic, how it differs from local, "regular" or "conventional" food, and whether or not organic food is more nutritious.

Defining "Organic"

My kooky hippie older brother and his hippie friends were right. Like many forward-thinkers, my brother and his friends were initially written off by mainstream society. Who would have thought their free-spirited, anti-establishment, back-to-nature philosophies from the 60s would pave the way for today's thriving organic food movement? I was very young at the time, but I remember my oldest brother's girlfriend once arguing with my mother about the medical industry brainwashing society into believing formula was healthier for infants than mother's milk. This girlfriend went on to become a doctor and his wife.

The environmental movement of the 1960s and 1970s laid the foundation for the increased support for the organic food movement today. Following grassroots advocacy for organic standards in the 1980s, the U.S. government passed the Farm Bill in 1990.[20] One of the purposes of the Farm Bill was to establish national standards for the marketing of certain organic agricultural products as organic. The act also established the criteria for certifying a farm or part of a farm as organic.

Organic food is grown on farms committed to environmentally friendly agricultural methods. For plant foods, the term "organic" means grown on certified organic land without synthetic fertilizers, chemicals, or pesticides.[21] Genetic modification and irradiation are also off-limits. For animals, the term "organic" means only organic feed for at least a year, and no antibiotics or growth hormones.

Despite the adoption of government standards, it's important to note that not all organic food is created equal. As a consumer, it's your business to be market savvy, whether you're buying food or a new bike rack for the car. Marketers frequently use misleading labels that muddy the meanings to increase sales. The United States Department of Agriculture (USDA) has implemented a set of labeling rules to clarify the levels of food purity.[22]

The USDA defines "organic" for products containing more than one ingredient as:

> **100% organic means that every ingredient in the product was raised and harvested in an organic environment as approved and certified by the USDA. It means that 70 to 95 percent of all the ingredients have been raised in a USDA approved manner. Any product containing ingredients with less than a 70 percent organic content can separately list each ingredient that falls into the USDA organic category, but the product may not display a label claiming the product as organic.[22]**

For foods containing just one ingredient, such as milk, eggs or fruit, an official USDA Organic label is displayed on the package or the fruit. When shopping for organic goods, always look for the USDA organic seal to ensure the food is certified organic. For meat and dairy, this seal ensures you're getting antibiotic-free and hormone-free products. Seafood has no formal USDA organic certification standards, so the term "organic seafood" doesn't mean much.

Is Organic Food More Nutritious?

The pendulum continues to swing on this topic. Recent studies have added fuel to the debate about the differences between organic and conventionally grown foods. According to a 2012 Stanford University report, an analysis of 237 studies of organic produce, meats, and dairy foods, concluded that organic foods are no more nutritious than their conventional counterparts. Advocates of organic foods, meanwhile, say that the study takes a narrow view of organic food choices, and that most people choose organic because they want to avoid pesticides, hormones, food additives, and other chemicals used in conventional farming.[23]

In April 2014, The Environmental Working Group, the nation's most effective environmental health research and advocacy organization, released its annual ranking of conventional foods with the most and least pesticide residues: the "Dirty Dozen" and the "Clean Fifteen." The rating is based on an analysis of 32,000 samples tested by the USDA and the FDA that are most likely to be contaminated with pesticides.[24]

I saw organic apples for the first time when I was in my teens. What struck me immediately was their appearance: they looked downright ugly and unappetizing. Because organic farmers don't use pesticides, in those days their fruits and vegetables often looked gnarly, were bruised, or had holes from worms. The organic fruits and vegetables were neither pretty nor perfect and they weren't waxed like fruits and vegetables in the supermarket.

Fifty years later perfection of shape, color, and texture remains the aesthetic standard to purchase a fruit or a vegetable. Organics have come a long way in appearance from those days; however, we still unconsciously make purchases based on aesthetics. So what is wrong with bumps or an odd shape in a vegetable? Is there less nutritional value? Does it taste different? The answer to both is no. In fact when you cut them up they all look and taste the same.

I recently came across a website created by a few students in Germany called uglyfruits.eu. The students are advocating for the consumption of ugly fruits and vegetables. In the USA alone up to 40% of the food we grow goes to waste because it doesn't meet the aesthetic standard. If ugly fruit became fashionable we would eliminate a ton of waste and bring the price of fruits and vegetables way down because there would be more supply.

Interestingly enough, the fruits and vegetables photographed on the website are anything but ugly. Nature's abstract designs of different shapes and sizes are captured and they are fascinating. What has been considered nature's ugly flaw displays nature's creativity.

Clean 15 & Dirty Dozen

This 2015 rating is based on an analysis of 32,000 samples tested by the USDA and the FDA.

Clean 15	Dirty Dozen
These are the foods we eat that are least likely to be contaminated with pesticides. You can buy these non-organic.	These are the foods we eat that are most likely to be contaminated with pesticides. Buy organic.

eggplant

kiwi

cabbage

cantaloupe

sweet peas-frozen

mango

couliflower

sweet corn

papaya

grapefruit

asparagus

sweet potato

pineapple

avocado

onions

apples

cherry tomatoes

nectarines

cucumber

peaches

celery

snap peas-imported

strawberry

bell pepper

spinach

potatoes

grapes

The History of Industrial Farming in America

To understand how we arrived to where we are with organic farming today, let's go back for a minute to the19th century when all food was grown organically without chemicals or pesticides. There was no need to label food organic because that is simply how farmers grew their crops. What changed? In the 20th century our country evolved rapidly. The population was increasing, and industrialized farming practices allowed our country to keep up with the growing demand. Food was no longer grown. Instead it was being manufactured.

Mechanical tractors became available in the 1920s and quickly replaced manual labor. [25] Chemical fertilizers and pesticides were introduced. The post World-War II agriculture industry saw many technological innovations like large-scale irrigation, fertilization, and the use of pesticides. Ammonium nitrate, used in weaponries, became an abundantly cheap source of nitrogen, one of the 17 nutrients needed to grow vegetables.

Nerve gas was adapted into pesticides. DDT, originally developed by the military to control disease-carrying insects among troops,[26] was so effective and economical that it was applied to crops, launching the era of widespread pesticide use. These developments enriched large food producers but damaged the environment.

Pesticide use enabled farmers increase the variety of crops they could grow throughout the year. They also saw an increased crop yield, which lowered prices for customers. The year-round supply of some foods further benefited consumers via increased supply and lower prices. [27]

Unfortunately, today this reciprocal exchange of supply and demand has fallen gravely out of balance.[28] The majority of local farmers in the United States have been replaced by a handful of corporations that now control how two million farmers feed the country's population of 300 million people.

Industrial farming has devastated the environment worldwide. [22] In 2006 the UN News Centre reported that cattle farms generate more greenhouse gases, as measured in carbon dioxide equivalent, than cars do.

The organic food movement of the 1990s changed how many Americans viewed food, their health, the environment, agricultural and marketing practices.

Consequently, livestock have become significant contributors to climate change.

Livestock now use 30% of the earth's entire land surface. Moreover, 33% of the global vegetative land is used to produce feed for livestock. As forests are cleared to create new pastures, meat production has become a major driver of deforestation, especially in Latin America, where some 70% of forests in the Amazon have been cleared for grazing.[29]

The Organic Farming Movement

During the 1960s the organic food movement gained meaningful traction and began to surface as a legitimate and serious food choice. In the 1970s, growing consumer interest in health and nutrition coupled with the increasing importance of preserving the natural environment stimulated the development of the organic market. Food co-ops, farmers markets, and small independent natural food stores began to crop up. The farm movement even made it to network TV. "Farm living is the life for me!" Does that ring a bell? You guessed it: Green Acres. How funny was that show?

The organic food movement of the 1990s changed how many Americans viewed food, their health, the environment, agricultural and marketing practices. The public was ready for a food change. The enormous success of organic food chains like Whole Foods and Trader Joe's proved that organic food could be profitable to retailers and food producers in the 21st century.

Local farming, also known as "The Farm-to-Table Movement", was an extension of what began in the 1960s and 1970s as well. In the 21st century local farming has gone far beyond the traditional farm in the country.

In New York City farming has hit the roof—literally. Whether the farm is soil-based or hydroponic, in which vegetables are grown in water rather than soil, new farms are spreading across NYC rooftops. In terms of rooftop commercial agriculture, New York is a leader at this moment. New York City is suddenly a farming community. Basil and bok choy are growing in Brooklyn. Tomatoes, leeks, and cucumbers are sprouting in Queens. Commercial agriculture is bound for the South Bronx. The NYC Planning Department recently revamped the city's zoning regulations to encourage green development, called "Zone Green" rules. [30]

Barry's Northeast Farm Tour

Having lived in New York City my entire life, I was enthused to discover urban agriculture alive and booming in the five boroughs of NYC, along with local farming throughout the northeast. Last summer, I set out to discover just how much local agriculture has grown in popularity in this region.

My first adventure was a small farm in Far Rockaway Queens, located two blocks from a beach popular with surfers. On a half-acre parcel was Edgemere farm. Edgemere is both a CSA (community supported agriculture) and a shared site for market gardeners and farmers looking to grow and sell their produce in New York City. The farm consisted of chickens, vegetables, herbs, and composting, which provided much of their nutrient rich soil.

Next stop, to my amazement, was a hidden gem called The Queens Museum Farm. This working farm, established in 1697 and located in Little Neck, NY, was literally a quarter of a mile off the Long Island Expressway, a road that I have driven my entire life. What a find! We were transported to another era when vegetables were naturally organic.

I then headed to Brooklyn, a hot bed for farming. In addition to farms on abandoned lots, Brooklyn is home to the largest rooftop garden on the Northeast: the Brooklyn Grange. Today you can find gardens on the rooftops of restaurants and public schools, providing both fresh ingredients and an education for children.

Not far north from the city streets lies Glynwood farm in Cold Spring, upstate New York. Glynwood is a 225-acre, organic, non-profit farm. Its mission is to support the community and ensure that farming thrives in the Hudson Valley. Glynwood is also a CSA that donates food to local farm-to-school efforts and area food banks. They raise and sell turkeys, chickens, cows, pigs, and more than forty different types of certified naturally grown vegetables.

My tour also revealed older cottage-industry farms kept alive by the dedicated local natives on the eastern shores of Long Island, New York. These farms are thriving today, providing fresh seafood, fruits, vegetables, and poultry to local outdoor farmers markets and to restaurants.

One Westhampton family has dedicated generations to their farm, raising chickens and growing organic eggplant, squash, tomatoes, watermelon, cantaloupe, carrots, beets, and gorgeous flowers. Amazingly, that farm gives all the food away. Anyone is welcome to stop by and pick vegetables.

On my final tour days, I also discovered that the seascape of Cape Cod, Massachusetts offers a myriad of hidden farms large and small. In Truro, I found a five-acre organic farm founded in 1984 with over 30 varieties of greenhouse tomatoes. In Dennis, off Route 28, Matt's Organic Garden has been providing local restaurants, natives, and tourists with organic vegetables for years. And nearby Barnstable is home to the naturally growing Cape Cod Organic Farm with wild crops, a farm stand, and pigs in the back.

Conventional vs.
Organic vs. Local

Differences Between Conventional, Organic, Locally Grown, And Genetically Modified Food

Conventional Farming

Applies chemical fertilizers to promote plant growth.

Sprays pesticides to eradicate pests.

Uses chemical herbicides to manage weeds.

Organic Farming

Employs manure and compost to fertilize the soil.

Relies on insects and birds, mating disruption, and traps to deal with pests.

Rotates crops, hand weeds, and mulches.

Cultivates land without synthetic fertilizers, chemicals or pesticides.

At the end of the day common sense is all you really need to realize that ingesting chemicals through food was not nature's intention. When you eat organic beef or poultry, you and your family are not ingesting the antibiotics and hormones that were given to the livestock on conventional farms.

Locally Grown

Locally grown means seasonal food that comes from small farms. Some say it applies only to foods grown within a 100-mile radius of where you purchase it; others stretch it to 250 miles. Local grocery stores and farmers markets now stock a wider variety of fresh fruits and vegetables than ever before. Consumers can easily purchase food that is certified USDA organic or uncertified locally grown.

Many small organic farmers choose not to become certified due to the high costs of the certification process. Buying local food also allows you to help your community's economy and helps reduce the environmental costs associated with food transportation miles. It's important to note that local food is not necessarily grown using

organic methods. If you buy your fruits and veggies from a local farmers market, you can often ask the farmer himself about his agricultural practices and the produce he's selling. The farmers market may not always easily fit your busy schedule, but taking 30 minutes to buy locally grown foods for your family is worth the time.

Here's where taste is a distinct factor. Nothing tastes better than fresh fruits and veggies picked directly from the farm just hours before they make their way to your house. The down side here is that produce is seasonal. Take advantage when items are in season. That's when food is at its cheapest and most flavorful. Eat fresh fruits and vegetables when they're at their peak. One of my favorites is tomato season. I crave them all winter: perfectly ripe heirlooms with a slice of fresh mozzarella, fresh basil, and a drizzle of extra virgin olive oil. There's nothing better!

Where I shop and what I buy varies depending on many factors. In the northeast, even in the winter, the local farmers market has items like apples, different varieties of squash, parsnips, turnips, cheese, eggs, and chickens, depending on where you live. For the spring, summer and fall I go for what is in season. There is nothing better than the day fresh strawberries —the first spring fruit— appearing at the farmers market. They're a real treat after a New York winter. My choice is to go organic whenever possible depending on cost and my budget.

The Cost of Buying Organic

One common concern with organic food is cost. Organic foods typically cost more than their conventional counterparts. Higher prices are due, in part, to more expensive farming practices. When it comes to price, frozen organic is a smart choice. Whole Foods has a good selection of organic frozen fruits and vegetables that fit into a tight budget. Frozen fruits and vegetables are also a great time saver. They are cleaned, chopped, ready to use, and can stay in your freezer for months.

One common concern with organic food is cost. Organic foods typically cost more than their conventional counterparts. Higher prices are due, in part, to more expensive farming practices.

Genetically Modified Foods

Genetically modified food comes from plants and animals that have had their DNA altered by genetic engineering techniques to make them more resistant to disease, insects, or other growing and breeding concerns. [32] In the USA, genetically modified food is not required to be labeled as such, and while genetically modified food has the potential to help solve world food supply concerns, critics worry about the unknown effects on our health and the environment.

Are the Foods in Your Kitchen Trying to Kill You?

Although healthy cooking with fresh ingredients is en vogue, there still remains a great deal of ambiguity around what is healthy and what is not.

In this section we explore a healthier relationship with the food kingdom.

Corn is Now America's Largest Crop

It's a Staple of the Global Food Supply

Originally cultivated in Mexico 7,000 years ago, corn is now America's biggest crop and a staple of the global food supply.[33] Hundreds of years ago American Indians grew corn with a variety of colors: red, yellow, blue, olive, and even black. We have recently learned that the black, red and blue corn are rich in anthocyanins, which have the ability to fight cancer, lower cholesterol and blood pressure, and reduce the risk of obesity.[34] We can still see this corn today around the holiday season, usually marketed by the name "Indian corn." It's used for decoration, not consumption. Instead most sweet corn mass-produced today was developed through genetic modification and radiation in the 1950s, and contains none of the anthocyanin benefits once inherent in corn.

Corn is America's most productive and subsidized grain. It's also one of the principle ingredients of the industrial food system today, and a formidable force in the American economy. For decades the Federal government has given corn growers incentives to grow as much as possible through the Federal farm subsidy system.[35] As a result, food products derived from this versatile crop have become pervasive in the American diet.

The saying goes, "You are what you eat." If your diet consists of processed food from a mainstream supermarket and processed food, then what you are is corn. Corn may not be clearly indicated on the ingredient list, but corn is in the feed used for beef and poultry, it's in bread, it's in the Lunchables meals you buy for the kids. It's in margarine, processed cold cuts, cakes, spaghetti sauce, jams and jellies, fruit drinks, and beer. And don't forget the ubiquitous high-fructose corn syrup used in soda and hundreds of other cheap, sweet products. With such widespread use, it is challenging to find processed foods that do not contain any corn ingredients at all.

Corn is low in saturated fat, cholesterol, and sodium. It's also a source of dietary fiber, thiamin and folate. But 82% of the calories in corn come from carbohydrates. This high-carb content is why corn can be used to make corn syrup, a low-priced sugar alternative. In fact, today's corn has a glycemic index level equivalent to that of a Snickers bar.[35]

Unless you are growing and eating your own food or living on a deserted island, it's impossible for you and your family to completely avoid corn in today's food options. Your best defense against the food machine inducing the obesity epidemic is cooking and eating at home using fresh, unprocessed ingredients.

The Controversial Gluten Topic

As recently as 15 years ago, hardly anyone had even heard of gluten, knew what the word gluten meant, or paid any attention to avoiding it. Today gluten-free diets are all the rage and boldly marketed on packaged goods everywhere.

What exactly is it? Gluten is a protein found in the grains of wheat, barley, and rye. Gluten makes pizza dough stretchy, gives bread its classic texture, and is used to thicken sauces and soups. That's why we love it—gluten is what makes our favorite foods irresistible.

[36]So what is the problem with gluten? To people with a chronic digestive disorder called celiac disease, gluten is truly evil. Their bodies regard even a tiny crumb of gluten as a malicious invader and will mount an abnormal immune response. The immune system response can damage or even destroy villi—the lining of the small intestine. Under normal conditions villi allow nutrients from food to be absorbed through the walls of the small intestine into the bloodstream. Celiac disease is very serious. Without healthy villi, nutrients are not absorbed properly, causing the individual to become malnourished, no matter how much food one eats. For people with celiac disease, a

Wheat

Barley

Rye

Processed foods with wheat

Here are examples of processed products not on the radar that contain some form of wheat, barley or rye:

- Canned, packet, and restaurant soups contain wheat flour as a thickener.
- Frozen and canned vegetables prepared in a sauce, as well as frozen creamed vegetables.
- Commercially prepared sauces, such as soy sauce, Worcestershire, teriyaki, and horseradish sauce, contain wheat unless otherwise stated.
- Desserts, ice cream, ice cream cones, sherbet, icings, meringues and puddings all contain wheat.
- Dip and gravy mixes contain wheat-based thickening agents. As a general rule most thickening agents such as starches contain wheat.
- Ground spices like curry powder contain wheat agents that prevent them from clumping.
- Instant drinks like instant coffee and tea all contain wheat. So do powdered drinks like hot-chocolate.
- Condiments like processed ketchup, mayonnaise, and mustard contain wheat agents.
- Many dressings contain wheat-enriched emulsifiers or stabilizers.
- Sausages, Lunchables, and prepared meat patties contain wheat.
- Imitation cheeses like cheese whizzes, and pasteurized cheese spreads contain wheat.
- Beer is usually made from barley, but wheat is also widely used as an ingredient.
- Sweets like licorice, chocolate, candy, and chewing gum all contain wheat.

gluten-free diet is essential. But for others a gluten-free diet is not necessary. An unnecessary gluten-free diet can result in an insufficient intake of vitamins, minerals and fiber.

Gluten Sensitivity

There are folks that do not test positive for celiac disease but still react poorly to gluten. Unlike celiac disease, gluten sensitivity doesn't damage the lining of the small intestine. Today, there is no accepted medical test for gluten sensitivity; however people with gluten sensitivity can experience the same side effects with symptoms as severe as those of celiac disease when they eat gluten.

Today the gluten-free business is booming. Food companies are cashing in on the mass confusion by hitting their labels with the latest health buzzwords whether they apply to the product or not. Now we have products screaming that they are gluten free that did not contain gluten in the first place. There's no such thing as gluten-free rice, apples or eggs. Of course they're gluten free! That's not remarkable, that's marketing.

Now, on the other hand, there are many food items that may contain sources of gluten, often in hidden or unexpected ways. Because wheat is used as a binder and thickening agent to add volume and texture in a wide variety of processed food products, it is very hard to avoid. If you are concerned about gluten, always read the labels of any processed food product you are buying to know for sure if wheat, barley or rye is used as an ingredient.

For people with celiac or an immune-mediated wheat allergy you can still enjoy cookies, breads and desserts via flour alternatives. I find rice flour to be an excellent substitute for wheat flour. It is commonly used in gluten-free baked goods to provide structure and substance, and is also a popular addition for its unique and slightly sandy texture. It can also be used as a thickener in sauces and for breading in crunchy fried dishes. It is available in white, which is made from polished white rice, and in brown, which is made from whole grain brown rice. Rice flour is low in sodium, saturated fat, and cholesterol. It's rich in calories, and contains a mixture of complex nutrients and carbohydrates.

Sources of Gluten

[146]The following are varieties and derivatives of wheat, and therefore sources of gluten:

- wheatberries
- durum
- emmer
- semolina
- spelt
- farina
- farro
- graham
- einkorn wheat
- malt in various forms, including: malted barley flour, malted milk or milkshakes, malt extract, malt syrup, malt flavoring, malt vinegar
- brewer's yeast

America
Loves Chicken!

Americans buy more chicken than any other food.[37] Chicken consumption per capita has increased nearly every year since the mid-1960s. But buying chicken is not like it used to be. Today more than ever labels are amplified and roaring with buzzwords. You see labels like "100% natural," "organic," "free-range," and "air chilled." Food labels are packed with information, but many of the claims and phrases found on chicken labels can be extremely confusing and downright misleading. Do you really know what you're buying?

Price is a huge factor. Marketers have discovered that more and more people will pay extra dollars per pound for chicken and products touting those terms because consumers perceive them as healthier, better tasting, smarter choices--and this brings peace of mind. How do you know if a food label is accurate or even true? Fortunately some of the terms and claims used on food labels are legally defined by the U.S. Department of Agriculture (USDA).

> Quick, Why did the chicken cross the playground?
> To get to the other slide.

Chicken Labels Glossary
Let's start with the misunderstood label "organic," and answer that burning question: should you buy organic?

Organic
Of all label terms, the "100% USDA organic" label is the only one that has legal backing from the U.S. government. It also carries a higher price than most other chicken choices. I've witnessed prices upward of $6 per pound at farmers markets in New York City.[38] But is it worth the price? Farmers who want to obtain the USDA organic label for

their products cannot use antibiotics, genetically modified organisms, or feed made from other animal parts. Organic chickens must be fed organic feed and provided with access to the outdoors.[37] When you see the USDA 100% organic label on chicken, it guarantees that the farmer has met the standards defined by the U.S. Department of Agriculture. In addition, researchers found a 33% greater risk of antibiotic-resistant bacteria in non-organic chicken, which may be related to the routine use of antibiotics in conventional chicken farming.[37] This is most likely due to the fact that among conventional poultry farms, thousands of chickens are crowded and housed very close together, so disease can spread quickly. Organic chicken is definitely a good choice.

Natural
"Natural" might be the most confusing of all labels. When it comes to the challenge of paying extra money for organic chicken, people may choose products that are labeled "natural" because natural is perceived as higher value or more nutritious. This is the most classically misleading marketing term of all time, in all food categories. The term "natural" has nothing to do with how a chicken is raised. It simply means that nothing has been added to the bird after slaughter. Antibiotics can still be used unless the label specifically says they weren't. In an effort to control some of the confusion around the label, "100% natural," the USDA requires marketers to say specifically what they mean when they use the term. In fact, a national survey revealed a trend that more consumers value the term "natural" than "organic." [39] Half of polled consumers said the "natural" label was either important or very important to them, whereas only 35% believed "organic" carried the same value. The reality, however, is that "natural" is neither a good value nor a good choice.

Free Range

"Free-range" is also a confusing label. Many people who choose a free-range chicken imagine the chicken clucking happily, eating grass and insects, and roaming around enjoying the sun and a country view. Yes, this is a lovely vision. But it's not the reality. The term "free-range" only means producers must demonstrate that the chickens have access to the outside. The interpretation of the word "outside" is what is in question. "Outside" can be a concrete parking lot.[40] The government only requires that outdoor access be made available for an undetermined period of time each day; that can be five minutes or five hours. The only way to truly know what the chicken producer means by their free-range claim would be by asking the farmer or calling the company. Again, the lack of regulation and transparency around the meaning of this term make it a risky choice for your dinner table.

Pastured

This means that the birds are actually allowed to forage on grass during the day. Sounds like what you would imagine the free-range label to mean. It's also much more expensive to raise chickens this way, because of the amount of space required. The space requirement limits the amount of chickens that can be raised at a time. These birds are raised the old-fashioned way and are available in the U.S. from family farmers who care about their animals and provide them with good, healthy diets and lifestyles. Without a doubt, "pastured chicken" is a very good choice.

Hormone-free

The USDA prohibits the use of hormones in raising chickens, so labels saying "no hormones" or "hormone-free" are pure marketing nonsense. This is an established regulation. This isn't a selling point for a particular brand. It's a reiteration that the USDA prohibits the use of all hormones in raising poultry. It doesn't tell you anything new or relevant about the food, so I can't endorse it as a label choice.[41]

Antibiotic-free

This is a very confusing category. There are many variations to the "raised without antibiotics" label. Practices can vary greatly from producer to producer. Today there is no standardized definition by the USDA for consumers to

Antibiotics are allowed in conventional chicken production but not in organic.

be absolutely sure what this label means. Antibiotics are allowed in conventional chicken production but not in organic. Labels like "no antibiotics administered" or "raised without antibiotics" refer to giving animals no antibiotics during their lifetime. It's not as good as organic, but it's still a good choice.[42]

Air-chilled

"Air-chilled" is a relatively new term in the United States, though it's been popular in other parts of the world for decades. The majority of chicken in America is "water-processed," meaning the meat is chilled in cold pools. The water has to be chlorinated to kill bacteria. In "air-chilling" the chicken skips the chlorine dip, as it is a more time-consuming process. The "air-chilled" system helps prevent the spread of bacteria by keeping all of the chickens independent, and saves tens of thousands of gallons of chlorinated water every day. With no water added, the air-chilled method keeps the bona fide chicken flavor and juices. No water is absorbed, so you get only the natural flavor of chicken. Many chefs report the air-chilled method produces a better tasting chicken. To give it a try, Whole Foods carries Bell & Evans air-chilled chicken. In my opinion, it's an excellent choice.[43]

Kosher

For Kosher chicken the labels are granted by religious authorities—not the government. A Kosher chicken must meet the requirements of Jewish law, and must be slaughtered according to Jewish law. A rabbi is not required as many people often believe, but the person who slaughters the animal must meet certain requirements of Jewish observance, knowledge, and trustworthiness. The kosher slaughter is done by hand to ensure the blood is drained, unlike conventional chicken machine processing procedures. The chicken is then soaked and salted multiple times within three days, a procedure that removes all the blood from the meat. The rabbis who supervise the Kosher meat processing plants are there to certify that the meat meets Kosher standards, not to bless the meat, as is commonly thought. This label doesn't indicate anything about how the birds were raised, so it's not my first choice. If Kosher birds are a priority for you and your family's diet, I recommend getting a bird that is also certified organic.[44]

Egg Facts
Cracked Open

Eggs Play a Distinct Role In Our Diets And Recipes

Egg yolks are one of the few foods that naturally contain Vitamin-D and are considered to be a complete protein. A complete protein contains the nine essential amino acids your body cannot produce naturally. An egg white is made mainly of protein, Vitamin-B3, riboflavin, chlorine, magnesium, and potassium, according to the Iowa Egg Council, an industry group.[45] The white contains about 57% of an egg's protein. Many nutritionists consider eggs a "super food" because of their nutritious value and health benefits. The color of an egg yolk is determined by the hen's diet. The more yellow and orange plant pigments there are in the grain fed to a hen, the more vibrant the color of the yolk will be.

Labels are comforting. They make us feel confident that we are making the right choice for our family's well being with every purchase. When I put eggs in my shopping cart with cartons that say "Organic" or "Free-range" or "Omega-3" I immediately feel like I'm doing my due diligence to feed my family healthy food. Unfortunately, the sad truth is that this mentality is pure fantasy. Most labels are far from being our friends. Part of what we'll discover by deciphering the egg-label jargon is the fact that not all eggs are created equal; some eggs are better than others.

Organic

"Organic" is a term that is defined by the USDA. Hens laying "organic" eggs are given feed that has little to no exposure to pesticides, herbicides, commercial fertilizers, or fungicides. Seeing "organic" on a label tells us the hens meet the requirements of free-range but nothing about the treatment or conditions to which the hens were exposed.[46]

Free Range

Egg cartons that say "free range" often mean that hens are un-caged and have access to the outdoors. Just as we saw in the free-range chicken section, the USDA standards for raising the birds are difficult to qualify. The same goes for our egg-laying hen friends. Outdoor frequency, length of time and conditions are not specified, and there are no standards as to what the hens are fed. Eggs aren't a good buy if "free range" is the only label, but if it's paired with "organic," you're in decent shape.[47]

Cage Free

Similar to "free range," don't be mislead about this label. Just because the hens aren't in cages doesn't mean they go outside or that they aren't crowded together outside a cage. The birds are un-caged, but where? It could be in an airplane hangar or a in a barn. There are no standards or government auditing processes to ensure compliance. Additionally, "cage free" tells us nothing about what the birds are fed. This label is ambiguous and doesn't tell you much, so it's not my first choice.[48]

Vegetarian Fed

This is important for you to know: chickens are not vegetarian by nature. They eat bugs, worms, and most anything else they are able to catch. Vegetarian feed refers to the chicken feed that is provided for the hens by the farmer. Labeling chickens and eggs as "vegetarian fed" might give

people the idea that chickens should be or are vegetarian, when in fact they are not. Actually, it suggests that the birds spend no time outside foraging.[47]

Omega-3 Enriched

Eggs inside cartons with "Omega-3" labels come from birds that have been fed a diet that was most likely high in flax seed, algae, vegetables high in omega-3 fats, insects, and lots of fresh green grass. Yes these eggs do contain more omega-3s than the others.[48]

Natural

This means absolutely nothing! There are no guidelines or definitions surrounding the term "natural." Basically a bird laid an egg. Anything that happened to that egg on its journey to your plate remains a complete mystery.[49]

Pasteurized

This label tells us that the eggs underwent a process called pasteurization to kill bacteria. It has nothing to do with the egg-laying hens roaming free in a pasture. If you eat or use raw eggs to prepare foods that aren't cooked, like homemade mayonnaise, this could be a label that would interest you.[49]

White vs. Brown Eggs

The breed of chicken that did the laying is what determines the color of an egg. Brown eggs come from dark colored hens and white eggs from white hens. There is really not much else different between the two, except I do find the brown eggshells are definitely harder to crack. Brown eggs tend to be more expensive, but not because they are healthier.[50]

Further Mysteries of Food Labeling Revealed

We talked about misleading labels such as "all natural" that pretty much mean nothing. Another labeling phenomenon is the missing ingredient. Processed food products may contain ingredients that are not written on the label. If you are unknowingly ingesting ingredients, this can cause a myriad of health issues should you have dietary restrictions or food allergies.

In November 2012, Perdue Foods of Bridgewater, VA issued a voluntary recall of its chicken breast nuggets after it discovered that the nuggets, which had undergone a recipe reformulation, contained milk that was not listed as an ingredient on the labels.[51] For those who are lactose intolerant this could be a huge concern, to say the least.

Also in 2012, The Kroger Company, a Cincinnati-based grocery store chain, recalled its house brand of French vanilla ice cream, stating that pecans, a known allergen, may be an ingredient that was not listed on the label. Kroger removed the affected items from store shelves.[52]

There are many other examples of processed food products containing ingredients that are not on the label. The biggest offenders in this category are genetically altered ingredients that have not been labeled as genetically modified organisms (GMOs). There is no required regulation today in the United States, and that is an extremely controversial topic. As parents it's more important today than ever before to question the information about food products put before you because the supermarket shelves are packed with dubious products disguised as food and nutrition.

Thankfully, awareness and change are on the horizon! Consumers are demanding it. And the state of Vermont is leading the charge.[53] On May 8th 2014, Governor Peter Shumlin signed a new law making Vermont the first state to require labeling of foods containing GMOs. Governor Shumlin stated, 'Vermonters have spoken loud and clear: We want to know what's in our food." As anticipated, the following month, four national organizations that would be affected by the new GMO labeling filed a lawsuit in federal court challenging the measure's constitutionality.

Ben & Jerry's jumped right in to support Vermont's new GMO labeling by renaming its most iconic flavor, Chocolate Fudge Brownie, as Food Fight Fudge Brownie. In support of Vermont's legal defense, a portion from each sale of Food Fight Fudge Brownie in its Vermont company-owned stores through July would go to support the fund.

To fend off the plethora of unhealthy products on the shelves today, your defense is cooking for your family using fresh ingredients whenever possible and limiting the amount of processed foods and ingredients on the menu.

Beef is Back

For decades red meat has been perceived as a food villain, causing beef consumption to decline since its peak in the 1970s. This perception arose from reports of health risks; disease scares in the media, high prices, and the environmentalist-vegetarian movement. But recently, red meat has been making a comeback. The high-protein, low-carb movement has returned beef to many tables, with affordable cuts perfect for braising, such as chuck and brisket, increasingly making their way into our shopping carts.

But is red meat good for us? Should you embrace the reversal and feed your family beef? Humans have been eating meat for thousands of years. [54] Traditional hunter-gatherer populations got most of their calories from meat, and our bodies are well designed to digest and absorb nutrients from it. Red meat is highly nutritious.[55] Beef is full of protein and a source of niacin, selenium, vitamin B6, Vitamin D and phosphorous. Beef is the best dietary source of iron and supplies Vitamin B-12, which is essential in the production of red blood cells.

The eating habits of the Stone Age have never been so popular and controversial as they are now. In 2013 the Paleo diet (also known as the "caveman diet") topped online searches as the most-Googled diet.

The United States Department of Agriculture (USDA) meticulously grades beef at the request of meat packers. Only beef that is USDA inspected may carry the USDA label. There are generally three USDA grades of beef that you would buy in a supermarket. In the order of highest to lowest they are Prime, Choice, and Select. The lesser grades you would typically find in frozen and processed food products are Cutter and Canner. The quality of USDA Select only slightly exceeds the quality of Cutter and Canner, yet some major chain stores will tout Select as a premium grade through catchy labeling.[56]

Grain-fed Beef vs. Grass-fed Beef

Now, more than ever, the source of your food matters. In today's beef marketplace, food-producing corporations have essentially taken over the once popular family-run ranches. The need for cheap, mass-produced beef by supermarkets, restaurants, and fast-food chains has unfortunately led to a nutritional deficiency epidemic in those beef products.[57] Most U.S. beef is raised on a grain mix composed mostly of cheap corn feed.[58] Just like humans eating high-carbohydrate foods, grain-fed cows fatten up fast – which is precisely the goal.

For the producer, giving animals growth hormones and antibiotics to stimulate growth on a diet of corn enables a quick turnaround from the ranch to the supermarket, leading to higher profits. The consumer lives in a land of plenty that provides far less than what we need to stay healthy.

As with everything in the market place, quality counts. Conventional USDA grain-fed meat is fairly nutritious; grass-fed beef, however, is even more nutritious. The grass-fed alternative is gaining popularity and becoming more readily available--but it is more expensive. A number of ranchers are feeding their herds the way they all did up until 50 years ago, switching to grass feed because grass is uncontaminated by growth hormones and antibiotics. Animals are free to roam in pastures to eat the food nature intended.

When cows eat the kind of food their bodies were designed to eat, they stay healthier and leaner. Grass-fed beef is naturally lower in fat. Plus, the saturated fat in grass-fed beef is good for you. Grass-fed has higher levels of omega-3 fatty acids, and cattle that eat grass have significantly lower chances of being infected with bacteria.[59] Grass-fed beef also contains more carotenoids, vitamin E, and minerals like potassium, zinc, and phosphorus than conventional beef.

Growing up in the 60s it was common in Brooklyn to have different types of food delivered to your house on a weekly basis. We had the milkman and the soda guy, and some of my neighbors even had potato chips and pretzels delivered. The local butcher delivered a variety of steaks, burgers, and chicken to our house every week. I looked forward to butcher day because my mom always made burgers for dinner.

Burgers were always a favorite meal both for me and for Roy. I considered trying grass-fed beef many times, but it was pricey, so I passed it up in favor of regular grain-fed beef. After watching the documentary King Corn, which explained the negative effects on humans of eating corn-fed beef, I decided to pay the extra dollars and try the grass-fed ground sirloin.[60]

The significant taste difference between this grass-fed burger and the burgers I'd been eating the past 25 years was obvious. The taste reminded me of the burgers I'd enjoyed as a kid. Although some people describe the flavor as being a little gamey, I believe grass-fed beef tastes better. And I'm not alone: a taste-testing experiment published by Slate chose grass-fed beef over several other options, including USDA Prime.[154]

The Problems with Processed Meats

A major theme throughout *Two Pans and a Pot* is avoiding processed foods whenever possible. This particularly means saying, "No," to processed meats. They are usually manufactured with a carcinogenic ingredient known as sodium nitrite. Manufacturers use it as a color enhancer to turn meats a bright red color so they look fresh and appealing. Unfortunately, sodium nitrite under certain conditions in the body can damage cells and turn into cancer-causing molecules. Nitrite-free bacon, hot dogs, and sausages are available at stores. In NYC I find them at Trader Joe's.[61]

Some of the additional additives you'll also consume with processed meats are:
- Salt (for taste, impact on meat proteins, shelf-life)
- Phosphates (for protein structuring and water binding)
- Chemical preservatives (for shelf-life)
- Monosodium glutamate, or MSG (for enhancement of flavor)
- Food coloring substances (synthetic and of plant origin)
- Corn syrup, dextrose, sucrose (flavoring agents and sweeteners)

Processed meats include most bacon, sausage, hot dogs, sandwich meat, packaged ham, pepperoni, salami, and virtually all red meat used in frozen prepared meals.

The Dangers of Dairy

I'm about to make a very bold statement about dairy that most people do not want to hear. In fact, I was one of those people in my former life. This conversation makes some people so angry they regard you as though you are trashing American culture. But here goes: dairy is the perfect food... if you are a calf.

My investigation into dairy started when my son was ten years old and began to suffer from allergies, which brought on asthmatic episodes. A mom in the park one day suggested that I cut out dairy. I looked at her as if she were crazy, but I was desperate, so I listened to what she had to say. The facts rolling off her tongue convinced me, and I took her advice. I also began my own investigative journey into the dairy industry's practices and dairy products.

I discovered this helpful friend was correct, that dairy products are mucous-forming[62] and can contribute to respiratory disorders, hay fever, and seasonal allergies.[63] Cow's milk is intended for baby cows. We're the only species that drinks the milk from another species after infancy. How on earth did that begin?

Americans Get 97% of Our Dairy from Cows. Why?

Is it taste? Generational traditions? Industrial accessibility? Yes, yes, and yes! The three dairy animals most familiar to Westerners--sheep, goats, and cows--were all domesticated around 8000 B.C.[64] Cows responded the best to centuries of breeding, which is why they're now relatively docile animals with high milk outputs.

Cow's milk fat content is similar to that of human milk, which makes it familiar to our palates. Its relative blandness makes it a blank canvas with a range of flavor profiles and consistencies for the creation of items like cheese and ice cream. This is why we rely on cow's milk. With the exception of goat's milk, most other milks, even if they taste good, are too hard and expensive to mass-produce.

Problems with Dairy

Products from cow's milk contain three components that are not found in other foods: lactose (milk sugar), whey protein, and casein (another protein).

Some people are lactose intolerant, which means they do not produce the enzyme lactase, which is needed to break down milk sugar. When lactase isn't broken down properly, it ferments in the intestines and causes digestive distress.

Cows are routinely given steroids and other hormones to plump them up and increase their milk production. These hormones can also negatively impact humans' delicate hormonal balance.[65] And don't kid yourself. If the cow you're eating received steroids and hormones, you're consuming those substances too.

Most cows are fed commercial feed, which can contain genetically modified corn and soy, animal products, chicken manure, cottonseed, pesticides, and antibiotics.

Most dairy products are pasteurized to kill potentially harmful bacteria. During the pasteurization process, vitamins, proteins, and enzymes are also destroyed. Enzymes assist with the digestion process. When they are destroyed through pasteurization, milk becomes harder to digest, putting a strain on our bodies' enzyme systems.

Alternative Milk Choices are Booming.

The market is now flooded with cow's milk alternatives like soy, rice, oat, almond, hazelnut, hemp, and coconut milks. Soy, rice, and coconut milks can probably be found at your local grocery store. Milk alternatives were created due to an increase in demand to accommodate different dietary restrictions, including vegetarians, vegans, and people with milk allergies or lactose intolerance.

Not only are milk alternatives easily found in supermarkets, but I've also begun to see yogurts made from coconut milk and almond milk in more and more supermarkets. In the non-dairy yogurt category, I've found coconut yogurt brands to have the closest taste and consistency to traditional dairy yogurt. Coconut milk is known to be high in fat; but it's still a good alternative for those allergic to dairy, soy, or nuts.

Soymilk is probably the most popular alternative to cow's milk. Made out of soybeans, with no casein or lactose, Soymilk is an excellent alternative for lactose intolerant sufferers. And because it's shelf-stable, it does not need to be refrigerated.

For those with soy intolerance or soy allergies, rice milk offers a suitable alternative. Made from brown rice, this milk is usually not sweetened, although rice milk flavors like vanilla or chocolate are available. Rice milk is very high in carbohydrates and low in protein.

Still new to the market, and perhaps harder to find, are oat and hemp milks. Both are relatively high in carbohydrates and a good alternative if you are allergic to dairy, soy, or nuts. Hemp milk is made from the hemp plant, which is high in omega-3s.

The Truth about Tuna

When it comes to healthy eating, fish has it all. And canned tuna gives you the biggest bang for your buck. It's rich in protein, low in fat and calories, and an excellent source of essential omega-3 fatty acids. Canned tuna is the second most popular seafood product in the U.S. after shrimp.[66]

Engrained in American culture for the past two centuries, tuna is as essential as pumpkin pie on Thanksgiving and as commonplace as mashed potatoes. In all its forms, tuna represents more than one-third of the total seafood consumed in the U.S. Canned tuna is a big business. On average, Americans eat nearly three pounds of canned tuna per capita every year. The government promotes tuna via school lunch programs. Tuna is also a dietary recommendation of the U.S. Department of Agriculture. Tuna continues to act as a staple of low-carb diets because it is low in fat and high in protein. Bodybuilders binge on it.

Throughout my life tuna has always provided a reliable food choice, a close friend I could count on when in doubt about what to have for lunch. Familiar and always satisfying, a tuna hero was (and still is) my go-to sandwich. When I was a kid growing up in Brooklyn, my house was the lunch destination on Saturday afternoons after basketball at the park. Those guys loved my tuna so much that they used to call me the "Tuna Down Kid." "Down" comes from the phrase, "whiskey down", which is New York City short-order lingo for rye toast. So basically it's a tuna salad sandwich on rye toast with lettuce and tomato.

The History of Tuna

The tuna industry actually began as a result of a downturn in the sardine industry. In the late 19th century and early 20th century, sardines were the popular American canned fish product. In 1903, Southern California canner Albert P. Halfhil's catch of sardines in San Pedro Bay dwindled. Halfhil was faced with a cannery of empty sardine cans and needed a way to fill them.[67]

The enterprising Halfhil began packing his empty sardine cans with albacore tuna. He discovered that albacore tuna "turned white and tasted delicious when steam cooked." America agreed. Halfhil sold 700 cases in that first year. By the outbreak of the First World War in 1914, production had reached 400,000 cases.

The tuna revolution took off during the war. American doughboys in Europe required an inexpensive, portable, protein-rich food, and canned tuna proved a perfect solution. Returning soldiers continued eating tuna, which ousted salmon as America's fish of choice by the 1940s.

Concerns about Tuna

Now we get to the disconcerting part of the tuna story. Worldwide industrial waste of the past two centuries has created a huge mercury problem in the fish we like to eat. Although mercury naturally occurs in the environment, the primary source of methylmercury, which is absorbed by larger fish in the ocean, is industrial waste and pollution. Forty percent of the mercury in the earth's environment is caused by power plants using coal to produce electricity.[68]

Through rain, snow, and runoff, mercury can wash directly into the earth's oceans, rivers, and lakes. When mercury gets into water and becomes exposed to certain bacteria, it undergoes a chemical transformation into methylmercury, which is absorbed by tiny aquatic organisms. When fish eat those organisms, the mercury levels begin to build up in their bodies. When larger, longer-living fish feed on smaller fish throughout their lives, ever-higher levels of methylmercury accumulate. Because it binds to the protein in fish muscles, cooking and heat do not reduce mercury levels.

The amount of mercury in fish varies depending on the type of fish. Factors that affect the build-up include their size, weight, age, what they eat, and where they live. Tuna can cruise up to 55 miles per hour, and are constantly in motion. To keep this speed machine going, the tuna eats up to 10% of its body weight daily, resulting in high mercury levels for the species. Depending on the variety, a tuna's weight can vary from 10 pounds up to 600 pounds.

Smaller, non-predatory fish with shorter life spans tend to have lower levels of mercury. Fish low in mercury include catfish, cod, flounder and sole, haddock, herrick, lobster, rainbow trout, wild and farmed salmon, sardines, scallops, and shrimp.

The tuna varieties with higher mercury content are bluefin, black fin, albacore, and yellow fin tuna. Other fish high in mercury include king mackerel, marlin, bluefish, shark, swordfish, and wild sturgeon.

Although tuna provides millions of people with nutrition, protein and livelihoods worldwide, they are more than just seafood. Tuna are one of the top predators in the marine food chain, and are one of the most important fish in our oceans; they play a major role in preserving a balance of the ocean's ecosystem. Because of the huge worldwide demand, however, they are also over fished and in danger—some varieties more than others.

Bluefin, the largest of all varieties, is particularly threatened because of its high demand and rewarding price tag. Bluefin, an eminent predator, resides at or near the top of the oceanic food chain; its size and speed protect it against most natural enemies. The Atlantic Bluefin plays a significant role in the ecosystem by consuming a wide variety of fish—herring, anchovies, sardines, bluefish, mackerel, and others—and keeping their populations in balance. Its extinction would have unpredictable cascading effects in the ocean's ecosystems and would give rise to serious consequences to many other species in the ocean's food chain.

Tuna on the Shelves Today

Bluefin Tuna. Bluefin tuna are the largest and can live up to forty years. Called the tiger of the sea, this top predator can grow to over 1,000 lbs. Bluefin tuna also happens to be delicious—the dark red flesh is highly valued by the sushi chefs of Japan and by food connoisseurs worldwide, making the premium cost skyrocket to thousands of dollars per pound at times of the year.[69] Despite the amazing speed of this tuna, it cannot escape the nets of the world's insatiable appetite. World populations of Bluefin are being caught faster than they can reproduce.

Yellow Fin Tuna. Yellowfin tuna populate tropical and subtropical oceans of the world. This tuna is migratory and capable of swimming great distances--even across an entire ocean. Far less expensive than Bluefin, this variety tastes nearly as good. Yellowfin is used in the raw sushi market and is often canned and labeled as Yellowfin. Yellowfin is the top tuna harvested by U.S. fishermen in the Atlantic. More than half of this catch comes from fisheries that operate in the Northwest Atlantic, Gulf of Mexico, and Caribbean. Because of the worldwide tuna demand, Yellowfin tuna are now close to being endangered.[70]

Skipjack Tuna. Skipjack tuna are found in most of the waters around the world. They are the smallest and most abundant of the major commercial tuna species. Tuna labeled "light" or "chunk light" are most likely skipjack. Skipjack makes up about 70% of the canned tuna market. Skipjack generally has the strongest flavor and highest fat content—it can taste fishy. Dried skipjack is known as Katsuobushi and is used in Japanese cuisine. It's also a fast-maturing fish, so the level of mercury in its flesh is lower. Currently this variety is not under threat.[71]

Albacore Tuna. Albacore is the most popular canned variety in America. It has the lightest flesh and the mildest flavor. Like skipjack, albacore is one of the smaller tuna species and is highly migratory. Albacore are also found around the world and can travel across an entire ocean. These fish are important commercially: along with skipjack, they are one of the two main canned tuna species and are labeled as 'solid white' tuna. While albacore is reasonably abundant in the Pacific Ocean, it's less abundant in the North Atlantic.[72]

Exercise and Building Strength For the Entire Family

The Foundation for Health and Longevity

The obesity rate among kids ages 6-19 has more than doubled in the past 30 years.[73] It currently almost quadruples the obesity level of the late 1960s.[73] Simply put, kids are sitting around far more today than they used to. According to the Kaiser Family Foundation, 8-18 year olds watch about 4.5 hours of television a day.[74] Combine television with social media and video games, add junk food and fast food to the mix, and you have the perfect ingredients for a rapidly rising health crisis.

In her position as First Lady, Michelle Obama declared war on childhood obesity, calling it a national epidemic. In February 2010 she announced the *Let's Move* campaign, a comprehensive initiative dedicated to solving the problem of obesity in our country.[75] *Let's Move* is designed to encourage healthier food in schools, better food labeling, and more physical activity for children. Its advocates include pop stars, large corporations, healthcare providers, and—most importantly—schools. In March 2013, Michelle Obama rolled out a health and fitness initiative in Chicago as the second phase. Over the next five years, *Let's Move! Active Schools* will provide grants to 50,000 schools across the country to develop physical education programs that will fight childhood obesity.[75]

Though the First Lady has elevated the awareness of the risks associated with childhood obesity and the benefits of exercise, it's not enough unless individuals respond. Now is the time to discover the immediate and long-term benefits of exercise. Now is the time to learn what foods your kids need to grow strong and resilient. Now is the time to equip your children to achieve and maintain physical, emotional, and mental health. The benefits of exercise extend far beyond the physical: exercise aids in the development of essential interpersonal skills, improves the quantity and quality of sleep, and enhances motor coordination.[75] Physical activity not only helps your child maintain a proper weight, but it can also teach the entire family a

lifetime of healthy habits. Children who exercise and play sports are more likely to continue exercising as adults.[75]

In 2005, an important report from the U.S. Centers for Disease Control (CDC) raised public awareness of the health benefits associated with regular physical activity. This CDC panel recommended that school-age children participate in at least 60 minutes per day, three days per week, of moderate to vigorous physical activity that is developmentally appropriate. Research has shown that increased levels of physical activity and fitness are associated with reduced

risk of disease in adulthood, including cardio-vascular disease, diabetes, selected cancers, and musculoskeletal conditions.[80]

Exercise and physical activity is so important to our well being that I'm amazed it is not a top priority for everyone. Growing up in the 60s my friends and I had two educations: in school and after school. We played in the schoolyard, on the block, and in the backyard. In my neighborhood we played until dark or until our moms called us in for dinner.

Anyone who resists the benefits of exercise and play might want to consider the undisputed fact that humans are meant to move.[12] Babies love to rock their bodies, flail their arms and kick their feet. Toddlers love to run around, dance to music, climb, jump and roll around. Older kids enjoy both organized and non-organized sports, and play-grounds. This is all great fun, and a fundamental ingredient for growth from childhood and throughout adulthood.

The Importance of Muscle Strength

Physical strength is just as critical and essential to human survival today as it was thousands of years ago. Of course, life in the twenty-first century doesn't necessitate lifting heavy stones, climbing trees, or fending off wild animals. Still, every movement we make requires muscle strength. When we walk, climb stairs, bend down, breathe, or digest food, muscle strength is needed to function effectively. Most of us take basic muscle strength for granted yet lacking this strength causes numerous problems.

The latest studies show that building strength is a key factor in health and longevity for everyone. Starting exercise at a young age promotes healthy muscles, bones, and joints. It lays a strong physical foundation and bolsters self-esteem.

The latest studies show that building strength is a key factor in health and longevity for everyone.[77] Starting exercise at a young age promotes healthy muscles, bones, and joints. It lays a strong physical foundation and bolsters self-esteem. Moreover, our children's physical strength lies within our control. Weight-bearing and resistance activities provide the stimulus to build and retain bone mass in the body. Activities such as cycling, gymnastics, skating, ball games, dancing, and supervised weight training will help build strength, and bone mass and density.[77]

Muscle tissue functions as body armor to build your child's defense against sickness and disease. By building muscle, the human body has the protein it needs in reserve to deploy during illness. The body then uses the protein to create white blood cells and antibodies to fight infection. In the 1970s a few myths about youth weight lifting spread through America like wild fire. They raised concern among parents and educators and created a stigma that continues to smolder in today's fitness culture. The two misconceptions are as simple as they are incorrect. The first is the belief that strength training may stunt children's growth; the second is that children under the age of 12 should avoid weight training all together.

There is simply no scientific evidence to support either of these statements. In fact, over the past 15 years all of the major fitness and medical organizations in the U.S. have recommended strength training for youth, as long as basic

In 2008 the U.S. Department of Health & Human Services released the following information:

[79]Regular physical activity in children and adolescents promotes health and fitness. Compared to those who are inactive, physically active youth have higher levels of cardio respiratory fitness and stronger muscles. They also typically have lower body fatness. Their bones are stronger, and they may have reduced symptoms of anxiety and depression.

Youth who are regularly active also have a better chance of a healthy adulthood. Children and adolescents don't usually develop chronic diseases, such as heart disease, hypertension, type 2 diabetes, or osteoporosis. However, risk factors for these diseases can begin to develop early in life. Regular physical activity makes it less likely that these risk factors will develop and more likely that children will remain healthy as adults.

Youth can achieve substantial health benefits by performing both moderate- and vigorous-intensity physical activity for periods of time that add up to 60 minutes (1 hour) or more each day. This activity should include aerobic activity as well as age-appropriate muscle- and bone-strengthening activities.[81, 82]

safety guidelines are followed and the kids are properly supervised.[77] Regarding the myth of age, children can begin to resistance training as soon as they are able to accept and follow directions—usually around eight years old.[78]

Adding Endurance and Flexibility

Along with muscle-strength, cardio-respiratory endurance is an essential component of your child's physical health. The heart and lungs work together to facilitate the oxygen and carbon dioxide exchange. Oxygen plays a vital role in the metabolism of our living organisms. Endurance is developed when kids regularly engage in aerobic activity. During aerobic activities the heart beats faster and breathing is heavier, which strengthens the heart and improves the body's ability to deliver oxygen-laden blood to all its cells.

So far we've discussed the benefits of strength training and endurance. The third element to comprehensive fitness for your children is flexibility. Kids need to stretch their bodies, especially during growth spurts. Flexibility allows muscles and joints to bend, to move gracefully, and perform effectively. According to the American Academy of Pediatrics, children become more agile when they stretch and move their bodies in a full range of motion.[83] Stretching also helps kids' bodies recover after exercise and reduce muscle tension. Plus, it feels good!

Although an obesity epidemic rages in our country today, it doesn't have to

infect your family. A nutritious diet and physical activity can prevent today's children from becoming overweight and remaining overweight throughout their lives. Diet and fitness trends come and go, but preparing healthy meals and encouraging physical activity for your children is a timeless solution. Having fun is what motivates children, so abstract ideas like healthy bones, longevity, and disease prevention will do little to encourage them. Show them how much fun being active is. Fun is the number one motivator in almost every aspect of a child's life.

Greek culture

There was a time when children of all ages naturally weight trained by simply helping around the home: carrying pails, digging or tilling the land, raking, and performing chores around the farm or house. Improving our well being through exercise and nutrition is ancient news. Exercise, athletics, and nutrition were a key part of education in ancient Greece. The first Olympic games took place in Greece in 776 BC.[76] They were held in honor of Zeus, the chief

god in Greek Mythology. When it came to overall health, early Greek culture believed that developing the body was as important as improving the mind.
Plato's Law specifically mentions how athletics played a critical role in Greek society. Greek youth worked out in the wrestling school called "palaestra" to determine who the serious Olympic contenders would be. The youths worked with athletic trainers who used long sticks to point out correct body positions.

The trainers paid close attention to balancing different types of physical exercise and the athlete's diet. The Olympic Games originally consisted of just one event, called the "stade" race. It was a short race covering the length of the stadium. Gradually, additional running events were introduced similar to today's marathons. Other popular sporting events that were added to the ancient games were boxing, chariot racing, wrestling, long jump, javelin throw, and discus throw.

Lose Fat, Get Cut
For Mom and Dad

Even if you are over the age of 40, you have the ability to lose fat, build muscle, and sculpt your body. There's no magic pill, no product to buy, no chicanery. The recipe is simple: eat right and exercise effectively.

I love to compare the weight loss process to Michelangelo sculpting marble. It wasn't until I visited the Academia Gallery in Florence to see the David live that I truly understood the magnificence of this work of art. As I walked down the corridor of unfinished torso sculptures called "The Prisoners," I witnessed the beauty of body parts breaking out of eight-foot marble slabs. A sculpted thigh, arm and shoulder coming to life with detailed veins and muscles all carved from solid stone as though oxygen was running through the rock. They looked like muscular bodies trying to escape their stone surroundings.

Beyond these brilliant pieces stands David. At 17 feet tall, he dwarfs each visitor with his power and beauty. I was in awe. Carved from 1501 to 1504, David began as a 20-foot-tall smooth, rectangle slab of Italian marble from a nearby quarry.

With hammer and chisel Michelangelo released the David from within this solid stone block. Hammer stroke by hammer stroke, strong lean biceps, taut triceps and polished abdominals emerged. David's perfect beauty, strength and presence materialized, celebrating the magnificence of the human form. The statue embodies Michelangelo's creativity and his ability to capture the intense human moment before David battles Goliath.

Chiseling Away the Belly Fat

Just as Michelangelo released David from within the confines of his outer marble material, you have the ability to re-sculpt your human form. Your marble exterior is made of both subcutaneous and visceral fat. Your hammer and chisel are lean, clean foods and an exercise regimen.

Subcutaneous fat lies just under your skin—the flab on your butt and thighs. Visceral fat surrounds your vital organs. That's right—the belly fat! All body fat is not the same.

The visceral fat stored deep inside in your abdomen endangers your health far more than the flab on your butt, thighs, or arms. And that's why your exercise routine will target visceral fat.

You gain abdominal fat as you age for a variety of reasons. It accumulates over time from eating high-fat and processed, sugary foods, and from the lack of physical activity.

This belly fat is also associated with many serious health problems: cardiovascular disease, type 2 diabetes, increased blood pressure, and insulin resistance. However, this toxic fat doesn't have to encroach on vital organs like your liver and pancreas. New research demonstrates that exercise and a lean diet are the keys to eliminating belly fat and preventing health issues. [84]

You can reduce visceral fat by engaging in aerobic exercise and changing the foods you eat. Add interval training with a few resistance exercises, and subcutaneous fat will begin to chip away, just like the David's outer marble, to reveal the muscle tone within your body.

In terms of a meal plan you'll want to rely heavily on fruits, vegetables, high fiber ingredients, whole grains, nuts, lean meats, and fish. It's critical to avoid sugary and diet drinks, processed foods, most dairy, cheese, and pasta. For this meal plan to work your body still need fats, so use oils that are high in monounsaturated and polyunsaturated fats, like extra virgin olive oil.

For cardio I never liked running because I became fatigued in minutes, got bored, and chalked it up to the fact that I just don't like to run. Then one afternoon while chatting at a café with Anne, a marathon runner, I had a major revelation. She told me that the first mile was the toughest for her. I was so surprised to find out that someone who runs over fifty miles a week struggles with the first mile. This conversation gave me a completely new outlook on running, swimming, biking, and weight lifting. It's tough for everyone! And if she could struggle past the initial warm up, I could too.

I'll paint a picture: you're working out, you're breathing heavily, your heart is pumping rapidly. Blood is streaming through your veins delivering oxygen to your calves, thighs, and torso to keep you moving. Beads of sweat are forming on your forehead, and your legs are burning. You feel like stopping but instead decide to power through the pain for a few more minutes. You begin to feel a rhythm; your arms, legs, and lungs synchronize. Breathing becomes manageable. You've entered the aerobic zone. Whether you're running, biking, or swimming, this moment where your heart, lungs, and muscles synergistically begin to work overtime is the moment you begin to burn fat and get cut.

If the feeling of the first few minutes of your workout is torture, you are not alone. That sensation of early fatigue is normal. It even happens to people who work out five times a week and to athletes in training. Rather than getting overwhelmed, understand what is going on in your body for those first few minutes. This is warm-up time; the fatigue is caused by your body's delay in delivering sufficient fuel to the muscles at work.

It's extremely important to fuel up before a workout because your body needs energy in order to maximize your work and get results. During exercise your working muscles burn glucose and muscle glycogen for energy. The carbohydrates you take in break down into the sugars glucose and fructose, which your body absorbs and transforms into energy. [140]The glucose not needed for energy right away is stored in your muscles and liver in the form of glycogen. Afterwards, your body stores any unused glycogen as fat.

This is why it is so important to push through that initial fatigue. Once you enter the aerobic zone and your body taps into muscle glycogen, you will level-set to where your energy delivery will allow your muscles to perform for longer periods of time. This process will ease with time and practice, and you'll burn fat and get fit.

So where does the energy to support working through your wall come from? No matter what exercise you do or which sport you play, carbohydrates provide the energy to fuel muscle contractions. Then, for the post-workout rebuild and repair of muscle you need high quality protein. When you work out, you are actually ripping muscle. Over the next 24 hours your body repairs it, which strengthens your muscles. So remember the post-workout recipe of protein, repair, and rest.

Eating Right: The Foundation of Losing Fat and Getting Fit

Here are some key food combinations for pre- and post-workout eating to help you power through to burn fat and build muscle. Mix and match to fit your tastes.

Pre-workout Power Fuel
- Hydrate: drink water, at least 8oz
- Veggie omelet
- Whole grain bread with almond butter and bananas.
- Greek yogurt with nuts, dried fruit and kiwi
- Quinoa with legumes.
- High-glycemic fruits like pineapple, apricots, banana, and mango, with cottage cheese.
- Greek yogurt fruit smoothie with granola.
- Oatmeal (not instant) with blueberries, almonds, and apple or pineapple.
- Apple and melon wedges with almond butter.

Post Workout Power Fuel
- Hydrate: drink water, at least 8oz.
- Organic dark meat chicken with steamed broccoli and kale, drizzled with olive oil.
- Three-egg vegetable omelets with avocado: use one egg yolk and drizzle olive oil over avocado.
- Wild roasted salmon with sweet potato and spinach with olive oil.
- Veggie tuna with hummus, spinach and whole wheat toast
- Sirloin (grass-fed preferred) with steamed collard greens and olive oil.
- Turkey breast with feta cheese, walnuts, and spinach.

The approach to weight loss in many diets revolves around reducing calorie intake. In a lose fat, get cut approach you maximize the amount of calories you burn. Calories are a measurement unit of energy. If your yogurt or sweet potato contains 100 calories, that number indicates the amount of energy your body is able to gain from eating the yogurt or sweet potato. Physical activity then burns calories. Walking and even breathing burns calories, but actively and intensely using your muscles burn even more calories.

Both cardio and strength training will increase your appetite because you've burned calories and exhausted your muscles. The brain knows that the body must repair and rebuild muscle tissue quickly. What your body craves is real nutrition and proteins to repair and rebuild your muscle.

I recommend looking into the book *South Beach Diet* by cardiologist Dr. Arthur Agatston for a simple and clear understanding of the effects of carbohydrates and proteins on the cells of the human body. It's worth the small investment. It worked for me.

Healthy eating combined with effective exercise will bring noticeable results. But don't think of it as a diet, a temporary change in eating habits. Think of it as a renewal. Once you commit, it's like putting on glasses with new lenses.

Eat clean and eat often—up to six times a day. When you work out and restrict your food intake at the same time, hunger becomes your archenemy, a gnawing feeling in between meals when your blood sugar levels drop. My cravings hit at 3pm every day, like clockwork. To stay ahead of the hunger, try eating more frequent, smaller meals throughout the day, dividing your daily allotment of calories into smaller portions.

The truth is, though, we aren't very good at measuring, counting, or cutting calories. It's easy to wind up concentrating more on the calories than on the actual food you're eating. And in actuality, the ingredients are what matter most. Plus, portion control is difficult to manage.

I have found, however, that when you have an exercise routine and stick to eating fruits, vegetables, lean meats, grains, fish, and nuts, you can eat as much as you want, as often as you want, and portion control will happen naturally.

High Intensity Interval Training: The Structure for Losing Fat and Getting Fit

Let's get specific about your exercise regimen. High intensity interval training is designed to put you on the path to lose weight and get cut—even as busy parents. With a combination of a couple weeks of healthy eating and Spartacus workouts, you will begin to see results. Your abdomen will begin to shrink because your abdominal fat cells are beginning to reduce in size. I lost 30 pounds in 60 days and proudly gave my abdominal muscles their public debut. Spartacus has become my lifestyle routine. Roy has also adopted Spartacus workouts, as have many of my friends. It's addicting!

If you are looking for a workout that combines cardio exercise and muscle strengthening, fits into your busy schedule, gets incredible results, and encourages you to eat clean, interval training may just be the ticket for you. This is not the socializing kind of routine where you can read a magazine while you workout or chat on the phone. Each session is short, and you'll need to focus and work hard but you will see your body change in ways you never thought possible. The routines are designed to incorporate aerobic, core, and strength training in the form of full body exercises. Kid-approved versions are available, too.

It's not complicated, either. This workout is all about alternating higher and lower segments of intense activity in intervals. Though simple, the results are remarkable.

High intensity interval training gets and keeps your heart rate up, which burns fat efficiently. According to the American College of Sports Medicine, more calories are burned in short, high intensity exercise than in long, lower-intensity, endurance exercise.[141]

Whether you are a seasoned athlete or new to exercise, interval training is the way to see results. You'll most likely experience a little pain at first, but you'll never be bored.

If you have never exercised in your life, begin slowly with a steady paced cardio exercise. Walking and biking, outside or in a gym, are great starting activities and from these you can progress to a low impact interval training program and advance from there.

If you've been doing the same jogging routine for months and haven't seen results, this might be a good time for you to mix it up. Try this instead: run your usual jog for five minutes, then turn up the pace and run hard and fast for one minute, and then go back to your usual pace. Repeat that a few more times. You just mastered interval training. Alternating the pace forces your body to exert itself more and increase your heart rate more than in your normal workout.

This technique of intense workout periods with short recovery segments keeps the workout intensity high.[141] High intensity interval training actually keeps you burning fat even after you leave the gym. During the high intensity intervals, your body isn't able to bring in enough oxygen to distribute to your muscles. Therefore, the oxygen must be replenished post-workout in order for your muscles to repair and build. This process causes you to continue to burn fat and get cut during the next 24-36 hours.[142]

Along with putting your body in a state to build lean muscle, interval training also develops your cardiovascular system. By pushing your heart rate up during periods of intense exercise, you'll increase your cardio ability and strengthen your heart. During the short rest intervals, you'll increase your recovery ability and thus recover more quickly in future workouts and gain endurance.

Constructing Your Own Exercise Routine

There are multiple ways to discover the best exercise routine. Many gyms will give you a free evaluation with a trainer when you join. If they don't, ask for it—you'll probably get it. If you are interested in interval training, let the trainer know. If you use a book or an online source, make sure you read the entire program or watch the whole video. After tons of research I actually found my Spartacus workout while thumbing through a Men's Health magazine at the airport—you never know when or where inspiration will appear.

If you are not a gym person, you don't need to join one. You can easily do interval workouts in your own home. You don't need special equipment. All you need is a timer and a positive attitude. Oh, and music for sure. Your body is a self-contained gym: running, biking, jumping rope, high knees, scissor kicks, planks, push-ups, or anything plyometric like jumping lunges will work.

Intervals are demanding. Even if you already workout, you will be sweating and exhausted the first few times you try intervals. By the second week, though, it gets easier; you feel stronger mentally and physically.

As you progress you can begin to incorporate other routines, like weightlifting, swimming, or yoga. What I love

If you are looking for a workout that combines cardio exercise and muscle strengthening, fits into your busy schedule, gets incredible results, and encourages you to eat clean, interval training may just be the ticket for you.

about Spartacus is that it is always there for me as a base to modify, and if I get caught up in life and miss a few weeks, I can easily go back to the beginning for renewal.

The Historical and Scientific Basis of Interval Training

If you're thinking this is an awesome new concept in exercise, it's not. Interval training was developed over seventy years ago to improve running performance in the mid-1930s. The development of this unique type of training was happening simultaneously in Sweden and Germany.

The German running coach, Dr. Woldemar Gerschler, was a pioneer attempting to base his training methods on solid physiological and psychological principles. For the physiology, he teamed up with cardiologist Dr. Herbert Reindel in search of a training method that would maximize the fitness and efficiency of the heart. His system focused on greater effort of intensity, followed by periods of rest or light running, this allowed for partial recovery before the next intense effort.

The Swedish coach Gosta Holmer developed a different style of interval training. His style of training called for the athlete to alternate between a fast and slow pace based on how he or she felt. The Swedish word for this

type of training is Fartlek or "speed play." Fartlek is still a popular form of training for runners today.[143]

Interval training faded during World War II, but re-emerged with Emil Zatopek, a Czechoslovakian distance runner best known for winning three gold medals at the 1952 Summer Olympics in Helsinki.[144] As advances in running continued, interval training was used to improve the speed and cardiovascular endurance in sprinting sports like soccer, football, basketball, hockey, tennis, and swimming.

In 1996, Izumi Tabata of the National Institute of Fitness and Sports in Japan published the results of his study on the effects of high intensity interval training. Tabata's evaluated an interval training protocol used by Japanese speed skaters.

His key findings:

• Athletes can achieve maximal oxygen consumption (VO^2) improvement with high intensity interval training

• High intensity interval training yields some anaerobic benefits that cannot be achieved with steady state aerobic exercise alone.[145]

Coaches and trainers have applied the Tabata protocol to many other exercises, including body-weight exercises such as pushups, pull-ups, and burpees. The new regimen involved eight 20-second rounds of intense effort aiming for as many repetitions as possible, each followed by 10 seconds of rest.

Circuit-training routines were then created wherein each station involved a different exercise and followed the Tabata-inspired protocol. Next came the incorporation of resistance training routines using barbells, dumbbells, kettle balls and other weights along with squats and thrusters. Many adaptations have recently become popular with the rise of PX90, Insanity, CrossFit and weight loss programs.

High intensity interval training has a long history of success, has research to confirm its effectiveness, and now comes in a variety of forms, allowing you to tailor an interval regimen to your own goals, interests, and resources. Combined with clean eating, I know of no better way to chip away fat, shape muscle, and bring out the David inside the marble of your body.

Physically Active Kids
Need More Nutritious Foods

Diet and exercise patterns that are established during childhood and adolescence may spell the difference between health and risk of disease in later years. Children are growing and developing teeth, bones, muscles and blood. During this time they need more nutritious food than adults, in proportion to their weight, especially during the growth spurt of puberty.[85]

Key nutrients that children need

Protein. Proteins are a primary component of our muscles, hair, nails, skin, eyes, and internal organs, especially the heart and brain. They are needed for growth and healthy red blood cells.

Iron. It's especially important for teenage girls to get enough iron. Girls commence menstruation at puberty, and with blood loss comes iron loss. It's important to ensure that girls absorb adequate iron from a variety of foods to avoid the unpleasant physical effects of iron deficiency, such as fatigue and shortness of breath.[86]

Iron deficiency anemia is one of the most common diet-related deficiency diseases. Adolescents are particularly susceptible to iron deficiency anemia due to their increased blood volume and muscle mass during growth and development.[86]

Calcium. The skeleton accounts for at least 99% of the body's supply of calcium. Gain in skeletal weight is most rapid during the adolescent growth spurt, during which approximately 45% of the adult skeletal mass is formed. All the calcium for skeleton growth comes from our diet.

We now know that healthy meals and snacks are essential for your child's proper growth and development. Use the list below to ensure that you adequately supply the most essential nutrients to your family.

Foods high in protein, iron and calcium

Protein: beef, chicken, fish, eggs, cheese, tofu, nuts, beans, and seeds.

Iron: clams, mussels, oysters, liver, beef, pork, chicken, turkey, lamb, squash, cashews, pine nuts, hazelnuts, peanuts, almonds, pumpkin seeds, beans, lentils, whole grains, dark leafy greens like spinach and Swiss chard, tofu, and dark chocolate.

Calcium: greens, broccoli, sardines, canned wild salmon, Swiss & gruyere cheese, almonds, sesame seeds, sunflower seeds, soy milk, yogurt, tofu, oatmeal, and oranges.

Foods to Raise a Healthy Brain

Brain health is central to total body health. Remember to account for the brain when cooking, educating, and encouraging your children and family to eat right. Building a healthy brain begins with nutrients that promote brainpower. For starters, blood sugar fuels your brain. This blood sugar is metabolized from carbohydrates, and your brain utilizes an astonishing 20% of the carbohydrates from the foods you eat. Your brain cells need two times more energy than the other cells in your body. In addition to blood sugar, your brain also depends on essential fats and an array of vitamins and minerals.

Complex Carbs vs. Simple Carbs

Carbohydrates are available to us in two forms: complex carbohydrates and simple carbohydrates. Complex carbs deliver optimum brain functionality from a steady supply of starches and sugars taken in from foods like fruits, vegetables, grains, and legumes. These carbs act like time-release capsules of energy. Simple carbs, on the other hand, work more like a quick injection of energy. These carbs are found in most processed, sugary foods and refined flour products. The effect of sugar from these products on the blood stream is fast and furious.

The Brain Power Trifecta

A healthy brain requires balanced levels of blood sugar, along with two other components: essential fats, and a group of four essential vitamins and minerals.

Balanced blood sugar

Antioxidants are one of the keys to balancing and maintaining your blood sugar. They help your blood circulate, they flush out waste, they protect your neurons from damage, and they build communication receptors between brain cells. [87] Common antioxidant-rich foods include kidney, pinto, and red beans, blueberries, strawberries, cranberries, blackberries, raspberries, artichokes, pecans, apples, and prunes.

Essential fats

Omega-3 fatty acids are crucial to eye and brain development. They also help to stabilize mood. Healthy fats are associated with learning because the nutrients promote good blood flow, allowing efficient delivery of oxygen to the brain. Common sources of natural omega-3 are oily fish like salmon, tuna, mackerel, sardines, and herring. It's also prevalent in flax seeds and nuts, especially walnuts.

Vitamin and minerals

Phosphorus: Aids in cognitive growth and development. Common sources are meat, nuts, dairy, legumes, broccoli, and peas.

Choline: An essential nutrient for brain development and memory function. Choline helps the brain communicate with the rest of the body. Common sources are eggs (especially the yolk), beans, Brussels sprouts, broccoli, peanuts, soybeans, potatoes, cauliflower, lentils, oats, sesame seeds, flax seeds, and grass-fed beef.

Lutein: An important phytonutrient that supports eye health and helps regulate overall brain function, cognition, vision, hearing, and speech. Common sources are foods with vibrant colors like beets, spinach, kale, and bell peppers.

Taurine: Another essential amino acid that is important in the health of our vision, brain, and central nervous system. Sources of taurine include chicken, turkey, cottage and ricotta cheeses, granola, oat, wheat germ, eggs, Parmesan cheese, and cod. [88]

The sugar spike from simple carbs creates a roller coast effect that operates as follows: The simple carbs convert to glucose, which in turn leads the pancreas to overproduce insulin. This excess insulin lowers your blood sugar, which causes your energy level to plummet, triggering a craving for more carbs, and the cycle starts all over again.

As you can see, complex carbs offer a steadier supply of blood sugar than simple carbs do and should be the preferred form of carbohydrates for brain health.

Just as an athlete needs nutritious foods to build his legs, arms, and chest muscles, our children need to eat the right foods to build strong, vigorous brains. Every animal you can think of—mammals, birds, reptiles, and fish—has a brain. But the human brain is unique. It gives us the power to speak, think, imagine, love, create, and problem solve. It is truly an amazing organ. As the old saying goes, "Staying sharp all day starts off with a good breakfast." It's as true today as the first time it was said. Today a better turn of phrase might be, "A balanced breakfast of protein and complex carbs fuels your brain all day long!"

Brain Building Foods

Avocado. Naturally rich in healthy fats (omega-3 fatty acids), avocado improves blood flow to the brain, a natural way to enhance brain ability. [89]

Blueberries. Commonly known for their disease fighting antioxidant powers, blueberries have ranked among the healthiest fruits for years. Blueberries also enhance your children's brainpower with B vitamins and folic acid—all needed for healthy brain development. [90]

Dark Greens. Full of folate and vitamins, spinach and kale are part of a healthy diet linked to lower odds of developing dementia later in life. [91] Drew Ramsey, author of 50 Shades of Kale, reported that "kale contains sulforaphane, a molecule that has detoxifying abilities, and diindolylmethane, which helps new brain cells grow." [92]

Eggs. Eggs are well known as a great protein source. Choline is another essential nutrient found in eggs that your body needs for cells to function normally.

Although choline was discovered in 1862, it wasn't identified as an essential nutrient for human health until just 10 years ago. Children have a developing memory center, which is forming during the first 6 years of life. Ensuring that they eat enough choline is essential, as it's an important nutrient in this development. [93]

Kidney Beans. Growing children and adolescents have increased needs for iron. One cup of kidney beans provides almost 30% of the daily-recommended intake for iron. Beans provide great energy from protein, complex carbohydrates and fiber, along with many vitamins and minerals; kidney and pinto beans have more omega-3 fatty acids than others. [94]

Lean Beef. Iron is an essential mineral that helps kids stay energized and focused at school. Lean beef is one of the best sources of iron. In fact, just a single ounce per day has been shown to help the body absorb iron from other sources. Beef also contains zinc, which helps with memory. [95]

Nuts and Seeds. Packed with protein, essential fatty acids, and vitamins and minerals, nuts and seeds may boost mood and keep your nervous system happy. Topping the nut list are walnuts, almonds, cashews, pecans, pine nuts, and flax, sunflower, chia, and pumpkin seeds. [96]

Oatmeal. Oatmeal provides glucose (blood sugar), your brain's basic and most essential fuel. It's also full of fiber, vitamin E, B vitamins, potassium, and zinc—all great for brain function, especially early at the start of the day. [97]

Salmon and Tuna. Omega-3 fatty acids contribute to healthy brain function. They are considered essential fatty acids because the body cannot synthesize them, and so they must be obtained from your diet. Salmon and fresh tuna are high in omega-3s. [98]

Whole Grains. Chock-full of B vitamins and folate, whole-grain bread also trumps white bread because it releases energy more slowly and steadily. The brain needs a constant supply of glucose, which whole grains provide. Most importantly, the fiber contained in whole grains helps regulate the release of glucose. Quinoa contains the highest protein content of all grains. [99]

Striking It Rich: Fats Explained

When you think of oil, what comes to mind? I think of fried chicken—crunchy on the outside, juicy and moist on the inside. I think of yummy sautéed veggies and fresh, lightly dressed salads. The list could go on forever; the possibilities of cooking with oil are endless. So many foods are made better with oil, with its subtle yet powerful impact on the taste, aroma, and wonderful crispy texture of our favorite foods. The smell of onions and garlic being sautéed in extra virgin olive oil makes me salivate.

For centuries, the world has squeezed olives, vegetables, fruits, and seeds to make oils. We rendered animal fats to make ingredients like butter, margarine, ghee, and lard. Fortunately it's a bit easier today. Instead of squeezing whole ingredients, all we have to do is choose the oils we need from a shelf in the market.

For years fats have carried a bad reputation due to reports about the unhealthy trans fats used in the mass production of processed foods, and their use in fast food chains. But not all fats are bad. In fact, some fats are essential for your family's health and development. Finally we are starting to become educated about the indisputable fact that our bodies need fats from oil to function smoothly, and to continue to stay healthy and fine-tuned. Fats occur naturally in the plants and animals we consume. It is one of the three essential nutrients the human body requires to sustain life. The other two are carbohydrates and protein.

Your Body Needs Good Fats To Stay Healthy

Fat contains essential nutrients your body uses to make tissue and manufacture proteins, nucleotides, and lipids. Consuming the wrong fats may be harmful to your health. The trick is choosing the good fats and oils over the bad, whether you are cooking in or eating out. Children whose diets include too many bad fats may have a higher risk of increased cholesterol levels, weight issues, and heart disease later in life.[100]

Gram for gram, fats are the most efficient source of food energy for humans. They have more than twice as much energy potential (calories) as protein and carbohydrates. Each gram of fat provides nine calories of energy for the body, compared with four calories per gram of carbohydrates or proteins.[101]

Good fats promote healthy skin, too. The early Greeks and Romans may have been the first cultures to enjoy the benefits of exfoliation. They used olive oil and sand to scrub their skin clean. In addition to giving skin its radiant appeal, the layer of fat just beneath the skin acts as the body's own insulation and helps regulate body temperature.

Know Your Fat:
Monounsaturated, Polyunsaturated, Saturated, and Trans Fats

Good fats:

• *Monounsaturated and polyunsaturated*

There are two types of polyunsaturated fat: omega-3 and omega-6. These are also known as essential fatty acids. Unsaturated fats help us produce good cholesterol, keep arteries clear, and reduce bad cholesterol, which is associated with heart problems.[102] Eating foods with unsaturated fats can help avoid these problems later in life.

• *Monounsaturated fats*

Monounsaturated fats are found in abundance in olive oil, canola oil, avocado, seeds, nuts, and nut butters. These healthy sources of fat also add flavor, help satiate your appetite, and protect your heart by lowering blood pressure. Work them into the family's diet with snacks like nuts and seeds instead of cookies, pretzels, crackers, ding dongs, or candy.

• *Polyunsaturated fats*

Polyunsaturated fats are found in flax seeds, flax seed oil, and walnuts. One type of polyunsaturated fat, omega-3 fatty acids, may be especially beneficial to your heart. Fatty fish are the best food sources for this essential fatty acid. Fish particularly rich in omega-3 fatty acids are salmon, sardines, mackerel, herring, trout, and fresh tuna.

Bad fats:

• *Saturated and trans*

Both kinds of fat increase the production of bad cholesterol and can reduce good cholesterol. Both can also increase the risk of heart disease later in life.[103] Be careful, though: not all saturated fats are bad; in fact your body needs these fats as well. Healthier versions of saturated fats come from lean red meat, skinless poultry, fish, and shellfish.

• *Saturated fats*

Foods high in saturated fats are often high in calories and low in essential nutrients. Milk and cheese products can be high in saturated fats. Pizza and dairy desserts, like ice cream and pudding, are among the top sources of saturated fat in the typical American diet.

• *Trans fats*

Trans fatty acids are chemically altered man-made fats found in partially hydrogenated oils. Although trans fats make food taste better, they are addictive and dangerous. Trans fats can also raise cholesterol and increase the risk of heart disease. They're used in the fast food industry because they're cost-effective, act as preservatives, add flavor, and can be reused. The tradeoff, of course, is that you're gambling with your health. Foods high in trans fat include cookies, crackers, cakes, muffins, pie crusts, pizza dough, margarine, vegetable shortening, cake mixes, pancake mixes, chocolate drink mixes, donuts, French fries, potato chips, candy, packaged popcorn, frozen dinners, and fast foods.

Prominent Oils

Smoke Points

When you are choosing which oil to cook with the most significant factor to consider is its smoke point, or the temperature at which any oil will start to smoke and break down. All cooking oils and fats react differently to heat. In general, the hotter they get, the more they break down and eventually start to smoke. Some oils should not be heated because they have a low smoke point, and their health benefits can be eroded in the heating process.

Grape Seed Oil

Touted for its anti-aging properties, grape seed oil is high in vitamin E and linoleic acid. Grape seed is a multi-purpose oil, and you can use is it for skin care, braising, frying, or baking. Grape seed oil is mild in flavor and has a high smoke point, making it good choice for cooking over high heat. If you are looking to move away from vegetable oil for cooking, this is a great replacement. Use it to dress salads and raw veggies or to make dips and sauces.

Extra-Virgin Olive Oil

Olive oil is probably the most popular and healthiest of all the cooking oils. When researchers began investigating why people in the Mediterranean region live longer lives than others, they found that this resulted largely from their healthy diet, [104] which includes heavy consumption of olive oil. Use it in dressings, drizzle on steamed vegetables, or sauté onions, garlic, and veggies in it. When you fry eggs, replace the butter with olive oil. You can also use olive oil to clean and moisturize your skin.

Canola Oil

Canola oil is beneficial for heart health, thanks to its fatty acid profile and omega-3s. Canola oil is good for light cooking, sauces, and even desserts. Canola's neutral flavor and high smoke point make it an excellent choice for braising, baking, and sautéing. Canola oil has a low level of saturated fats and is the most cost effective for frying.

Walnut Oil

Rich in omega-3 fatty acids, vitamins B1, B2, and B3, vitamin E, and niacin, the health benefits of walnuts were first identified in 1931.[105] Interest has grown over the past decade. Walnut oil has a rich, nutty flavor that is best used uncooked in cold sauces and salads, tossed in pasta, or brushed on grilled fish or meat just before serving. It can also jazz up desert recipes with a nutty flavor!

Avocado Oil

Avocado oil is one of the few plant oils not obtained from a seed. Instead, it is pressed from the fruit of the avocado. Buttery in taste, it contains monounsaturated fat and supplies lutein, an antioxidant that improves eye health. Considered to have highest smoke point of any plant oil, you can use avocado oil for high-heat cooking. It's also yummy when added to salad dressings or drizzled over crusty bread and melons.

Peanut Oil

Peanut oil has a high smoke point, which makes it perfect for pan-frying and deep-frying foods. Wonderfully pleasant and sweet, peanut oil is low in saturated fats, has healthy proportions of monounsaturated and polyunsaturated fats, is free from cholesterol, and contains linoleic acid, an omega-6 essential fatty acid.

Sesame Oil

Essential to Asian cooking, especially stir-fry, sesame oil has a rich, nutty flavor. Sesame oil consists of oleic acid (the heart-healthy fatty acid found in olive oil) and linoleic acid. It also contains sesamin, an antioxidant that helps keep the oil and foods that are made with it from spoiling.

Flaxseed oil

Flaxseed oil is a good source for omega-3s, but due to its low smoke point it should not be used for cooking over heat. It is best mixed into foods after they've already been cooked, like oatmeal. You can also use it in smoothies or as a salad dressing.

Coconut oil

New to many people but gaining popularity, coconut oil contains a saturated fat called lauric acid. It has been shown that lauric acid increases the good HDL cholesterol in the blood to help improve cholesterol ratio levels. Coconut oil has a high smoking point, so it's great for sautéed dishes. Coconut oil is renowned for being a healthy, flavorful alternative to butter in many types of baked goods. Just remember that coconut oil contains more calories than butter.

Sunflower Oil

Sunflower oil has become very popular over the past few years as a substitute for other cooking oils because of its healthy properties. Sunflower oil is an excellent source of vitamin E, a powerful antioxidant proven to reduce heart disease and promote healthy skin and hair. Other important nutrients in sunflower oil include magnesium and folic acid. Sunflower oil is versatile and extremely light in flavor, so the oil doesn't overpower the rest of a dish's ingredients, making it ideal for sautéing.

If you want simple, start simple. Don't expect to easily create simplicity from complexity.

—Steve Jobs

Buying *Two Pans and a Pot*

Simplicity Leads to Excellence

It was two months into Roy's first semester at The Culinary Institute of America in Hyde Park, New York. He was home for the weekend. In celebration, I had planned to impress the chef in training with a fabulous home-cooked dinner. But when I opened the cabinet, every pot and pan I owned was gone. Who on earth, I wondered, would come into my house and only steal pots and pans?

Imagine my surprise when I told Roy what had happened and he admitted that he was the culprit. No, he hadn't lent them out or sold them off; he had thrown them in the garbage. I was livid. I hadn't seen him in two months and within two hours I was panless and potless. He proceeded to explain that most cookware materials are hazardous to our health, and that CIA recommends that all their chefs cook strictly with stainless steel.

There was a new culinary sheriff in town. It took me a moment to simmer down and see the humor in the situation. The fact was that the cookware he tossed out was old and not very good. Roy said the Teflon pan was proven to be toxic, especially when chipped. If nothing else, it proved to me my hard-earned money was being put to good use. He was clearly learning at CIA.

To cook each recipe in "Two Pans and a Pot"—and most other recipes you'll come across—all you will need are three cookware items: a roasting pan, a sautoir pan (also called a frying pan), and a stockpot. With less equipment you'll get more use out of each item, develop efficiency

Stainless Steel "grades"

18/0 stainless steel:
- Contains no nickel
- Does not conduct heat well
- Cannot use on stovetop
- Magnetic
- Rust resistant
- Will not hold up or clean well
- Less expensive

18/8 stainless steel:
- Middle of the road
- Stove top cooking not recommended
- Non-magnetic
- Rust resistant

18/10 stainless steel:
- Non-magnetic
- Can use on stovetop
- Better shine
- Better rust resistance & hardness
- Durable
- Low maintenance
- Doesn't react with foods / healthier
- Rust resistant
- Worth the investment
- Will last forever

with the equipment you do have, and find your kitchen less cluttered. It's easy to fill cupboards with items and equipment that promise to make your life easier but fail to deliver. I've found that you can de-clutter your kitchen and still have everything you need within easy reach. Plus, buying fewer pieces allows you to buy higher quality cookware.

Royal and I recommend stainless steel cookware. Before we get into the reasons for this, let's talk about the composition of stainless steel. Stainless steel is an alloy that starts with basic iron. The iron is then compounded with up to eight alloys, depending on the quality. The major alloys in stainless steel are chromium and nickel. Chromium provides protection from rust and corrosion and improves durability. Nickel adds a polished look, additional rust resistance, and hardness. Because these metals are not the best conductors of heat, either copper or aluminum is added to the bottom of the pan or pot to increase the ability to conduct heat evenly.

There are also varying thicknesses in stainless steel pots and pans, and you should go for the heavier gauge. Heavy-gauge pans deliver heat more evenly, and their bottoms are less likely to dent, warp, or burn your food. And if your stovetop is electric, flat bottoms are particularly important.

When you're shopping for your pots and pans you'll see that stainless steel pans are graded based on metal ratios: 18/0, 18/8, and 18/10. The first number is the percentage of chromium, which is usually 18%. The second number is the amount of nickel, which comes in 0%, 8%, or 10% grades. The higher the nickel content, the better the quality of the stainless steel. A simple way to test for nickel is to place a magnet against the pan. If the pan is magnetic, it is 18/0, containing no nickel. If it's not magnetic, the pan is 18/8 or 18/10.

Stainless steel cookware is virtually indestructible. It can handle extreme temperatures. It won't chip. It is resistant to rust, stains, and corrosion. You cannot easily dent or scratch it. It is easy to clean and dishwasher safe. The nickel in the alloy will also keep the stainless steel pans looking like new for a long time, with very little maintenance.

And with stainless steel there's no need to worry about the metal reacting with foods, especially acidic foods like tomatoes. The smooth non-porous surface allows the pans to be easily sanitized, so killing germs and preventing

Stainless Steel Cooking Rule N° 1

Always, always, properly preheat your pan
Stainless steel is a versatile material. It allows you to quickly whip up scrambled eggs for breakfast or slow-cook braised short ribs for a winter family dinner. The first secret to cooking with stainless steel is simple: stainless steel pans must be preheated before you put food in the pan. If you've ever tried to make scrambled eggs in a stainless steel pan without preheating it, I'll bet the eggs stuck to the pan. Want your eggs to slide across the surface like an Olympic ice skater? Preheat the pan and allow the butter or oil to heat up before you pour in the eggs.

How do you know when a pan is hot enough?
Place the pan on a burner over medium-high heat. Give the pan a minute to warm up, and then add a drop of water to your pan. If it bounces and sizzles away, it's not hot enough yet. When you add a drop of water to the pan and it moves like mercury and doesn't sizzle away, your pan is hot enough. Now add the oil. Wait until the oil is hot enough. You'll be able to identify this point because the oil becomes streaky like ripples on a lake. Now you're ready to sear, sauté, or fry. Follow these two steps, and you'll never have issues with food sticking to the pan. Before long, you'll instinctively know when the pan is hot enough.

residue is easy. Thorough cleaning is important because it thwarts the microscopic growth of bacteria caused by leftover food particles. The hard, non-porous surface also prohibits the absorption and transfer of odors and tastes like onion and garlic from one recipe to another.

Buying Two Pans and a Pot

The beauty of buying separate pieces of cookware rather than a full set allows you to pick and choose the pieces you like and that you feel most comfortable using. You have less clutter in the cabinet and more money to spend on quality pieces. Buying pots and pans separately also allows you the flexibility to choose different weights or handle angles for flexibility in your hand. It doesn't matter if the pieces don't match. This is about function, efficiency, and cooking to feed your family. Plus an eclectic mix of different cookware, adds character to the kitchen. Go for the best quality you can. It's worth it in the end because your two pans and a pot will last a lifetime.

The Roasting Pan

Roasting pans are designed to withstand very high heat in the oven. Make sure to invest in a quality pan that will not warp when you use it on the stovetop as well. A quality-roasting pan on your stovetop is perfect for sauces and gravies, or for sweating vegetables.

Depth is also important. Shallower pans cook foods more quickly, but that's not always what you want. For our one-pan roasting technique a deeper pan is the key to roasting meats and vegetables in their own juices. Ever have smoke come out of your oven while you roasted? That is most likely because the juices bubbled up splashed around and wound up on the bottom of your oven! That's why we like a deeper pan.

Many roasting pans come with non-stick roasting racks. Don't choose a pan based on the rack; roasting racks can be bought separately and are relatively inexpensive. The most common rack is the "V" rack, which holds the roast high. If you prefer a rack that holds the roast lower in the pan there is the "C" rack. Your third option is a flat rack, which is more versatile than the other two. Roasting racks are great. I love mine for roasting duck, which always ends up delicious, perfectly cooked, and crispy on all sides.

As far as shape goes, a rectangular roasting pan is generally the most effective choice. Try to buy one that has its corners rounded: it's easier for scooping items out, like sauce or gravy, and makes tasks like whisking easier. When it comes to roasting pans, size matters. Make sure there's enough space to allow air to circulate around your food in the pan. This ensures even, effective roasting.

Roasting pans also differ in the design of their handles. Traditional French-style roasting pans have riveted handles that horizontally extend out from the pan's sides, making them easy to grip. A similar style has handles that curve in toward the pan, making it a little harder to grip but requiring less room in the oven. The last notable type has folding handles, which also use less room in the oven. I've found that these handles can be hard to grip when you are wearing oven mitts.

The Sautoir Pan

Our second pan of choice is the multi-functional sautoir (saw-TWAH) pan, with a tight fitting lid. This simple French design is perfect for braising and pilaf. It also combines the talents of the sauté pan and the stewing pan. The definitive benefit over the sauté and stewing pans is that the sautoir pan typically has a heavier bottom, which cooks more evenly. It also has higher, straighter sides that contain splatters during stir-frying and pan-frying, and liquids during braising or poaching. After all, safety in the kitchen is paramount when you have kids.

Like all high quality stainless steel cookware, the sautoir pan delivers delicious caramelization and deglazing to create five-star flavors.

The Stockpot

The third item in our trio of stainless steel simplicity is the multipurpose stockpot. I find it funny that a lot of people own stockpots but never make stock. When Roy was growing up, I was one of those people. I loved using the stockpot for braising on a Sunday afternoon, or for cooking chicken soup on a cold winter weekend, but never for making stock.

So you're probably wondering, "What's the best size?" For family cooking the 10-quart stockpot is the most useful size. It's the biggest "small" pot for the job. The 10-quart stockpot can handle your large weekend jobs, yet is small enough for the quick-steamed vegetable, rice, or pasta dishes.

This pot gives you lots of flexibility. Use it for steaming or blanching vegetables, or for cooking stews, rice, chili, pasta, or even lobsters. Its size and depth suit it perfectly for anything that requires a lot of liquid. The stockpot unlocks the culinary kingdom of ingredients and flavor. The stainless steel quality measurement is the same for this pot as for the two pans: 18/0, 18/08, and 18/10.

I prefer a wide stockpot to a tall and narrow one. A wider pot allows you to see and maneuver the food better and is without a doubt easier to clean. If you have a smaller kitchen with less storage space, you might consider the tall style. Both types of pot will give you great results.

When it comes to stockpots, handles matter. A lot. The stockpot can get pretty heavy when it's filled with chicken soup or chili. Look for handles that are easy to grip, especially using potholders. The most common handles are flat, thick, or round. When you are in the store browsing for a stockpot, pick up the pot you are considering with pot-holders for a test run.

Stainless Steel Cooking Rule N° 2

For goodness sake, let the meat brown correctly
The second secret to cooking like a chef in stainless steel pans is browning meat properly. The most common mistake we all make is turning the food too soon, before it browns nicely. Stop messing with the food, and let your ingredients actually cook until they are dark golden brown and stick a little to the pan. When you let the food brown this way, the Maillard process begins, proteins are released, and starches caramelize, turning to sugars.

The brown liquid and dark bits that stick to the bottom of your pan, collectively called fond, are a goldmine of flavor. Fond delivers the enticing, heady aroma that fills your home with love. That brown stuff, desired by professional chefs, provides the flavorful foundation of braises, sautés, sauces, soups, stews, pilaf, and gravies.

This happens because the drippings from the proteins, fats, and carbohydrates stick to the pan, brown, and convert into more complex compounds. You're not just cooking the food—you're actually changing its flavors and adding to it as you let the foods brown properly. In other words, when it comes to browning, sticking is key. No sticking means no browning, and no browning means no flavor.

The chef's knife
is the culinary
paintbrush,
the cutting board
the pallet,
and nature's ingredients
the medium of choice

The One Knife Chef

Why is the chef's knife the only blade you'll need?

Every night at 6 p.m. the mad rush begins, just like rush hour. Only the rush hour takes place in your kitchen, not on the road. It's dinner hour—the daily test of your efficiency, patience, and multitasking skills. The 8-inch chef's knife is the essential kitchen tool for maximum efficiency. It allows you to multitask with confidence rather than waste time switching knives to chop, cut, clean, dice, or disjoint large cuts of meat. Plus, there's less to clean up.

Going with only one chef's knife also leaves room in your budget for a knife of the highest quality. Don't let a high price turn you off; it's worth the investment. It will last a lifetime, like a family heirloom.

Just as a great meal begins with fresh ingredients, production of a superior knife begins with high quality materials. Roy and I go with the forged 8-inch carbon stainless steel chef's knife. The heavy and durable blade sharpens easily, holds a sharp edge, and won't rust, tarnish, or discolor. The carbon adds strength to the steel

Just as a great meal begins with fresh ingredients, production of a superior knife begins with high quality materials.

To the chef, knife quality is crucial. Sharp knife in hand, the chef becomes an artist whose hands and imagination shape the culinary kingdom. The chef's knife is the culinary paintbrush, the cutting board the pallet, and nature's ingredients the medium of choice.

The only other knife you need is a serrated utility knife for slicing breads, roasts, and hard-crust foods. Ever try slicing fresh bread with a non-serrated knife? It's like trying to cut a watermelon with a seashell. It's dangerous because you can easily cut yourself. Be safe and use the right tool. A bread knife's serrated edge does most of the work for you. It's not essential to get the most expensive bread knife, leaving you more savings to put toward a nice carbon stainless steel chef's knife.

The History
of the Chef's Knife

I'm always fascinated by the history and evolution of the basic culinary tools that are still used in our kitchens today. In the roasting section we'll talk about how the caveman discovered how to cook meat. Learning how to divide the food amongst the clan not only set a tone for structure, it initiated the division of responsibility between men and women. [106] At first they used sharpened stones or finely honed edges of seashell to cut the roasted meat into portions for the cave clan. Later, stone knives were polished and attached to wood or bone for handles. [107]

The big leap in culinary evolution came with the discovery and harnessing of metals. Around 3,000 BCE in Southwest Asia people began to use copper metal knives. [108] Once our early ancestors figured out how to combine copper with tin, the Bronze Age was born. It probably took around a thousand years or so for this new discovery to reach Europe, where it was most likely used to create weapons and armor for conquering nations. With this new technology the local chef was also able to develop metal knives for cooking and eating, which revolutionized the culinary technique of cutting ingredients—Ah! We just uncovered the birth of the original foodie movement!

Next was the arrival of the Iron Age. The Greeks harnessed iron to make quality, efficient steel weaponry, armor, and knives. The Germans became efficiency masters in their production methods, and the Japanese developed the Samurai sword. Germany and Japan, the two primary producers of cutlery today, were also the key regions for sword production. Thus, the history of the sword is also the history of the chef's knife.

The chef's knife can be traced back to 1731 when Peter Henkel founded and manufactured cutlery for what would become the worldwide knife empire that still exists today.

How to Use Your Knife

Safety and Precision Knife skills

For safety in precision cutting, we suggest the simple guiding hand technique. As you grip the object you're going to cut, tuck your fingertips slightly under. Tuck your thumb back from your fingertips. The knife blade should then rest against the knuckles, allowing you to cut with precision while protecting your fingers. The photos below illustrate this technique on a variety of ingredients we cook with in Two Pans and a Pot. With a little practice you'll be slicing and dicing in no time.

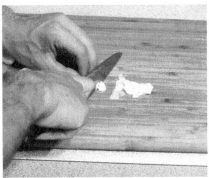

How to Begin Your Family's Culinary Journey

There is magic that happens in the kitchen, a transformation of delight and intrigue when it comes to mixing ingredients. Aromas fill the air, steam rises, and sizzling sounds resonate while delicious scents of sautéed onions and garlic enter our imaginations. Nature's brilliant offerings from around the world are at your fingertips. Crunchy vegetables, delectable fruits, grains, herbs, poultry, and fish spirited with life are all brought together by you, the cook, to create meals that nourish your family.

We begin with fundamentals. People put down cookbooks and skip recipes because they lack familiarity with ingredients and cooking techniques or fear the process will take too long. Once you master the basic techniques, become more acquainted with ingredients, and gain confidence, you will be able to follow most recipes.

The Process: Intuitive Cooking

I've met a lot of overwhelmed home cooks who lack confidence in their natural abilities. I'm here to tell you that cooking isn't as hard as it may seem, and that you already possess all the instincts required to make balanced, tasty meals your family will love. You just have to log a few practice hours and trust your potential. The human species wouldn't have survived this long if we did not inherently

know how to feed ourselves. I promise you, the skills are there, buried inside you, no matter how disastrous past cooking attempts may have been. I'm here to help you unlock your culinary kingdom.

I don't want to teach you how to memorize recipes. I want to show you how to cook using your instincts and what you already have on-hand in your kitchen. Cooking in this manner allows you greater freedom to produce more nutritious meals. These time-tested, simple, and efficient techniques will also allow you to spend more time with your family around the table. Plus, passing these techniques down to your kids will lay the foundation for them to build their own culinary kingdoms. Imagine your children intuitively using brain-building ingredients to cook meals for their own families. Cooking together will strengthen you both as individuals and as a family unit.

I'm convinced that we are all capable of intuitive cooking. It might be hidden in your subconscious, but I believe it's a characteristic that each one of us inherently posses. Cooking is an outlet that enables you to be creative and produce a finished product that sparks lively dialogue. More than that, feeding our children and partners is a fundamental part of the human experience and part of the DNA that sustains our family units. I've personally given this a great deal of thought as a single parent and as a novice cook, mainly because I've learned that not all people like to cook. For a lot of people the thought of cooking beyond the basic tuna sandwich can prove intimidating. But this is perception, not reality. The thought of running a 26-mile marathon may seem completely out of reach to some seasoned runners. But it's not truly out of reach; it's doable—just like intuitive cooking.

Perceptions often prove unnecessarily limiting. For example, in 1954, the world believed that no one could run the mile in less than four minutes. However the current world record is 3 minutes, 43.13 seconds, set by Hicham El

Guerrouj of Morocco on July 7th 1999 in Rome, Italy. Just as the fastest sprinters in the world do not let perceptions limit them, we must push past our own perceptions and believe that successful intuitive cooking is possible. Hicham shows that anyone with enough determination and passion can be just inches away from experiencing huge successes and breakthroughs in their lives.

What we put in our minds ultimately determines how well we do. This section of the book will help you build and reinforce the fundamentals and inspire your intuitive cooking sense. The days of fretting over missing a step in a recipe and delivering a disastrous dish are behind you. Enjoy this guide as a way to free yourself from the restrictions of by-the-book cooking.

When preparing meals, most of the time you'll cook based on what's in the fridge on any given day. Today we are trained to follow a recipe's exact ingredients, measurements, and processes. Throw that notion out with the onion-skins! How many times have you stood in front of the refrigerator staring at the items on the shelves waiting for something inspirational to hit you? This is the critical time to free your creative and confident inner chef to create an awesome meal.

All you need are three cooking techniques: roasting, braising, and pilaf. I will teach you each method as a comprehensive cooking principle. Each principle reduces prep time, cooking time, clean up, and expense. Using these techniques, along with fewer pots, pans, and ingredients, you will become an efficient cook.

Getting Started with Vegetable Trios
Whether you're building a website, responding to an email, or deciding what's for dinner, how and where to start is often the most difficult part—a real brainteaser at times. Having a process enables you to begin with confidence every time.

When it comes to cooking, there is a process you can follow which also allows you to be creative and make every dish your own. From Oso Bucco to jambalaya, a mixture of three to four aromatic vegetables is used to create different types of soups, stews, gravies, sauces, braises and classics from around the globe. The tastiest dishes from around the world commonly begin with a trio of simple, sautéed plant ingredients—a true gift from nature's garden.

In the French cuisine it's called mirepoix, a combination of finely diced onions, celery and carrots sautéed in butter.

The Italian cuisine has a similar version called saffritto. They swap out the butter for olive oil and often add garlic. In Cajun cuisine it's the Holy Trinity. They use green peppers instead of carrots as the base flavor for dishes like gumbo and etouffees. Likewise, a Spanish sofrito consists of onions, tomatoes, garlic and parsley cooked in olive oil.

The concept also shows up in the cuisines of Asia. Many Indian dishes start with a combination of onion, garlic, ginger, and some variety of hot pepper. In Thailand, curry pastes begin with a combination of lemongrass, shallots and chilies. In China the trio is scallions, garlic and ginger.

What I love about trios is that they put you into a cooking process that is so easy to master that, once you know it, you can enjoy cooking and let your creative juices flow. You are set free to experiment with a variety of herbs and spices, vegetables and proteins.

Being creative in the kitchen is a process that cultivates cutting edge ideas and recipes. These chopped up plant trios give each dish its cultural identity and flavor profile. Chefs from around the world use the trio technique to marry flavors to create their signature dishes as well as infuse new concepts. From Italy to China, these ancient recipe starters can guide your intuitive magic wand of one-pot cooking.

For delicious home cooking you have the freedom to choose the trios that fit your lifestyle with the ingredients you have on hand. You can just as easily use your trio whole, fine or roughly chopped. That is what I love about intuitive cooking; you cannot make a mistake, and you always have a place to start.

Trios truly are your chef window into the culinary kingdom, and I'm excited to get you started. Here are some distinctive combinations that are sure to awaken flavors in your kitchen and joy throughout your house:

Cajun/Creole: celery, bell peppers, onion
Chinese: scallions, ginger, garlic
Cuban: garlic, bell peppers, Spanish onion
French: onion, celery, carrots
Greek: lemon juice, olive oil, oregano
Indian: garlic, ginger, onion
Indonesian: coconut, chili peppers and fish
Jamaican: garlic, scallion and thyme
Southern Italian: tomato, garlic, basil
Spanish: garlic, onion, tomato
Thai: basil, ginger, and lemongrass
West African: chili pepper, onion, tomato

Cooking Techniques

Master one roast and you can master any roast. Create one braise and you can create any braise. Dominate one pilaf and you can dominate any pilaf.

A recipe is a list of ingredients with step-by-step directions, whereas a cooking technique involves preparing ingredients for any recipe. A cooking technique is transferable from one recipe to another. Mastering techniques and applying them to multiple dishes leads to efficiency. And efficiency leads to better productivity, allowing you extra time in the day to sustain a more balanced lifestyle for you and your family.

In our Western culinary culture, most home-cooked dishes base their methods on French cooking techniques simply because the French were the first to document and methodize cooking procedures. Techniques for preparing food in Western cuisine are beating, chopping, creaming, crimping, deboning, de-seeding, dicing, filleting, glazing, grating, peeling, rolling, shredding, skinning, slicing, tenderizing, and zesting. Techniques for cooking foods are baking, boiling, braising, broiling, frying, grilling, roasting, poaching, sautéing, steaming, and stewing.

Timing

Good timing is an essential skill in many areas of life. Ask any musician about timing; they'll tell you on-point timing is paramount. If you've ever tried karaoke you know that the music doesn't follow you—you have to follow the music. The timing of a joke can determine whether the audience laughs at the punch line or not. Comedian Steven Wright is a consummate timing master in his unassuming monotone delivery: "Last night I went to a 24-hour grocery. When I got there, the guy was locking the front door. I said, 'Hey, the sign says you're open 24 hours.' The clerk replied, 'Not in a row.'"

Getting a feel for good timing is important to success in the kitchen as well. Timing develops quickly with practice until it becomes intuitive. Remember the first time you

drove a car by yourself? You had to think about every little thing: steering, checking mirrors, using turn signals. But now you just do these things without thinking. Learning to trust your instincts when you cook is just like that: the more you try, the easier and more natural it will feel, the more you'll trust your instincts, and the more confidence you'll gain. When preparing a meal, you'll instinctively know how to cook it, at about what temperature, for about how long, and what the dish should look like when it's done.

When preparing ingredients let's look at production line theory. To increase your speed in the kitchen the first step here is to read your menu all the way through and determine what kind of prep work is involved. It's going to be a lot faster if you do the same motion whenever possible. For example, if you're peeling a cucumber, peel all the fruits and vegetables you'll need for the meal at the same time. If you're dicing carrots, go ahead and cut all the vegetables you'll need, like your onions, fresh herbs, and garlic.

When you are doing the same motion you will accomplish the task at hand more quickly because you aren't putting the knife down in between cuts. Remember, saving time is all about effective prep work paying off. After all your ingredients are diced chopped, cleaned, and prepped you'll feel like a super star. Save even more time by doing the prep the day or evening before.

French efficiency: mise en place

Ever wonder how restaurants are able to serve so many different dishes at the same time? The real secret to their efficiency and success in the kitchen goes back to the manufacturing principles of mise en place.

Mise en place roughly translates as "put in place." In a nutshell, mise en place means preparing all ingredients before you start cooking. It boils down to efficiency. Prepare your work environment so that once you start cooking, you don't have to stop to do anything other than add the next ingredient.

To increase your speed in the kitchen the first step here is to read your menu all the way through and determine what kind of prep work is involved. It's going to be a lot faster if you do the same motion whenever possible.

There are three simple steps to mise en place:

Tools: Ensure you have all of the necessary tools called for in the dishes you're making before you get started. This includes pans, pots, a roasting tray, grater, peeler, dish towel, etc. Review the menu all the way through, and note all the tools. If something is called for at any point, make sure you have it handy.

Ingredients: Ensure you have all your ingredients for the menu on hand. It sounds so simple, yet how many times have you discovered after you've started that you are missing an item? Pay special attention to ingredient notes while organizing your mise en place. Clean, wash, peel, cut, dice, chop, grate, or mince all of the ingredients needed so they're all ready to go before you start cooking.

Clean as you go: The old me would say, "To keep the kitchen clean—eat out." Now, I'm all about "Clean as you go," which greatly reduces clean up time at the end of the meal. The last thing you want to do after a fantastic meal is clean dishes, right? Clean-as-you-go keeps the work area clean and organized at all times while preparing meals. This includes cleaning up spills, wiping down surfaces, removing waste, and washing used bowls, pots, and pans. A clean kitchen makes the cooking even more enjoyable.

A good example of how you've already used *mise en place* in your kitchen is the simple task of making an almond butter-and-jelly sandwich for your little one. Without thinking about it, you naturally round up all the ingredients needed put them on the table or counter and get them ready for assembly. You round up the jars of almond butter and jelly, the bread, a knife, possibly a cutting board, and a plate. You gather all the makings before you even think of putting the sandwich together. Sound easy? It is! So why not apply the same natural thought process to all your cooking?

Believe me, put *mise en place* into action, and you will discover that life in the kitchen will be smoother, more gratifying, and more creative. Mise en place will truly help you to become a superior cook, there's not a doubt in my mind. Now you will be able to focus on the most fun part of preparing a meal; cooking it. Turn your kitchen counter into the mise en place learning center and begin teaching your little sous chefs to help you!

Cooking Together as a Family

Cooking with your children removes the boundaries between education and life. The kitchen is a natural laboratory where kids relish learning. Cooking is a great teacher because it's a tactile, visual, and auditory experience.

When children help prepare a meal, they often become agreeable, inquisitive, and creative, taking ownership and pride in what they are doing. This is a great way to establish an open dialogue, which will benefit both you and your children. Cooking together opens up a communication style that allows give-and-take, comforting and nourishing a child's soul and brain.

The world is abundant with choices and opportunities. Cooking with your children is a superb choice. It contributes to their self-worth and shows them how much fun can come from taking on a new adventure. When you focus on the positive, your child will learn to do so as well and enjoy positive relationships, whether in business with coworkers or in life with loved ones. Communication and building relationships are critical to have joy in the real world. Above all, children must be confident in a parent's love, acceptance, and understanding. When this is present and evident, most children can cope better with the challenges life will present them.

Our children today are growing up digitally with a very different worldview than the one we once had. Traditional job roles still exist, but a new trend is emerging: to be self-employed, own your own business, and pursue creative activities. Those who succeed today are good at finding niches and gaps in the market and driving towards them. "Security" and "consistency" aren't buzzwords in their employment vocabulary. As you raise your own children this is important to understand. Outside-the-box thinking, problem solving, socialization, and creative assertiveness are important elements of success for the current generation of leaders we're raising. Cooking with your children will help them develop these skills.

Cooking nourishes all developmental areas: cognitive, physical, mental, social and emotional. At the

kitchen counter, children learn comparative words as they measure and pour liquids. They develop problem-solving skills through experimentation, and observe cause and effect when they transform raw food ingredients into a remarkable meal. Cooking has the potential to support learning in diverse areas of your child's life. Kids who actively cook with their parents are challenged to exercise skills in the areas of reading, following directions, fractions, counting, money, vocabulary, shapes, colors, chemistry, nature, social studies, geography, health, and nutrition.

Cooking also inspires children's curiosity and creative thinking. Kids become curious and will ask you questions like, "Where does broccoli come from?" Be prepared to explain your broccoli's origins, and how it's grown. (Tip: this is far easier to do if you purchase your broccoli from a local farmer.) As you and your child experiment with different ingredients, dishes, and cooking techniques, you encourage risk-taking and openness to new experiences. And don't be surprised if your child pushes you to think outside of your box!

Most importantly, the cooking learning process creates lifelong memories for your children—and maybe even for your children's children one day.

Family Meals

With our busy schedules, sitting down together for a family meal just doesn't seem to be a priority. Instead, in the guise of making life easier, the pattern often finds everyone departing to his or her choice of entertainment. Computers, social media, video games, and television are all culprits. Socializing with friends and homework, too. **Any parent would say that their children's well-being is top priority. However, siting down for a healthy meal together has become less of a priority.**

Two Pans and a Pot builds and reinforces your culinary confidence by teaching you three techniques: braising, roasting, and pilaf. Learning the principles behind these simple cooking methods will enable you to master most recipes and create delicious, nutritional dinners quickly, even on busy nights. These three efficient techniques are designed for cooking big batches that can be easily frozen. We know kids love to help in the kitchen, and the benefits are enormous. Utilize your new sous chefs over the weekend and cook nutritious meals to enjoy throughout the week.

Benefits of Family Meals

Research has shown that in families that frequently eat together, the children benefit in numerous ways.[109] Kids are happier, healthier, and feel more secure. They get better grades and are less likely to be overweight, smoke, drink, or use drugs. Unsurprisingly, results from recent studies about consistent family meals show that these children tend to have better relationships with their parents and their siblings.[110]

In other words, the more often you eat together as a family the better emotional, mental, and physical health they will enjoy. The result of cooking and sharing meals, whether it's breakfast, lunch or dinner, is priceless. The rewards for building these dining habits for your family far outweigh the challenges you face to do so. I'm here to make it easier for you to get there, having walked the path myself.

Here are three statistics ascribed to one family ritual—family mealtimes. Children of families that share at least three meals a week are

- 35% less likely to engage in eating disorders
- 24% more likely to eat healthy foods
- 12% less likely to be overweight[111]

In families that eat dinner together regularly, the children—even teenagers—actually want to do so more often. Here are a few more ways that family meals benefit everyone at the table:

- Family meals provide a sense of unity and identity. Family meals become a vehicle for carrying on valued family traditions and favorite dishes for celebrations. To this day my older brother still has to have a seven-layer chocolate cake on his birthday.

- Family meals give us the opportunity to talk about family happenings, to share the news of the day, to laugh together, to compliment the chef for a delicious meal, and to give each other undivided attention that produces a peaceful sense of belonging.

- Experimenting with flavor profiles from around the world is a brilliant way to explore your family's cultural and ethnic heritage. It's a great way to teach your children about new cultures, too.

- Family meals give regular structure and routine to both the day and the week. When kids know that they can expect a reliable schedule, it increases their sense of security, deepens their sense of feeling loved, and improves their sense of wellbeing.

- Family meals provide a meaningful opportunity to teach your kids about healthy eating and exercise. It also presents you with a forum in which you can encourage courtesy and manners that are valued in society (but, let's be honest, are not widely practiced today).

Kids love telling and hearing stories about themselves as babies. They love stories about you, their grandparents, aunts, uncles, and other ancestors. These moments that intertwine past, present, and future deepen the roots and strengthen the branches of your family tree, providing much-needed water and sunlight.

The water sounds like this: "Tell us the story about how you and dad met."

The sun shines in questions like, "Tell us about the day I was born."

Telling these stories around a family meal binds everyone together. There's no better place to share your children's history with them than at the family table, over a delicious meal.

Our Family Meals at Fire Island

As you have probably gathered by now, family mealtime is very dear to my heart. For the first 10 years of Roy's childhood, we spent weekend summers sharing houses with family friends and their kids on Fire Island. Living in Manhattan during the hot summers can get pretty hairy, and while we love New York, there's nothing like a summer weekend at the beach. There were many summers when this was a financial stretch, but Roy didn't have siblings and I felt these community experiences early on in his life were connectors that would help him build a strong sense of family and community for his future.

To give you an idea of why I felt so strongly about this, let me offer a quick sketch of Fire Island, in case you aren't familiar. Imagine a place with no cars, no need to lock your doors or have a TV. It's a place where kids can walk freely to the beach, the town, or the bay. It's a step back in time to when life was simple. It begins with a 45-minute ferry ride from Bayshore, Long Island. As soon as you board that boat, you begin to decompress in the warmth of the sun's rays on your face.

The ferry arrives at the dock and you are met by the serenity, peace and beauty of nature. Without cars, everyone still uses red wagons to cart stuff around. The salty and sweet sea air smells of cleanness and healing. At night the stars and planets hang so low in the sky that you feel like you could reach out and almost touch them. The word "paradise" comes to mind. The last time I went was over 10 years ago, and the magnificence of Fire Island still remains bold in my memory. Even time cannot dull the importance of the summers I spent there with my son.

On Fire Island everyone calls our type of house a group house, or a "grouper." Sharing and playing well with others

Imagine a place with no cars, no need to lock your doors or have a TV. It's a place where kids can walk freely to the beach, the town, or the bay. It's a step back in time to when life was simple.

is a key component for a grouper. Kids as well as adults have to share and compromise over toys, who showers when, cooking, and cleaning duty. Everything is a coordinated effort, even taking the kids to the dock to fish or to the beach to dig holes in the sand. You are no longer just a parent to your own but a guardian to all. If your kid wants to go the beach, they all want to go.

In every house there's an adult early riser. In our case, it was your friend here writing this book. Each morning, I'd pile the kids into the red wagon, venture down the block to the market and let them shop for breakfast. The real excitement for the kids was to sign their name on our house account.

Rainy days were always a huge cooking event. We made everything from cookies, cakes, and breads to homemade ice cream. One rainy day Roy came up with the idea to make Italian zeppoles. With no recipe, Internet connection or Wi-Fi, we all had fun experimenting with ingredients and deciding together which combination was just right. On Fire Island there are blueberry bushes everywhere, so it was the kids' job to pick enough to meet their snacking needs and to keep us eating blueberry pancakes all summer long.

Dinners were the most fun of all. As you can imagine, feeding six adults and five or more kids (friends always showed up) dinner from Friday night to Sunday was like orchestrating the three-ring spectacular at Barnum Bailey Circus. We always made it work. The kids loved to chip in and help: going to the market, shucking corn, peeling vegetables, mixing ingredients, ripping lettuce, and painting shells to decorate the table. When it came to helping and working in the kitchen, the kids banded together, jumped in, and were often willing to eat foods they would never have tried at home.

This was not only an amazing experience for Roy, but I too discovered things I didn't yet know as a parent. These times reinforced the importance of family meals and working together in a larger extended community. Most interesting of all was that the kids wanted to participate in conversations at the kitchen table whether it was breakfast, lunch, or dinner. It was a hoot. We had Clark telling tales about sand crabs and Keithy chiming in or Jennifer, the oldest, cheering the others on. The kids told stories about last year while the parents listened proudly.

It was clear that the kids observed each other and wanted to learn how to cooperate and navigate their social situations for the weekend. Jennifer the oldest, had all the kids following her around like puppies. If Jennifer was setting the dinner table, all the kids wanted to help her set the table. Those kids loved Jennifer, she was their rock star. Her parents said that at home they had never observed her assuming such a leadership-oriented role among her peers. It was a whole new, wonderful side of their daughter that had been unlocked in the context of our family community. It goes to show you how important it is for children to socialize in groups of kids that are a range of ages. Jennifer loved the attention. She also loved explaining, teaching, and sharing with all the kids. No doubt there were hectic moments too, but the kids always managed to work through it and play together again.

It was around mealtimes I witnessed the most unity and happiness. To be together on Fire Island with each other brought out the best in all of us. Family meals gave us the opportunity to talk about house happenings, news of the day, laugh, compliment the chefs for a delicious meal and give each other undisturbed time and attention that produced a peaceful sense of belonging.

Herbs and Spices

Herbs and spices are the determining factors that magically transform dishes and delineate one cuisine from one another. *The flavor that makes your heart beat faster isn't only combinations of meats and vegetables; it's due in large part to the herbs and spices added by the chef. When we are thinking about Italian, Greek, or Mexican dishes it's perfectly natural to think of the food ingredients that create cultural flavors and forget about the serendipitous influence behind the scenes: herbs and spices.*

What if I told you that you could unlock the culinary world kingdom of flavors by using fewer than four herbs and spices? Once you learn how to create these flavors, you will be the cooking sensation of your family and friends. Your kids might even nickname you "Flavors." Here's where you learn and experience how to combine our three techniques of roasting, braising, and rice pilaf with herbs and spices. Open your culinary world and build flavors from places like France, Italy, Spain, Asia, the Mediterranean, and right here in the USA.

First, let's explore a little background information and noteworthy history about herbs and spices. What's the difference between herbs and spices, anyway? Most of us tend to lump them together. Simply put, herbs are the fresh or dried leafy parts of the plant, while spices are created from the plant seeds. Spices are always dried and can be found ground or in seed form. Herbs can be fresh or dried.

The fresh or dried conundrum: which is better? Well, that depends on what you're making! When it comes to cooking there are many variables and decisions one can make. It reminds me of my father teaching me how to drive a golf ball. There was just so much to know: keep your left arm straight, don't sway, twist, bend your knees, keep your head down, eye on the ball. I was ten years old and thought he was crazy, how was I supposed to concentrate on all that and hit the ball at the same time? Then my dad said, "Kid, as long as your keep your head down, eye on the

ball, you'll connect. Once he said something simple, I listened and hit that ball for real. Of course it sliced into the wrong fairway, but I smashed that ball 200 yards. And that is exactly how you'll connect to the culinary kingdom. You just have to put your head down and take that first swing.

So when should you use fresh herbs and when should you go for dried? When we use fresh herbs, we want to experience the full flavor of the herb, which is best accomplished by adding the herbs at the end of the recipe. As with fresh basil on top of garden tomatoes or dill over roasted vegetables, adding a fresh herb keeps the flavors bright and intense. Fresh herbs are perfect at the end of sauces, soups, and salad dressings.

Dried herbs, on the other hand, infuse your dish during cooking, which is why they are typically added early on and play an important role in our cooking techniques. We often use dried herbs and fresh herbs in combination— dried herbs to infuse flavor, and fresh herbs at the end for freshness and presentation.

Fresh herbs are more expensive than dried. Some dishes, like pesto, call for fresh herbs only. When you need to use fresh herbs, buy a bunch even if the dish calls for a small amount. Tie the left over herbs together and hang them upside down. That's how easy it is to make dried herbs to add to your pantry.

The fresh or dried conundrum: which is better? Well, that depends on what you're making! When it comes to cooking there are many variables and decisions one can make.

Most of us use dried herbs and spices instead of fresh because they are easier to store, last longer, and are always in season. Dried herbs and spices will lose their potency over time, and should be replaced at least once a year. Just like driving a golf ball, keep it simple. Trust your instincts and over time and with practice you'll inherently know when to use dried or fresh herbs.

Branching out from salt and pepper not only takes your culinary skills around the world, but it also adds historic health benefits from within those pinches of this and dashes of that. Every time you enhance your culinary creations with herbs or spices, you supercharge your meal with nutrients, all without adding a single calorie.

Herbs and spices have been known throughout history for their medicinal value, at times being used more prominently in that capacity than for their flavor-enhancing abilities. They hold abundant antibacterial properties and are rich in phytonutrients, B-Vitamins, and trace minerals. True sea salt, for instance, contains 93 trace minerals.[114] Most herbs and spices contain more disease fighting antioxidants than fruits and vegetables.[115] Remember the section where we spoke about the industry breeding nutrients out of our food? Herbs and spices are the only ingredients left that still hold the nutritional power they had centuries ago.

History

Spices played an integral role in the expansion of early empires. To this day, they conjure up images of exotic places, historic figures and dangerous voyages in the search to find them. For centuries Greece and Rome dominated Western civilization, but both empires were dependent on Arab traders for spices from the East. For hundreds of years, spices were the world's most important commodities. Like oil today, spices drove the world's economy. Many men's fortunes were made in the pursuit of spices.

At one point in French history rent could be paid in peppercorns.[112]

Like gold and silver, spices were used as currency. They were responsible for many voyages of discovery, including the trip Christopher Columbus took at the end of 15th Century. He sailed west in search of India to find spices and accidentally landed in the New World.

In search of fame and fortune, Portuguese explorer Ferdinand Magellan set out from Spain in 1519 with a fleet of five ships seeking a western sea route

to the Spice Islands. The fleet encountered many battles on the voyage, and only one ship returned home three years later. Although the ship contained a treasure of valuable spices from the East, only 18 of the fleet's original crew of 270 survived. Magellan himself didn't survive the voyage, but his expedition proved that the globe could be circled by sea, opening the world to Western Europe. The history of herbs and spices is literally the history of the expansion of Western civilization.[113]

The Magic Wand of Eleven Healthy Herbs and Spices

1. Cayenne Pepper

This hot spice may possibly be the healthiest of all. It not only heats your food; it heats up your body and raises your body temperature, which helps burn fat. It supplies vital nutrients to the heart, improves blood circulation by thinning the blood, removes toxins from the blood, and rebuilds blood cells.[116]

2. Cinnamon

This ancient spice has one of the highest antioxidant levels of any spice. Cinnamon is highly effective at helping to stabilize blood sugar levels, making it very beneficial for those with diabetes. Sweeteners cause your pancreas to release large amounts of insulin, which can lead you down an unhealthy road. This spice reduces our insulin requirement by increasing its effectiveness. Sprinkle this on anything to enhance sweetness, guilt free.[117]

3. Cumin

The health benefits of cumin for digestive disorders have been well documented throughout history. It can help with flatulence, indigestion, diarrhea, nausea, and morning sickness. Cumin is exceptionally rich in iron, making it a great natural supplement for blood health. Increased iron makes the blood richer in hemoglobin, the substance that transports oxygen to all the cells of the body.[118]

4. Oregano

Oregano's essential oil is well known in natural health communities for its antibacterial properties. Along with garlic, oregano oil can effectively be used to help fight infection. Oregano contains high amounts of omega-3s, iron, manganese, and antioxidants.[119]

5. Nutmeg

Nutmeg contains eugenol, a compound that may benefit the heart. It was one of the key spices that gave the Spice Islands their name. Medicinally, nutmeg has strong antimicrobial properties that have been found to kill a number of cavity-causing bacteria in the mouth.[120]

While technically neither herbs nor spices, garlic and ginger are worth mentioning here for both their health benefits and their use in ethnic flavoring by chefs around the world.

Ginger

Cinnamon

Sea salt

Rosemary

Garlic

Thyme

Cayenne Pepper

Turmeric

Nutmeg

Cumin

Oregano

6. *Rosemary*

Rosemary has long been believed to have memory-enhancing properties. In 1529, an herbal book recommended taking rosemary for "weakness of the brain."[121] Today, research has found that rosemary contains compounds with properties that may protect against the normal memory loss that happens with age.

7. *Sea Salt*

Sea salt is very different from table salt: sea salt is healthy for you. It is not refined or processed but is created naturally by drying seawater in the sun. Sea salt retains its natural mineral content from the seawater. Sea salt helps to regulate the heartbeat and lower high cholesterol.[122] It contains dozens of minerals and trace elements that help hydrate your cells. The best varieties have a gray or pink color.

8. *Thyme*

Thyme's active compound is known for treating bronchitis, sore throats, chest congestion, laryngitis and asthma. Thyme is so effective at relieving inflammation that it is used as an ingredient in cough drops and mouthwashes.

9. *Turmeric*

This is the spice that makes your food turn yellow. It is loaded with antioxidants that help destroy free radicals. It also has wonderful anti-inflammatory properties. Turmeric's yellow-orange pigment comes from curcumin, the main active compound in this super-spice. Curcumin's anti-inflammatory benefits are comparable to drugs like hydrocortisone.[121]

10. *Garlic*

Garlic is well known for its health benefits and antimicrobial properties. Fresh garlic is thought to play a role in preventing food poisoning by killing bacteria like E. Coli and salmonella. The anti-clotting properties of ajoene found in garlic help prevent the formation of blood clots in the body. Garlic is also known to have anti-inflammatory and anti-histamine properties.[123]

11. *Ginger*

A number of studies have documented ginger's stomach-soothing capabilities. In addition to easing nausea and vomiting, the spice appears to reduce motion and morning sicknesses. Ginger helps bolster the immune system. It also decreases bacterial infections in the stomach, and helps your body battle coughs and throat irritation.[124]

Cooking With Flavor Profiles From Around the World

During one holiday season, Roy and I shared a house in Vermont with close friends who have three children, ranging from 6 to 12 years old. The kids were extremely excited that we were coming, and their parents let them know that we'd be cooking dinner Saturday night. Talk about being put in the spotlight! I love these kids. They are so funny, curious, and, of course, energetic. What I also know is that Nick doesn't like chicken or vegetables, Sophie doesn't like vegetables or spicy food, and Haley likes pasta with butter, but not much else. And Aunt Amy is really picky.

Roy and I decided we would make our braised "West African Short Ribs with Kale and Sweet Yams" dish but swap out the short ribs for chicken (even though we knew chicken wasn't high on Nick's list). It was a bold decision, considering their taste buds, and we weren't 100% sure their parents had ever experienced West African flavors, either.

Saturday morning, during our supermarket run, we separated into adult/kid teams with lists to buy all the ingredients for the braise, plus food for snacks and for breakfast and lunch on Sunday. Around 3pm, Roy and I started prepping. Fortunately, the kitchen was well stocked with cooking tools. In fact, the house had a large roasting pan with high sides, perfect for braising. There was no cover, so we improvised with tin foil.

Within minutes brilliant aromas of food sizzling, searing, and caramelizing swirled through the air. Sounds of cutting and chopping filled the cabin. It didn't take long before everyone was curious and intrigued by the scents coming from the kitchen. A few hours later we were ready for dinner. The kids set the table, candles were lit, and Roy and I plated each dish. Tender, juicy chicken fell off the bone while perfectly cooked kale, delicious sweet potato cubes, and chickpeas topped with West African flavored juices were heaped on each plate.

Within minutes brilliant aromas of food sizzling, searing, and caramelizing swirled through the air. Sounds of cutting and chopping filled the cabin. It didn't take long before everyone was curious and intrigued by the scents coming from the kitchen.

The moment of truth arrived, it was show time. We all sat down, made a toast, and waited to hear the reviews from the three children and their parents. After their first bite there was a moment of silence; Roy and I looked at each other in anticipation. A few seconds later Nick voiced his verdict: "Really good!" Dinner was a huge success! Afterward, Lisa and Todd just had to know what spices we had used.

Flavors are determined by our taste buds, which detect sweet, sour, bitter, and salty. There is also a fifth, lesser-known flavor: umami (a savory taste). And we recognize different cultures and their unique cuisines by their flavors.

Now we'll discover what flavors define a specific cuisine. These flavor profiles evolved over hundreds—and in some areas, thousands—of years. Just as each culture speaks a different language with different dialects, within cultures people have adapted different ways to prepare food, even when many of the ingredients worldwide are quite similar. If we can reduce the numerous flavors and techniques down to their core, we create a basis of understanding and reproducing the cuisine of a specific culture.

The flavor profiles I share in this book will allow you to create familiar cultural dishes using ingredients already in your pantry, your cupboard, and your fridge. Letting your meal inspiration come directly from your ingredients at hand is a technique I call ingredient-based cooking.

Ingredient-based cooking allows you to move away from recipes, freeing you to create fast, healthy, delicious meals. The most discouraging part of following a recipe is not only the running around to get all the ingredients, but also that you often buy items you'll never use again, an extra cost that nobody needs. As parents we often have trouble finding our keys, let alone having time for an ingredient hunt.

Like owning a personal culinary magic wand you'll use simple combinations of herbs and spices to unravel the world of flavors. Here's a perfect example using the rice pilaf technique: if you add basil, oregano, olive oil, and garlic to the rice, you will have created a wonderful, fresh, Italian-flavored rice pilaf. Now change it up. If you add garlic, ginger, Chinese five spice, and sesame oil instead, you will have created a fresh, Asian-flavored rice pilaf.

The flavor profiles I share in this book will allow you to create familiar cultural dishes using ingredients already in your pantry, your cupboard, and your fridge.

The Flavor Profile Chart on the next page details cultural ingredient flavor profiles from around the world. Use the last column for the shortcut version, or as some like to call it, the "cheat sheet" to begin your worldwide culinary journey. Once you discover how easily switching a few ingredients or herbs and spices transports your dish across the continent, your curiosity will inspire you to experiment even further. It's like a combination lock for your bicycle. You only need to remember four numbers to unlock it for your next journey. From there it's just a matter of mastering basic culinary techniques. Once you learn how to braise in Italy you'll know how to braise in Asia.

International Flavor Profile Chart

Region	Flavor Profile	Quick & Easy Shortcut
Cajun	dark roux, onions, celery, green pepper, tomatoes, parsley, cayenne, Cajun spice blends, blackening seasonings, lemon, scallions, Andouille sausage, crab, shrimp	cayenne, tomatoes, Cajun spice, sausage
China	onions, shallots, scallions, Chinese five-spice, ginger, cumin, anise, basil, garlic, sesame seeds, hot chili peppers, rice vinegar, Hoisin sauce, oyster sauce, soy sauce, rice, bamboo shoots, bok choy, udon and soba noodles	oyster sauce, bok choy, sesame seed oil, ginger
Egypt	cumin, coriander, cloves, mint, cardamom, cinnamon, dukkah, garlic, fava beans, ghee, rice, black lentils, pasta, onions, tomato, spinach, artichoke, lamb, beef, legumes, hummus	dukkah, mint, tomato, garlic
French	onions, chives shallots, thyme, tarragon, Herbs de Provence, bay leaves, chervil, capers, red and white wine, Dijon mustard, mushrooms, celery, carrots, cream	Herbs de Provence, butter, shallots, red wine
Germany	bay leaf, dill, coves, chervil, parsley, thyme, chives, anise, ginger, cinnamon, juniper berries, caraway, cardamom, anise, basil, sage, oregano, potatoes, asparagus, cabbage, beets, beef, goose, bratwurst, beer	bay leaf, cloves, cabbage
India	tandoori spices, garam masala, curry, cardamom, cumin, coriander, cilantro, garlic, saffron, dried chilies tamarind, fennel, yogurt, coconut milk, basmati rice, chickpeas, spinach, chicken, goat	curry, turmeric, cumin, chic peas
Israel	anise, bay leaves, chives, coriander, dill, fennel, parsley, baharat, cumin, couscous, cinnamon, beets, olives, olive oil, almonds, avocado, spinach, lemon, dates, pomegranate, pita bread, chickpeas, sesame paste, bulgur, lamb, za'atar	za'atar, couscous, caraway, cumin
Italy	onions, garlic, basil, oregano, sage, thyme, rosemary, red pepper flakes, capers, extra virgin olive oil, Balsamic vinegar, red wine vinegar, tomato, veal, broccoli rabe, mushrooms, artichoke, eggplant, pasta, pine nuts	tomatoes, garlic, basil, oregano
Japanese	miso, sesame seed oil, sesame seeds, rice vinegar, sake, soy sauce, wasabi, daikon, turnip, cucumber, eggplant, cabbage, scallion, bamboo shoot, ginger, ponzu, panko, seaweed, shrimp, tuna, soy bean, tofu	miso, ginger, soy sauce, rice wine vinegar
Mandarin	ginger, garlic, green onion, black bean sauce, five-spice powder, chili sauce & paste, oyster sauce, Rice vinegar, Sesame oil, soy sauce, mushrooms long-grain rice, egg noodles, chicken, shrimp, tofu, bok choy, Chinese eggplant	oyster sauce, garlic, sesame seeds, 5 spice
Mediterranean	oregano, lemon, olives, rosemary, bay leaves, thyme, dill, olive oil, lamb, garlic, lemon, feta cheese, tomatoes, red onions, spinach, eggplant, fish, rice, grains, honey, pistachio nuts, figs	lemon, oregano, dill, cumin
Mexico	cumin, chili powder, hot sauce, green peppers, oregano, lime, garlic, onions, celery, cilantro, tomatoes, scallions, black beans, cheddar cheese, avocado	jalapeno pepper, cilantro, garlic, lime
Morocco	cinnamon, cumin, saffron, ground ginger, paprika, aniseed, sesame seed. Couscous, onions, garlic, parsley, green coriander, marjoram, preserved lemons, honey, olives, olive oil, chicken, lamb, dilo dough, eggs, chickpeas, tomato, green pepper	cumin, cinnamon, ginger, onion
North Africa	cardamom, cinnamon, cloves, coriander, cumin, red pepper, dill, mint, thyme, barley, cabbage, carrots, eggplant, garlic, onions, peppers, spinach, chickpeas, lentils, dates, lemons, sesame seeds, walnuts, chicken, mussels, yogurt, olive oil	mint, lentils, turmeric, saffron
Portugal	parsley, hot chili powder, chili oil (piri-piri), cumin, rosemary, mint, oregano, bay leaf, saffron, fennel, coriander, cinnamon, cloves, pepper, curry powder, nutmeg, paprika, and of course, garlic	chili oil (piri-piri), fennel, saffron, bay leaves
Spain	olive oil, garlic, sweet onion, rosemary, pepper, tomato, paprika, capsicum, saffron, lentils, fava beans, garbanzos beans, cauliflower, olives, shrimp, pork chops, razor clams, lime, chili, jalapeño peppers, habanero peppers, eggs, avocado	garlic, onion, pepper, paprika
Thai	lemongrass, fish sauce, garlic, Thai chili peppers, coconut milk, ginger, palm sugar, Jasmine rice, Thai Basil, cilantro, Chinese broccoli, cabbage, cumin, nutmeg, Chinese five-spice, onion, red & green curry pastes, chicken, duck, tamarind, Kaffir lime	Thai basil, coconut milk, ginger, lemongrass

Seasonal Produce Chart

Spring

March, April, May

Artichokes
Asparagus
Belgian Endive
Broccoli
Butter Lettuce
Cactus
Cayote Squash
Chives
Collard Greens
Corn
Fava Beans
Fennel
Fiddlehead Ferns
Green Beans
Manoa Lettuce
Morel Mushrooms
Mustard Greens
Pea Pods
Peas
Purple Asparagus
Radicchio
Ramps
Red Leaf Lettuce
Rhubarb
Snow Peas
Sorrel
Spinach
Spring Baby Lettuce
Swiss Chard
Vidalia Onions
Watercress

Summer

June, July, August

Beets
Bell Peppers
Butter Lettuce
Chayote Squash
Chinese Long Beans
Corn
Crookneck Squash
Cucumbers
Eggplant
Endive
Garlic
Green Beans
Green Soybeans
   (Edamame)
Jalapeno Peppers
Lima Beans
Manoa Lettuce
Okra
Peas
Radishes
Shallots
Sugar Snap Peas
Summer Squash
Tomatillo
Tomatoes
Winged Beans
Yukon Gold Potatoes
Zucchini

Fall

Sept, Oct, Nov

Acorn Squash
Belgian Endive
Black Salsify
Broccoli
Brussels Sprouts
Butter Lettuce
Buttercup Squash
Butternut Squash
Cauliflower
Chayote Squash
Chinese Long Beans
Delicata Squash
Diakon Radish
Endive
Garlic
Ginger
Jalapeno Peppers
Jerusalem Artichoke
Kohlrabi
Pumpkin
Radicchio
Sweet Dumpling Squash
Sweet Potatoes
Swiss Chard
Turnips
Winter Squash

Winter

Dec, Jan, Feb

Belgian Endive
Brussels Sprouts
Buttercup Squash
Collard Greens
Delicata Squash
Kale
Leeks
Sweet Dumpling Squash
Sweet Potatoes
Turnips
Winter Squash

Braising

Braising is the cornerstone of comfort food cooking. Preparing delicious meals for your family doesn't get any more streamlined than this: prepare, sear, and braise with minimal mess and cleanup. One-pot cooking at its finest. Braising is a versatile cooking method open to a vast spectrum of ingredients. Braising transforms inexpensive, tougher cuts of meat into fall-apart-on-your-fork dishes rife with a complex flavors.

Braising relies on a small amount of slow-simmering liquid, and a tightly sealed pot. The liquid can be a creative mixture—broth, wine, juice, etc.—yielding a synergistic marriage of flavor. The moist heat inside the pot breaks down connective tissue and triggers the meat to release its gelatin into the cooking liquid, adding body to the sauce. Through a slow-simmering process flavor permeates deep into the meat, retaining all nutrients and even making some nutrients more readily available for the body to use. The sauce created by braising is exceptional.

Braising: One-Pot Cooking At its Finest

Braising is a particularly simple technique in which less expensive, tough cuts of meat transform into the most flavorful dishes that will ever adorn your table.

Into our wired world that seems to become more complicated everyday comes the art of the uncomplicated: braising. Braising is a particularly simple technique in which less expensive, tough cuts of meat transform into the most flavorful dishes that will ever adorn your table. My favorite meal of all time is braised short ribs. If your family has never experienced beef short ribs, you're missing out on one of life's great pleasures. I'm not exaggerating.

For the braising recipes in this section you'll use your sautoir pan with its tight-fitting lid. The sautoir is the ultimate multi-tasking cookware tool. It perfectly combines the functions of the frying pan, the sauté pan and the braising pan. Efficiency in one-pot magic!

Braise in the oven or on your stovetop. I prefer braising on the stovetop instead of in the oven, because you can braise year round, even on the hottest days. Using this technique in the summer months allows you to incorporate fresh herbs and vegetables to create delectable, healthy meals.

For braising cuts of meat the ribs, brisket, shanks, short ribs, shoulder, and chuck cuts are the best options because these cuts will become so tender that they fall off the bone. These braising choice cuts are the active muscles that have more fat. Along with beef you can braise lamb, pork, veal, chicken, or fish.

Braised fish is delicious; however, because it is more delicate than tough cuts of meat, stick with the large, firmer varieties. Swordfish, halibut, salmon, cod, tilapia, and monkfish are your best choices because they are heartier fish.

Some famous braised dishes you're probably familiar with include osso bucco, lamb shanks, braised brisket, and the oh-so-delicious braised short ribs. Braising is absolutely the easiest technique there is to create mouthwatering dishes that every one of your family members will love. You cannot go wrong. Even

if you burn toast four times a week, this technique will forgive you. Whether you're braising beef, chicken, or lamb, once your meat is in the sautoir, walk away and forget about it for a few hours. And, if you accidentally overcook your dish by half an hour, no worries. The longer the meat braises, the better.

This method also allows you to cook remarkable tasting dishes with very few ingredients. Didn't have a chance to go shopping? As long as you have a main meat in the fridge—even if it's frozen—all you need are some onions, carrots, maybe a bay leaf, some salt and pepper, and a liquid such as beer, wine, or even maple syrup. Don't worry about cooking family-friendly meals with beer and wines; during braising the alcohol evaporates.

Need a good idea for leftovers? Braising is the premiere technique to select on a Sunday afternoon to create a mouthwatering dinner that transforms into a variety of meals during the week. What everyone loves most about this technique is the delicious sauce that comes with every braise. Serve leftover braises on just about anything; the dish will be amazing and easy to make on the fly. Potatoes, couscous, risotto, quinoa, barley, rice or pasta will transform your braise into a new dinner each evening. This is your ticket to freedom from the weekday 6 p.m. dinner rush.

With very few ingredients, braising allows you the ability to switch cuisines in seconds. You feel like turning tonight's chicken dish Asian? Use ginger, Chinese five-spice, and hoisin sauce. Done! This method allows you to create cuisines as diverse as Vietnamese, Moroccan, Italian, British or Southern simply and without fail. You cannot make a mistake with this technique, and it will always taste amazing. Braising allows you to be creative in the kitchen with very little experience. So go! Braise! Have fun!

Learn to Make One Braise
You Can Make Any Braise

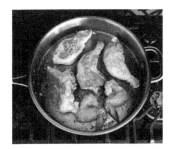

1
Sear the meat

Season the meat or fish with kosher salt and freshly ground black pepper on all sides. Preheat a sautoir pan over a medium-high heat, add 1 tablespoon canola or grape seed oil and let the oil heat for a minute, until it looks wavy. Add the meat or fish; hear the sizzle. Sear for 6-8 minutes without moving, then flip and continue searing on both sides until nicely browned, around 10-12 minutes.

Time saver: do not remove the meat from the pan, move aromatics to the bottom so the meat or fish is on top.

2
Add the aromatics

Add your aromatic vegetables, herbs and spices; sauté over medium heat for 5-10 minutes, until all ingredients are browned, without burning. Deglaze the pan by adding vinegar, wine, lemon, or broth; scrape off the fond (drippings and pieces stuck to the bottom of the pan) and stir.

3
Add the liquid

Pour in the stock; the meat or fish should be about ¾ submerged. Tightly cover the pan, bring to a boil and reduce heat to low (option: place in the oven at 325°F).

4
Braise it

Cook for 1-4 hours. Cook times vary depending on cut and size; see the chart for cook times. Add root vegetables, dried fruit, and white or sweet potatoes the last hour; add greens and vegetables the last 45-30 minutes of cooking time. For a thicker sauce, reduce it by removing the cover, turning the heat up a little and cooking uncovered for the last 30-45 minutes.

Swap out meats, vegetables, and spices from any dish to create new intuitive dishes. Experiment. You can't go wrong with braising. The meat will always be tender and fall off the bone. Use chicken instead of beef, or lamb instead of pork; the only difference will be your braising time.

A Quick Guide to Braising Times
Approximate cook times for meat weights between 2-5 lbs.
Approximate cook times for fish weights between 1-2 lbs.

- *Chicken parts will cook the fastest —braise for 1 hour*
- *Beef chuck—up to 2.5 hours*
- *Beef ribs—up to 3.5 hours*
- *Lamb shank or leg—up to 4 hours*
- *Pork shoulder falling off the bone —up to 4 hours*
- *Monk fish—45 minutes*
- *Cod fish—10-15 minutes*

West African Beef
with Kale and Sweet Yams

4	pounds short ribs, bone in or 3-4 pounds
	cubed boneless beef chuck.
1	tablespoon canola oil.
1	large onion, chopped.
5	garlic cloves, chopped.
1	teaspoon turmeric.
1	teaspoon ground cinnamon.
1	teaspoon ground cumin.
2	tablespoon apple cider vinegar.
2	cups beef stock.
½	cup dates, pitted and chopped.
2	yams, peeled and cut into 1-inch cubes.
1	(15-ounce) can garbanzo beans, drained and rinsed.
½	bunch red kale, chopped.
¼	cup chunky peanut butter or ¼ cup ground peanuts.
	Kosher salt and freshly ground black pepper, to taste.

COOK
3 hours 30 minutes
– 4 hours
SERVES
6-8

❶ Season beef with kosher salt and pepper and set aside.

❷ Preheat a sautoir pan over medium-high heat, add canola oil and heat for about one minute, until oil looks wavy.

❸ Add beef and sear on both sides, until nicely browned, about 10 minutes.

❹ Stir in onion, garlic, turmeric, cinnamon and cumin, moving the beef on top. Sauté 5-10 minutes until the onions are soft; add vinegar and deglaze, scraping off the bits stuck to the pan.

❺ Pour in the beef stock, cover pan and bring mixture to a boil; reduce heat to low (option: place in the oven at 350°F).

❻ Cook for 2 hours, add dates and continue cooking for another 1-1½ hours or until the meat is falling off the bone. No worries if cooked longer, as the beef will become even tenderer.

❼ Add the yams, garbanzo beans, kale and peanut butter and cook 30 minutes longer.

❽ Let rest for about 10 minutes before serving.

German Pot Roast

1 tablespoon canola oil.

3-4 pounds boneless beef chuck, cut into 1-inch cubes.

2 sweet onions, quartered.

3 garlic cloves, crushed.

5 carrots, quartered.

½ tablespoon dried dill.

2 tablespoons red sherry vinegar.

1 tablespoon juniper berries.

2 cups beef broth.

1 (12-ounce) can beer.

2 apples, peeled, cored and quartered.

3 russet potatoes cut into 2-inch chunks.

1 pound (about ½ small head) white cabbage, shredded.

Kosher salt and freshly ground black pepper, to taste.

COOK
3 hours -
3 hours 30 minutes
SERVES
6-8

Preparation

1 Preheat a sautoir pan over medium-high heat, add canola oil and heat for about a minute, until it looks wavy. Season beef with kosher salt and pepper and sear on both sides, about 10 minutes.

2 Add onions, garlic, carrots, dill, and juniper berries and move them to the bottom of the pan so the beef cubes are on top; cook until onions are soft, 5-10 minutes. Add sherry vinegar, deglaze, scraping off the bits stuck to the pan.

3 Add beef broth, beer and apples, cover and cook on the stovetop over low heat or in the oven at 350°F for 2 ½ – 3 hours.

4 Add potatoes and cabbage, cover and cook for 30-45 minutes; remove cover, let rest for about 10 minutes and serve.

Thai Beef Brisket

1	tablespoon canola oil.
3-4	pounds beef brisket, cut into 1-inch cubes.
2	shallots.
4	cloves garlic.
1	tablespoon ginger.
1	teaspoon Thai bird chilli pepper.
3	tablespoons curry powder.
2	tablespoons apple cider vinegar.
2	cups beef stock.
2	star anise cloves.
1	pound fresh string beans.
1	cup coconut milk.
1	cup fresh basil.
	Kosher salt and freshly ground black pepper, to taste.

COOK
3 hours -
3 hours 30 minutes
SERVES
6-8

Preparation

1 Preheat a sautoir pan over medium-high heat, add canola oil and heat for about a minute, until it looks wavy. Season beef with kosher salt and pepper and sear on all sides, about 10 minutes.

2 Add shallots, garlic, ginger, Thai chilli pepper and curry and move them to the bottom of the pan so the beef cubes are on top. Sear until onions are soft, about 5 minutes. Add the apple cider vinegar, deglaze, scraping off the bits stuck to the pan.

3 Add beef stock and anise cloves; cover and cook on the stovetop over low heat or in the oven at 350°F for 1½ hours. Add coconut milk and cook 1 hour longer.

4 Remove cover and cook for 30-45 minutes; add string beans and cook for another 15 minutes.

5 Turn off heat, add basil and let rest for about 10 minutes before serving.

Mykonos Citrus Chicken with Kale and Turnip

COOK
1 hour 30 minutes
- 2 hours
SERVES
4-6

1 large skinless chicken cut into 8 pieces.
1 tablespoon grape seed or canola oil.
1 large sweet onion, chopped.
1 tablespoon dried oregano.
1 tablespoon fresh thyme.
4 cloves garlic, chopped.
1 tablespoon apple cider vinegar.
2 cups chicken broth.
½ cup prunes pitted.
3 turnips, peeled and cut into 2-inch chunks.
1 pound kale, stemmed and chopped.
½ grapefruit peeled and diced.
1 lemon, peeled and diced.
2 tablespoons fresh mint, chopped.
   Kosher salt and freshly ground
   black pepper, to taste.

Preparation

❶ Season chicken with kosher salt and pepper on both sides.

❷ Preheat a sautoir pan over medium– high heat, add oil and let it heat a minute until it looks wavy. Place chicken in the pan and sear it until golden brown on both sides.

❸ Add onion, oregano and thyme and move them to the bottom of the pan so chicken is on top. Sauté for 5-10 minutes, until onions caramelize; add garlic and sauté 2 more minutes. Add cider vinegar to deglaze, scraping off bits stuck on the bottom.

❹ Add chicken broth and prunes; bring to a boil, cover and cook on stovetop over low heat or in the oven at 350°F for 30-45 minutes.

❺ Add the turnips, kale, grapefruit and lemon and cook for 30-45 minutes uncovered.

❻ Serve garnished with mint.

Southern Chilli Glazed Chicken

2   chipotle chillies, seeded and finely chopped.
1   cup ketchup.
4   tablespoons apple cider vinegar.
4   tablespoons blackstrap molasses.
2   cups unsweetened apple sauce.
1   cup chicken stock.
1   large chicken, cut into 8 pieces and skin removed.
1   tablespoon canola or grape seed oil.
1   large sweet onion, chopped.
3   turnips, peeled, each cut into 8 wedges.
1   bunch Swiss chard, stemmed and chopped.
4   scallions, chopped.
        Kosher salt and freshly ground black pepper, to taste.

COOK
1 hour 30 minutes
SERVES
4-6

> **Preparation**

❶ In a large bowl, whisk together chillies, ketchup, apple cider vinegar, molasses, apple sauce and chicken stock; set aside.

❷ Season chicken with kosher salt and pepper on both sides.

❸ Preheat a sautoir pan over medium-high heat, add oil, and let heat for a minute, until it looks wavy. Add chicken and sear until golden brown on both sides.

❹ Add chopped onion and move to the bottom of the pan so that the chicken is on top of onions; sauté for 5 -10 minutes.

❺ Add the chicken stock mixture, bring to a boil, reduce heat to low, cover and braise for 45 minutes.

❻ Add the turnips, braise, covered, for additional 30 minutes. Add Swiss chard and braise for 15-20 more minutes.

❼ Garnish with scallions and serve.

Asian Chicken with Rice Noodles and Dried Fruit

1   large chicken, cut into 8 pieces and skin removed.
1   tablespoon sesame oil.
2   green onions chopped.
1½   cup shitake (or crimini) mushrooms.
3   garlic cloves, chopped.
1   cup chicken stock.
½   cup prunes.
½   cup soy sauce.
¼   cup brown sugar.
1   pound string beans.
½   pound rice noodles.
6   heads baby bok choy washed.
½   cup basil, shredded.
    Salt and freshly ground black pepper, to taste.

COOK
1 hour 30 minutes
- 2 hours
SERVES
4-6

Preparation

1 Season chicken with salt and pepper on both sides.

2 Preheat a sautoir pan over medium-high heat, add sesame oil and let the oil heat for a minute, until it looks wavy. Sear chicken until golden brown on both sides.

3 Add onions, mushrooms and garlic and move them to the bottom of the pan so chicken is on top; sauté for 5-10 minutes, until soft.

4 Add chicken stock, prunes, bring to a boil, add soy sauce, brown sugar and reduce heat to low. Cover and cook on stovetop or in the oven at 350°F for 1 hour.

5 Remove cover and cook for 15 minutes, until liquid is reduced; add string beans and rice noodles and cook for 10 minutes. Add bok choy and cook 3-4 minutes, until wilted.

6 Turn off heat and let cool for a few minutes; sprinkle with basil and serve.

Japanese Miso Braised Pork

4 pounds boneless pork shoulder.
1½ tablespoon sesame seed oil.
1½ tablespoon apple cider vinegar.
3 cloves garlic minced.
1½ teaspoon fresh ginger minced.
1 Serrano chilli pepper, seeded and chopped.
1 teaspoon Chinese five spice powder.
¾ cup shiro (white) miso.
3 cups vegetable broth.
⅓ cup soy sauce.
2 tablespoon brown sugar.
1 Granny Smith apple, peeled, cored and diced.
1½ heads fresh broccoli, cut into florets.
½ pound fresh shitake (or cremini) mushrooms, sliced.
Kosher salt and freshly ground black pepper, to taste.

COOK
3 hour 30 minutes
- 4 hours
SERVES
6-8

Preparation

❶ Rub pork shoulder with kosher salt and black pepper.

❷ Preheat a stock pot on medium-high heat, add oil and let heat for a minute, until oil looks wavy. Sear the pork until browned on all sides and deglaze with cider vinegar, scraping all bits stuck on the bottom.

❸ Add garlic, ginger, chilli pepper and five spice powder, move to the bottom of the pan and sauté 1-2 minutes.

❹ In a small bowl, whisk miso paste with 3 tablespoons water until smooth, 1-2 minutes.

❺ Add vegetable broth, soy sauce, brown sugar, and miso mixture to the pan; bring to a boil, scraping the bottom of the pan to dissolve any leftover bits.

❻ Reduce heat to low, cover, and cook for 2 hours; add diced apple and cook for another hour, until the pork is very tender.

❼ Add broccoli and mushrooms and cook 20 more minutes.

Miso
strengthens
the immune
system

Honestly, I never knew about miso until Royal came home from CIA and starting cooking with it. That was when I found out what a powerhouse of concentrated flavor it was, and that it had the ability to add depth to so many dishes. I did some investigation to find out that fermented foods like miso have incredible health benefits too.

Used in Asian cultures for centuries to strengthen the immune system and as a probiotic, Miso paste soon became a staple in our kitchen. We hope it becomes a staple in yours. You'll find miso paste sprinkled throughout the recipes in the book to enhance flavor and add volume to sauces, broths, dressing, and vegetables.

A ubiquitous staple in Japanese and Chinese cuisines for over 2,500 years, Miso paste is fermented from soybeans, a part of the legume family. The health benefits of miso are nothing less than extraordinary. [150]It is a high source of fiber, contains all the essential amino acids (making it a powerful complete protein), is high in antioxidants that protect against free radicals, and is a great vegetable source of B vitamins.

Use white miso (shiro) in place of dairy and cream in soups. Blend light miso with vinegar, olive oil, and herbs for salad dressing.

Pork Vindalloo

1	large onion, finely chopped.
3	Tablespoon fresh ginger, peeled and finely chopped.
4	garlic cloves, chopped.
2	Serrano peppers, finely chopped.
1	tablespoon plus 1 teaspoon canola oil.
3-4	pound boneless pork shoulder, cut into 1 ½ - inch cubes.
2	Tablespoon curry powder.
1	(16-ounce) can diced tomatoes, drained.
2	cups chicken stock.
6	new potatoes, skins on, cut into chunks.
1	pound fresh spinach.
1	bunch cilantro.
	Garam masala spice mix.
	Kosher salt, to taste.

COOK
3 hour 30 minutes
- 4 hours
SERVES
6-8

> **Preparation**

❶ In a food processor puree the onion, ginger, garlic, and peppers with 1 teaspoon oil; set aside.

❷ Season pork with kosher salt on both sides. Preheat sautoir pan medium-high heat, add remaining tablespoon oil and let it heat for a minute until oil looks wavy. Sear pork until golden brown; add curry powder and diced tomatoes and sauté for 3-5 minutes.

❸ Add chicken stock, bring to a boil, and reduce heat to low. Add pureed onion mixture, cover and braise on stovetop or in the oven at 350°F for 2 ½ -3 hours.

❹ Remove cover, add potatoes and cook for 30 minutes; add garam masala and spinach and cook until wilted, about 8 more minutes.

❺ Turn off heat and let cool for a few minutes. Sprinkle with cilantro and serve.

Vindaloo is Tangy and Hot

Vindaloo is a tangy and hot Indian curry from the region of Goa. Its slight edge of sweetness gives it a dazzling balance of flavors.

Traditionally a chicken or lamb dish served with potato we mixed it up a bit and used pork.

Hailing from West India, Goa is India's smallest state. Originally a colony of Portugal, Goa was taken over by India in 1961. This dish pays homage to Goa with its ancient history and pervasive Portuguese influence—from food, to architecture, to language.

Spring Pork Stew

2 tablespoons miso.

3 cups vegetable broth.

2 tablespoons olive oil.

1 onion, peeled and chopped.

4 large carrots, peeled and chopped.

4 cloves garlic, minced.

4 ½ pounds pork shoulder, bone-in.

1 tablespoon dried thyme .

2 tablespoons white wine.

4 zucchini, diced.

2 cups crimini mushrooms, quartered.

1 cup frozen peas.

2 tablespoons parmesan cheese, freshly grated.

1 teaspoon lemon zest.

2 tablespoons fresh basil, thinly sliced.

Kosher salt and freshly ground black pepper, to taste.

COOK
3 hours
- 3 hours 30 minutes
SERVES
6

Preparation

1 Mix miso in a cup with a little broth to liquidity and set aside.

2 Preheat a stock pot over medium-high heat, add the onions, carrots and garlic until softened, about 3-5 minutes.

3 Add pork shoulder, thyme, wine and vegetable broth; bring to a boil, stir in miso and reduce to low heat. Cover pan and braise for 3 hours on stovetop or in the oven at 350°F.

4 Add zucchini and mushrooms and cook for 20 minutes; stir in peas, remove cover and turn off the heat. Let rest for 5 minutes.

5 Serve topped with lemon zest, freshly grated parmesan and basil.

French Lamb Shoulder Chops

2 tablespoons olive oil.

4-6 shoulder blade lamb chops, about 1-inch thick.

1 cup white wine.

1 large onion, chopped.

4 cloves garlic.

4 large carrots peeled quartered.

3 sprigs fresh thyme, chopped.

3 sprigs fresh rosemary, chopped.

¼ cup tomato paste.

3½ cups chicken broth.

2 tablespoons Dijon mustard.

1 cup lentils, rinsed.

2 turnips, peeled and cut into 8 wedges each.

1 tablespoon fresh tarragon, chopped.

COOK
3 hours
SERVES
4-6

Preparation

❶ Preheat a sautoir pan over medium-high heat, add oil and heat for a minute until the oil looks wavy. Season the lamb chops with kosher salt and pepper and sear in batches, until browned on both sides, about 10 -15 minutes; transfer to a plate.

❷ Add ½ cup white wine to deglaze the pan, scraping up all bits.

❸ Add the onions, garlic, carrots, fresh thyme, and rosemary and sauté for about 5-7 minutes. Stir in the tomato paste, remaining ½ cup white wine, and chicken broth.

❹ Return lamb and juices to the pot and bring to a boil; reduce heat to low, stir in Dijon mustard, cover and cook on stovetop or in the oven at 350°F for 2 ½ hours.

❺ With about 1 hour of cooking time left, add the lentils.

❻ Add turnips and cook for 25 minutes uncovered. Stir in tarragon, turn heat off and let rest for a few minutes before serving.

Spanish Lamb Shanks with Black Olives

4-5 pounds lamb shanks.

1 cup rice flour.

1 tablespoon grape seed or canola oil.

1 tablespoon sherry vinegar.

1 large sweet onion, chopped.

2 large carrots, diced.

1 jalapeno pepper, remove seeds, chopped.

4 cloves garlic, chopped.

2 tablespoons fresh rosemary, chopped.

⅛ teaspoon cayenne pepper.

1 tablespoon paprika.

1 (16-ounce) can whole tomatoes, drained.

½ cup red wine.

2 cups beef broth.

/4 cups niçoise black olives.

2 cups frozen peas.

Kosher salt and freshly ground black pepper, to taste.

COOK
3 hours –
3 hours 30 minutes
SERVES
4

Preparation

❶ Lightly flour shanks and sprinkle with kosher salt and black pepper.

❷ Preheat a sautoir pan over medium – high heat, add oil and let it heat for a minute until oil looks wavy. Add the shanks to the pan and sear until golden brown on all sides; transfer to a plate and set aside. Deglaze pan with sherry vinegar, removing any bits stuck to the pan.

❸ Add onions, carrots, jalapeno pepper; sauté a few minutes, then add garlic, fresh rosemary, cayenne and paprika and sauté for a few more minutes.

❹ Mix in tomatoes, add wine and broth; return shanks to the pan, cover and bring to a boil. Reduce heat to low, cover and cook on stovetop or in the oven at 350°F for 2 ½ – 3 hrs.

❺ Remove cover, add olives and cook another 30 minutes uncovered to reduce and thicken. Stir in peas, turn off the heat and let sit 5-10 minutes before serving.

Lamb Shawarma with Feta Topping over Warm Pita Bread

COOK
3 hours 30 minutes
SERVES
8-10

For the shawarma:

2	tablespoons olive oil.
2	tablespoons unsalted butter.
3-4	pound boneless lamb shoulder.
1	large white onion, quartered.
2	large carrots cut into 8 pieces each.
1	tablespoon ground cumin.
5	cloves garlic, minced.
3	cups beef broth.
2	tablespoons molasses or honey.
	Juice of 1 lemon.

For the feta topping:

1	red onion, thinly sliced.
1	cup red wine vinegar.
1	cup fresh flat-leaf parsley, stemmed and chopped.
1	large cucumber, diced.
1	red tomato, diced.
1	tablespoon olive oil.
1	cup feta cheese.
1	cup Greek yoghurt, to serve.
	Kosher salt and freshly ground black pepper, to taste.
	Pita bread, warmed, to serve.

Preparation

1 In a small bowl, combine onion and vinegar and set aside.

2 Season lamb with kosher salt and pepper.

3 Preheat a stock pot over medium-high heat, add olive oil and butter and sear the lamb on all sides, about 15 minutes.

4 Add onion, carrots, and cumin, cook 5-7 minutes; add garlic and cook for 3 minutes longer.

5 Pour in broth, bring to a boil and add molasses and lemon juice. Reduce to low, cover and cook on stovetop or in the oven at 350°F for 3 hours. Uncover to reduce and cook for another 30 minutes, until lamb is very tender.

6 Transfer lamb to a plate and shred using two forks.

7 In a bowl, combine parsley, cucumber, tomato and olive oil; season with salt and pepper, crumble in the feta cheese and toss lightly.

8 Layer shredded lamb on top of warm pita bread, spoon some topping and yogurt over it, roll up the pita and serve.

Balance
comes
in many forms

Your child's first adventure into learning physical balance was to stand and walk. His or her second was most likely learning how to ride a bicycle. Balance comes in many forms throughout life: physical, relational, psychological, emotional, plus balancing meals and exercise, balancing work, family and fun.

In Chinese culture, it's called Yin and Yang, the two opposite principles in nature. Usually in pairs, such as sun and moon, or passive and active, the nature of Yin and Yang lies in the interchange of the two components.

Human existence consistently and unconsciously pushes and pulls at emotional and physical extremes. It's what keeps us in check. Being aware of the need for balance in your daily life leads to finding equilibrium and fulfillment.

For a toddler, physical balance enables independence and curiosity; later in life, however, the loss of physical balance can eliminate independence. The best preventative for immobility and fragility is to exercise throughout your life.

Italian Monkfish with Dill Pistou

For the fish:
2   pounds monkfish tails.
¼   cup rice flour.
2   tablespoons butter.
6   sprigs fresh thyme.
3   sprigs fresh rosemary.
1   large white onion, finely chopped.
2   large gloves garlic, minced.
2   cups chicken stock.
2   small cartons cherry tomatoes.
¼   cup olives, pitted and chopped.
1   bunch fresh chives, chopped.
½   tablespoon olive oil.
      Kosher salt and freshly ground
      black pepper, to taste.

For the dill pistu:
½   bunch fresh dill.
1   cup walnuts.
½   cup olive oil.
      Juice of 1 lemon

COOK
1 hour
SERVES
4-6

> **Preparation**

❶ Dust the monkfish in flour, sprinkle with kosher salt and freshly ground black pepper.

❷ Preheat a sautoir pan over a medium heat, add butter, thyme and rosemary and brown the fish.

❸ Add onion and garlic and cook for about 4 minutes, until softened.

❹ Add chicken stock, bring to a boil, reduce to low heat, cover, and braise on stovetop or in the oven at 350°F for 45 minutes.

❺ For the dill pistu, puree dill, walnuts, olive oil and lemon juice in a food processor and set aside.

❻ In a bowl, mix the cherry tomatoes, chopped olives and chives with a little olive oil; set aside.

❼ Transfer fish to a plate and let sit a minute.

❽ Top with dill pistu and tomato mix and serve.

Oceans

I recently watched Dr. Sylvia Earle's Ted Talk, "My wish: Protect our oceans." Ms. Earle's passionate voice begins by poignantly informing us that over the past 50 years 90% of large fish in the earth's oceans have been consumed by us, and half of the coral reefs so critical to the earth's ecosystem have disappeared.

Ms. Earle's 18-minute Ted Talk inspired the Mission Blue global initiative. Dr. Earle urged people "to use all means at your disposal—films, expeditions, the web, new submarines—to create a campaign to ignite public support for a global network of marine protected areas; Hope Spots large enough to save and restore the blue heart of the planet." [51]

In order for the human race to see and experience the ocean as it truly is, Ms. Earle partnered with Google Earth to go under water, visit MissionBlue.org.

Cod with Black Bean Sauce

½ cup rice flour.
1 tablespoons Chinese five spice powder.
2 pounds fresh cod, cut into 4-6-ounce pieces (also amazing with flounder, halibut or shrimp).
3 tablespoons olive oil.
2 tablespoons rice wine vinegar.
3 cloves garlic, minced.
1 red onion, finely chopped.
1 tablespoon fresh ginger, peeled and minced.
6 carrots, peeled and minced.
1 bunch scallions, trimmed.
1 bunch broccoli rabe.
2 cups chicken broth.
3 tablespoons black bean sauce.

COOK
50 minutes
SERVES
4-6

Preparation

❶ In a bowl, combine flour and Chinese five spice powder and dust cod with the mixture.

❷ Preheat sautoir pan with 2 tablespoon oil. Add cod and sear until golden brown; remove from pan and set aside. Add vinegar and eglaze the pan, scraping up all bits.

❸ Add remaining tablespoon oil, garlic, onion, ginger, and carrot to the pan. Reduce heat to low and sauté until paste-like, about 10-13 minutes.

❹ Add scallions, broccoli rabe, broth and black bean sauce and bring to a boil; reduce heat to low, cover and cook on the stovetop or in the oven at 350°F for 15 minutes.

❺ Add cod and cook for 10-15 more minutes.

Cajun Shrimp with Sausage

1½ pounds shrimp, deveined (wild preferred).

1   fresh lemon.

1   tablespoon canola or grape seed oil.

1   pound spicy sausage (Italian or merguez), remove skins, cut into 1-inch pieces.

2   sweet onions, chopped.

3   cloves garlic, crushed.

3   cups chicken stock.

2   tablespoon Old Bay seasoning.

1   cup wild rice.

1   bunch collard greens, chopped. Kosher salt and freshly ground black pepper, to taste.

COOK
1 hour 15 minutes
SERVES
4-6

Preparation

1 Squeeze juice of the lemon over shrimp and season with kosher salt and fresh pepper.

2 Heat oil in a sautoir pan over medium–high heat, sear shrimp for 2 minutes and remove.

3 Add sausage and sear 5 -7 minutes, until browned.

4 Add the onion and garlic and move them to the bottom of the pan so the sausage is on top; sauté for 3-5 minutes until onions are translucent.

5 Pour in chicken stock and add Old Bay seasoning; bring to a boil, reduce heat to low.

6 Add the rice, cover and cook for 45 minutes, then stir in collard greens; cook for another 20 minutes.

7 Lastly add the shrimp and cook for another 3 minutes.

8 Serve immediately.

Roasting

Roasting may be one of the easiest cooking techniques. Your oven does most of the work while you spend time with the kids. Your effort comes primarily before the actual cooking begins.

Foods for roasting are prepared simply. Whole or partial chickens are spiced, and tenderloins, hams, beef, and fish are rubbed with seasonings. Vegetables are sliced, diced, cubed, or left whole. And then they cook until done, mostly hands-free, leading to deep and hearty flavors.

Roasting
The Very First Form of Human Cooking

The control of fire by early humans was a turning point in the cultural aspect of human evolution. It allowed humans to cook food and obtain warmth and protection. The ability to cook food improved caloric efficiency and supplied energy for our hungriest organ, our brain. In Catching Fire: How Cooking Made Us Human, Richard Wrangham, a professor of biological anthropology at Harvard University, says the adoption of cooking by our early ancestors profoundly shaped human families and relationships, making hearth and home central to humanity and perhaps even driving humans into the traditional family household that exists today. [125]

After the invention of fire the earliest form of cooking was most likely the direct heat from this revolutionary new product. The roasting rack hadn't been invented yet, so most likely food morsels accidentally dropped from the hunt directly into the fire. Our caveman ancestors ate the scraps after they had been heated and discovered that they tasted better than the raw meat. I imagine this was the inspiration for the first home cooked meal.

Next our new caveman chef probably experimented with placing large pieces of meat next to the fire to heat up. Since this only cooked the meat on one side, the primitive chef figured he needed to turn dinner around to cook the other side. This poor guy probably ended up with blisters on his fingers along with dinner that was charred on the outside and raw on the inside, but the new cooking technique was enjoyed by all.

Eventually, somebody thought of putting the meat on a stick and then turning it over the fire to cook the meat more evenly. The news of the new technique spread through-

out the land and spit roasting was born.

Spit roasting was state of the art cooking for thousands of years. For millennia people kneeled before a fire turning meat on a stick. Eventually, someone came up with the idea to cook food more quickly and more evenly in a box with walls that would absorb the heat from the fire. The news of the new technique spread throughout the land, and our third cooking revolution was born: oven roasting. No more spits, no more turning.

Roasting meat is still the most appealing dish to our senses, and it's easy to see why. Nothing beats a steak, charred crusty on the outside, perfectly medium-rare on the inside. These dishes beckon to you from the roasting pan as you walk by, tempting you with their aromas and juices.

The thought of roasting conjures up images of family dinners, holiday meals, and warm, cozy winter weekends. The aroma satisfies the spirit, enhancing the simplicity and value of life's basic necessities, all captured, honored, and celebrated by roasting.

Roasting is a nutritious approach to cooking high-protein foods with good carbs to help you and your family stay lean, strong, and energetic. We could learn a thing or two from our early ancestors in this regard. Hunting a two-ton animal took strength, endurance, and agility. Yoga is great for the soul but not much help in hunting a wooly mammoth. Cavemen were the first sustainability adapters. They utilized all of their resources and all the parts from their kill. They ate the meat, clothed themselves with the hides, and adapted the bones as tools. Waste was not part of their culture.

Fast-forward to your 21st century kitchen. What single technique for cooking meats

and vegetables can you master tonight, and use again and again, without following a recipe? You guessed it: roasting! Roasting transforms nature's magnificent creations grown and raised from the earth into golden bites of comfort, love, and nutrition for our families.

The technique for roasting vegetables is especially simple. All you need are your favorite vegetables, oil, salt, and pepper. Want to experiment? Add herbs and spices. What makes roasted vegetables mouth watering is cooking them at high temperatures. The delicious process of caramelization kicks in, which causes the natural sugars to oxidize and results in a sweet, nutty flavor with a

Roasting is a nutritious approach to cooking high-protein foods with good carbs to help your family stay lean, strong, and energetic.

golden-brown color. Roasting is also ideal for dense vegetables like potatoes, beets, and winter squash. It concentrates the natural sugars and intensifies flavor while retaining nutrients.

For meat I try to go with nutrient-dense food like grass-fed beef, organic free-range chicken and pork, and wild-caught fish whenever possible. Choosing your ingredients wisely is paramount. Organic and grass-fed meat is never naturally low-priced in today's marketplace. When the budget is a concern, I flip-flop ingredient portions, serving more root veggies and less meat. I always enjoy a cooking challenge where instincts combined with experimentation create delicious new dinners.

Your Roasting Guide

The guide is approximate times for medium. Cook times vary depending on the size/thickness of meat cut, the type/size of your oven, and the size/quality of the roasting pan used. For rare, cook to the lower times or a little under; for well done cook to the higher times.[126]

CATEGORY	CUT	WEIGHT	TEMPERATURE	TIME MINUTES PER LB.
Beef	Rib Bone in	4 to 6 lbs.	325°	23 to 24
	Rib boneless	4 to lbs.	325°	28 to 33
	Round or rump	2 1/2 to 4 lbs.	325°	30 to 35
		4 to 6 lbs.	425°	45-60 minutes total
Chicken	Whole	5 to 7 lbs.	350°	2 to 2/12 hrs. total
	Breast halves bone in	6 to 8 ounces	350°	30 to 40 minutes total
	Breast halves boneless	4 ounces	350°	20 to 30 minutes total
	Legs or thighs	4 to 8 ounces	350°	40 to 50 minutes total
Turkey	Whole	8 to 12 lbs.	325°	2 3/4 to 3 total
Unstuffed 15 to 17 minutes per lb.	Whole	12 to 14 lbs.	325°	3 to 3 3/4 total
	Whole	14 to 18 lbs.	325°	3 3/4 to 4 1/4 total
Stuffed 20 to 22 minutes per lb.	Whole	18 to 20 lbs.	325°	4 1/4 to 4 1/2 total
Pork	Loin bone in or boneless	2 to 5 lbs.	325°	20 to 30
	Crown	4 to 6 lbs.	325°	20 to 30
	Tenderloin	1 1/2 to 2 1/2 lbs.	425°	30 to 40 minutes total
Ham	Fresh bone in	5 to 7 lbs.	325°	22 to 25
	Fresh bone in	10 to 14 lbs.	325°	18 to 20
Lamb	Leg, bone in	5 to 7 lbs.	325°	20 to 25
	Leg bone in	7 to 9 lbs.	325°	15 to 20
	Leg boneless	4 to 7 lbs.	325°	25 to 30
Veal	Shoulder boneless	3 to 5 lbs.	325°	35 to 40
	Leg rump or round boneless	3 to 5 lbs.	325°	35 to 40

ROASTING METHODS	BENEFITS	TEMPERATURE / TIME
High/Low	Delivers a seared crust for golden color, texture, and flavor with a shorter roasting time.	Preheat oven to 450°F-500°F. Sear 15-20 minutes. Reduce heat to 325°F
Slow Roasting	Delivers juicy, tender, succulent flavor, and uniform cooking throughout with a longer roasting time.	Preheat oven to 275°F and cook at 275°F

Master One Roast
You Can Master Any Roast

1
> **Season the Meat**

Preheat the oven to 500°. Place the meat in the roasting pan. Season the meat using kosher salt and freshly ground black pepper, spice rubs, and fresh or dried herbs.

2
> **Season the Vegetables**

Wash your fresh vegetables. Cut into uniform pieces, quartered, or leave them whole—a real time saver. Place the vegetables in a large bowl and drizzle them with oil. Sprinkle with kosher salt, herbs and spices. Stir all around with your hands so that each piece is coated.

3
> **Combine the Ingredients**

Add the onions, garlic, ginger, carrots, potatoes, or root vegetables around the meat and pour ½ cup of juice or water in the pan. This will prevent the vegetables from burning and sticking to the pan.

4
> **Roast it**

Place the roasting pan in the oven and cook for 15-20 minutes at the high temperature. Then lower the temperature to 325°F and roast until done. This is the high-low technique. Remove from the oven and let rest 5-10 minutes. (See cook times chart for guidance.) For other vegetables such as broccoli and greens add to the roast during the last ½ hour of roasting.

Three Methods of Roasting

Whichever method you use, make sure to cook the food uncovered so that the hot, dry air can deliver the heat directly to the food without steaming it.

Method 1: Low heat

Cook slowly using an oven at 250 degrees to 325 degrees Fahrenheit. This temperature range is best for large or tough cuts of meat that contain a lot of connective tissue that needs to be broken down. Barbeque is a prime example of this method of slow-and-low roasting.

Method 2: High heat

Cook at high temperatures, 400-550 degrees if the cut is small enough to be finished cooking before the juices escape.

Method 3: Combination

This method combines high heat and low heat. Use high heat at either the beginning or the end of the cooking process, with most of the cooking done at a low temperature. This method gives a golden brown color, texture, and crust.

In roasting, the meat is generally removed from the heat before it is finished cooking and left to sit for a few minutes, while the inside cooks further from the residual heat. During roasting, meats are frequently basted on the surface with the juices created from the meat in the pan to reduce the loss of moisture by evaporation and to add flavor.

French Lemon Roasted Chicken with Vegetables and Gravy

2   large sweet onions, quartered.
4   cloves garlic, chopped.
1   pound parsnips, peeled, sliced in quarters lengthwise, then quarter.
1   pound carrots peeled, sliced in quarters lengthwise, then quarter.
5   celery stalks, peel top layer, cut in half lengthwise, then quarter.
1   large apple, peeled cored, slice into eigths.
4   tablespoons olive oil.
1/4   cup orange juice or water.
4   pounds whole chicken (option: swap chicken for turkey breast).
2   lemons.
1 1/2 tablespoon herbs de Provence.
3   sprigs rosemary.
       Kosher salt and freshly ground black pepper

For the gravy
2   cups chicken broth.
2   tablespoons rice flour.

COOK
1 hour 30 minutes
– 2 hours
SERVES
4-6

Preparation

❶ Preheat oven to 450°F.

❷ Place onions, garlic, parsnips, carrots, celery and apple in a roasting pan, drizzle with 2 tablespoons olive oil, juice of ½ lemon and season with kosher salt and pepper. Mix well and spread evenly in the pan; pour in ¼ cup orange juice or water.

❸ Place the chicken, breast side up, over the vegetables.

❹ Rub chicken all over with 1 tablespoon olive oil and the juice of half a lemon; season with herbs de Provence, kosher salt and pepper. Cut a lemon in half and put both halves inside chicken cavity, along with rosemary sprigs. Sprinkle herbs de Provence over vegetables.

❺ Put in the oven and roast for 10 minutes at 475°F reduce to 375°F and roast for 60-90 minutes.

❻ Raise heat to 425°F and baste chicken with the juices from the pan every 5 minutes for 10-15 minutes. Remove from the oven and let rest.

❼ Transfer chicken and vegetables to a large serving tray or plate.

❽ To make the gravy, heat the roasting pan on the stovetop, add chicken broth and bring to a boil. Stir in rice flour and cook, whisking occasionally, for 10 minutes. Serve with the roasted chicken and vegetables.

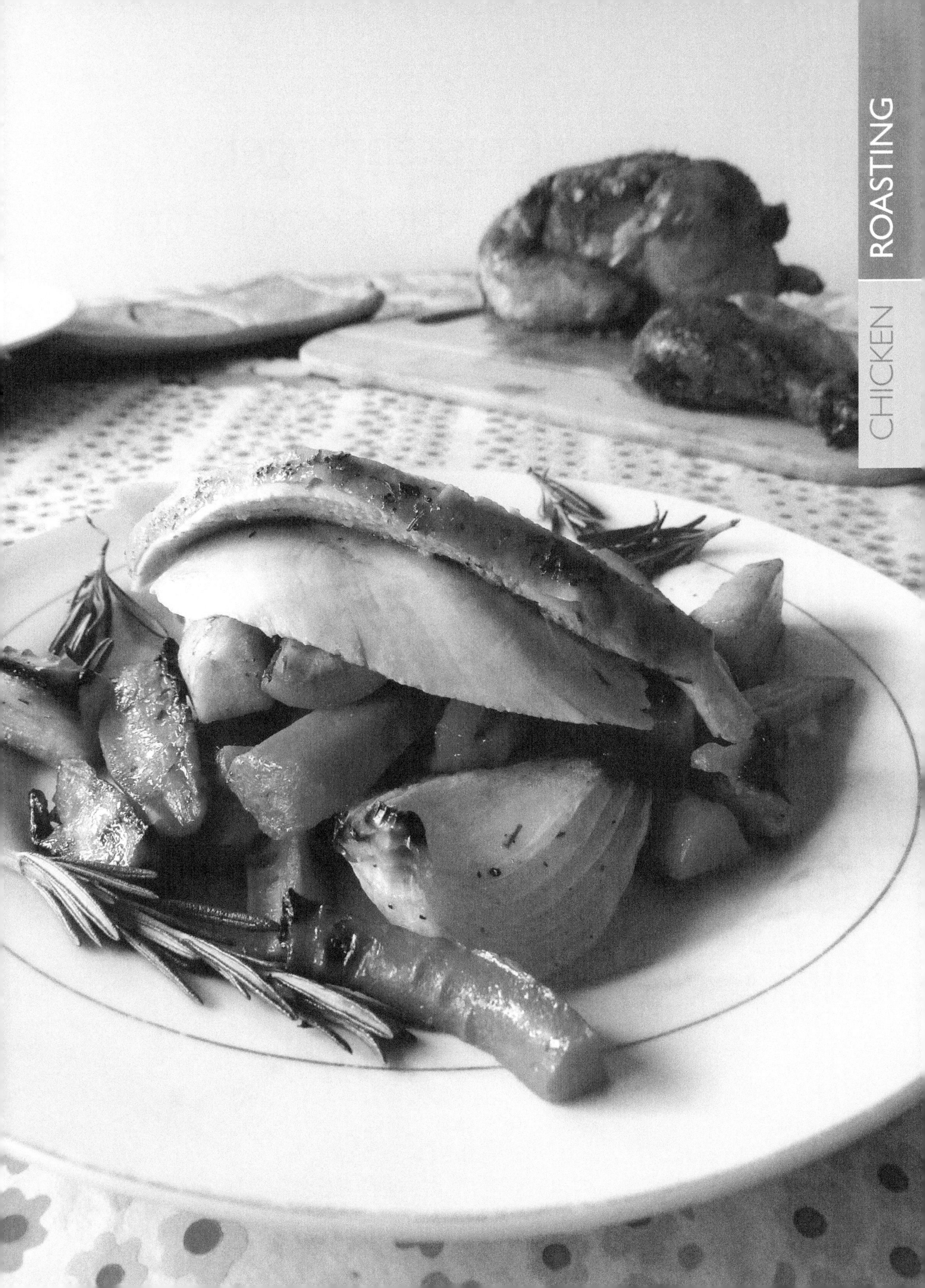

Dijon Chicken Fingers with Balsamic Sweet Potato and Fennel

COOK
1 hour 10 minutes
SERVES
6

2	cups panko bread crumbs, toasted.
2	sweet potatoes, scrubbed and cut into 2-inch cubes, skin on.
6	tablespoons olive oil.
1	tablespoon balsamic vinegar.
2	teaspoons honey.
2	large fennel bulbs, stalks removed, cut into 1½ -inch slices that are joined at the base.

2	eggs.
4	tablespoons Dijon mustard.
3	tablespoons dried tarragon.
1	cup brown rice flour.
3-4	pounds chicken breasts, sliced thin.
⅓	cup pumpkin seeds, roasted (optional).
⅓	cup feta cheese. Sea salt and freshly ground black pepper to taste.

Preparation

❶ Preheat the oven to 400°F.

❷ Place panko in a rimmed baking sheet and toast for a few minutes, in the oven, until browned, taking care not to burn. Transfer to a large plate, toss with 2 tablespoons olive oil and set aside.

❸ Increase oven temperature to 425 °F.

❹ Place sweet potato in a roasting pan; drizzle with 2 tablespoons olive oil, season with sea salt and black pepper and mix.

❺ In a medium bowl, whisk together balsamic vinegar, 2 tablespoons olive oil with the honey; add a pinch of salt. Place fennel bulbs in the bowl and toss with the mixture, then add to the pan with the sweet potato. Roast for 30 minutes; remove from oven and set aside.

❻ Meanwhile in a bowl, whisk together eggs, Dijon mustard and tarragon.

❼ Place rice flour on a large plate.

❽ Season the chicken with salt and pepper; dip in the flour, then the egg mixture and coat with Panko; place on a V rack.

❾ Place the V rack in the roasting pan with the sweet potato and fennel, return pan to the oven and cook for 20-30 minutes. After 10 minutes, drizzle chicken strips with a little olive oil (If you don't have a V rack, simply place the chicken in a separate roasting pan or cookie sheet).

❿ To serve, plate sweet potato and fennel, sprinkle with pumpkin seeds and crumbled feta cheese, and add chicken on top.

Hot Shot Wings

COOK	SERVES
1 hour 10 minutes	8

1   tablespoon canola oil.
4   pounds chicken wings, tips cut off.
2   limes cut into 8 wedges,
     to garnish the wings.

For the hot sauce:

3   tablespoons white miso.
3/4 cup soy sauce.
1/2 cup rice wine vinegar.
/4   cup your favorite hot sauce.
1/4 cup water.
4   tablespoons honey.
6   cloves garlic, crushed.
2   tablespoons fresh ginger, minced.
1/8 teaspoon black pepper.
2   bay leaves.
1/2 teaspoon chilli flakes.

For the dipping sauce:

/4   cup soy sauce.
1/2 cup rice wine vinegar.
/4   cup your favorite hot sauce.

> **Preparation**

❶ Preheat oven to 400°F and line a roasting pan with aluminium foil; coat lightly with canola oil and set aside.

❷ Wash and pat-dry the wings with paper kitchen towels, then place in a large bowl; set aside.

❸ Whisk miso with 3 tablespoons water for about 1 minute, until smooth.

❹ In a small pot, combine miso and the rest of the ingredients and bring to a boil. Reduce heat to medium-low and cook 3-5 minutes.

❺ Pour sauce over the wings and mix to coat well. (Option: place in fridge for an hour to marinate).

❻ Arrange wings in rows in the prepared roasting pan; drizzle with any extra sauce left and place in the oven. Cook for about 1 hour, turn the heat up to 475°F and cook for 5-10 minutes longer, until browned.

❼ Remove pan from the oven, let cool for a minute, then transfer wings to a plate, squeeze juice of 2 lime wedges over the wings. Garnish with lime wedges.

❽ For the dipping sauce, whisk together soy sauce and hot sauce with the rice wine vinegar.

Cajun Paprika Roasted Chicken

2	tablespoons brown sugar.
2	tablespoons paprika.
3	tablespoons tomato paste.
2	tablespoons warm water.
4	tablespoons olive oil.
1/4	teaspoon cayenne pepper.
	Juice of half a orange.
4	pounds fresh chicken, quartered (organic preferred).
1	tablespoon grape seed oil.
2	Yukon gold potatoes, skins on, cut in half.
2	sweet potatoes, skins on, cut in half.
3	parsnips or turnip, diced.
1	large sweet onion, quartered.
2	tablespoon Old Bay seasoning.
2	tablespoons fresh rosemary, chopped.
	Sea salt and freshly ground black pepper.

COOK
1 hour 15 minutes
SERVES
4-6

> **Preparation**

❶ Preheat oven to 425°F.

❷ In a medium bowl, combine sugar, paprika, tomato paste, water, 2 tablespoons olive oil, orange juice and cayenne pepper together and rub chicken with the mixture to coat generously.

❸ Lightly coat a roasting pan with grape seed or canola oil and place chicken in the middle of the pan.

❹ In a large bowl, toss vegetables with Old Bay seasoning, rosemary and 2 tablespoons olive oil; season with salt and pepper and arrange vegetables around the chicken.

❺ Cook for 1 - 1 ½ hours, remove from oven and let sit 5 minutes before serving.

Pushups
you can do them anywhere

Pushups are the old-school exercise that has never lost its cachet: you can do pushups anywhere, anytime, at any age. Pushups task your shoulders, chest, back, biceps, triceps, and core all in one exercise.

Do variations as you improve: hands together, hands far apart, decline/incline position, and clapping. Hold the plank position with elbows straight and bent for additional abdominal work. Using the weight of your own body is an intense workout.

Pork Loin with Parsnips and Pears

3   pears, peeled, cored and quartered.
1   apple, peeled, cored and quartered.
2   turnips, skinned and sliced.
2   large sweet onions, sliced thick.
2   tablespoons olive oil.
2   pounds pork loin.
1   tablespoon dried rosemary.
2   tablespoons dried thyme.
1   tablespoon garlic powder.
½   cup apple juice.
½   cup raw walnuts.
    Juice of ½ lemon.
    Kosher salt and freshly ground
    black pepper, to taste.

COOK
1 hour 10 minutes
SERVES
4-6

Preparation

❶ Preheat oven to 375°F.

❷ In a large bowl, lightly coat pears, apple, turnips and onions with olive oil and lemon juice, season with kosher salt and pepper; place in a roasting pan.

❸ Roast for 45 minutes, remove the pan from the oven and turn oven temperature up to 400°F.

❹ Rub loin with olive oil, kosher salt, rosemary, thyme, garlic, and pepper; pour apple juice into the pan and lay loin on top of the fruit and vegetables. Sprinkle with walnuts and return pan to the oven; roast for 20 minutes, turn to broil and broil for 3 minutes to brown.

❺ Remove from oven and let rest for a few minutes before serving.

Center Cut Pork Chops with Roasted Tomatoes and White Bean Salad

4   clusters vine cherry tomatoes, approximately ½ pound each.

3   tablespoons olive oil.

4   center-cut thick pork chops.

2   lemons.

4   teaspoons fennel seeds.

4   tablespoons butter.

8   large fresh sage leaves.

I   (15-ounces) can white (cannellini) beans, drained and rinsed.

I   red onion, sliced.

4   cups fresh arugula.

I   small block of parmesan, for grating.

COOK
1 hour 10 minutes
SERVES
4

❶ Preheat oven to 450°F.

❷ Place tomatoes on a roasting pan; drizzle with 1 tablespoon olive oil and season with salt and pepper. Place in the oven and roast for 25-30 minutes; remove and set aside to cool.

❸ Rub chops with the juice of 1 lemon, salt, pepper, fennel seeds, butter and sage leaves.

❹ Place in the oven and cook for approximately 15-20 minutes, until the pork chops are golden brown.

❺ Combine beans and sliced onion in a large bowl, mix in remaining olive oil and the juice of the second lemon, add arugula and toss together.

❻ Once the pork is done, let it cool for 3 minutes.

❼ Serve on a bed of bean salad, topped with freshly grated parmesan and a cluster of roasted tomatoes.

Potatoes
The World's
Fourth-Largest
Food Crop

The origins of the potato date back to the Inca Indians of the Peruvian Andes mountains, where they were the first to cultivate this tuber around 8,000-5,000 BCE.

The potato first arrived in Ireland in 1589. Eventually, European farmers found potatoes easier to grow than other staple crops, like wheat and oats. Potato expansion was encouraged by the discovery that potatoes contain many vitamins needed to support sustenance.

One of Vincent Van Gogh's first great works of art was The Potato Eaters, completed in 1885. Van Gogh empathized with peasant life and observed it so intently that he wrote to his brother Theo, "I have become so involved in it that I rarely think of anything else."

The Potato Eaters failed to become successful in his lifetime; however, today the painting is considered a masterpiece.

Sticky Ribs with Thyme Baked Potato

1   rack of pork ribs, about 3 ½ - 4 pounds.

1   tablespoon olive oil.

8   sprigs fresh thyme.

4   russet potatoes, washed and halved, skins on.

     Sea salt and freshly ground black pepper

For the sauce

¼   cup apple cider vinegar.

1   cup ketchup.

⅛   cup molasses.

⅛   cup Worcestershire sauce.

1   tablespoon garlic powder.

2   tablespoons honey.

1   tablespoon ground cumin.

½   tablespoon chilli powder.

½   cup water.

COOK
2 hours
SERVES
6-8

Preparation

1 Preheat oven to 350° F.

2 In a small saucepan, mix together all sauce ingredients; season with kosher salt and black pepper and add ½ cup of water. Gently heat, stirring, for 1-2 minutes and set aside.

3 Season potatoes with salt and pepper and drizzle with olive oil; and mix to coat. Wrap each potato and a sprig of thyme in aluminium foil and place on a baking sheet.

4 Lay down heavey tin foil on the bottom of the roasting pan, pour in 1/4 cup of water. Place ribs in the pan and coat both sides with the sauce. Cover the pan tightly with aluminium foil and place in the oven, together with the potatoes. Cook for 1½ hours.

5 Remove potatoes from the oven, remove tin foil and put back in the oven and cook ribs without aluminium foil for 30 minutes longer. Baste the ribs every 10 minutes, as they brown. For the last 10-15 minutes raise temperature to 425°F.

6 Before serving, warm up potatoes in the oven.

Pecan Crusted Salmon with Basil Cream and Asparagus

For the salmon

1 ½ -2 pounds salmon filet.
1   cup pecans.
½   teaspoon paprika.
1   tablespoon garlic, chopped.
2   tablespoons ginger, chopped.
1   tablespoon Bragg's aminos or soy sauce.
1   tablespoon honey.
1   tablespoon olive oil.
2   pounds asparagus, trimmed.
    Juice of ½ lemon.
    Sea salt and freshly ground
    black pepper, to taste.

For the basil cream

¾   cup cashews.
1   cup coconut milk.
2   tablespoons apple cider vinegar.
½   cup olive oil.
1   cloves garlic.
1   teaspoon black pepper.
1   teaspoon sea salt.
2   cups fresh basil, stemmed.
3-4 scallions, chopped.

COOK
15-20 minutes
SERVES
4-6

Preparation

1 Soak cashews in water for 15-20 minutes, then drain.

2 Meanwhile, preheat oven to 425°F.

3 Place salmon filet in a roasting pan and squeeze lemon juice liberally over the filet.

4 In a food processor, coarsely chop pecans; add paprika, garlic and ginger and pulse a few times to mix together.

5 In a small bowl, mix Bragg's aminos, honey, olive oil and pecan mixture together and spread evenly over the salmon filet; add asparagus to the pan and cook for 15-20 minutes, or until salmon is fork-tender. Remove from oven, let sit for a minute, and then cut into 4-6 pieces.

To make the Basil cream

1 In a food processor, combine drained cashews and the rest of the basil cream ingredients, except for the scallions, and process to a smooth puree. Pour into a small bowl and stir in the scallions.

2 To plate, lay 4 asparagus spears in a row, drizzle with basil cream and place salmon on top.

Sticky Pepper Shrimp with Watermelon Avocado Salad

2   heads broccoli, cut into florets.
2   tablespoons olive oil, divided.
1   cup jasmine rice.
7   tablespoons soy sauce.
2   tablespoons hoisin sauce.
2   tablespoons maple syrup.
3   tablespoons jerk seasoning.
6   cups watermelon, diced
     (option: use 2 peeled and thinly sliced
     apples when melon is out of season).
2   avocados, peeled and diced.
2   pounds shrimp, cleaned and
     deveined (wild caught preferred).
½   pound arugula.
½   cup feta cheese.
     Juice of ½ lemon.
     Sea salt and freshly ground
     black pepper, to taste.

COOK
1 hour 10 minutes
SERVES
4

> **Preparation** >

❶ Preheat oven to 425°F.

❷ Place broccoli in a roasting pan, drizzle with 1 tablespoon olive oil and lightly sprinkle with sea salt and black pepper; place in the oven for 5-10 minutes, while you prepare the shrimp.

❸ While broccoli roasts, cook jasmine rice following package directions.

❹ In a small bowl, combine soy sauce, hoisin, maple syrup, jerk seasoning, lemon juice and 1 tablespoon olive oil; whisk until thoroughly mixed together.

❺ Remove roasting pan from the oven, coat each shrimp with the mixture and place in roasting pan with the broccoli. Cook for approximately 10-15 minutes.

❻ Meanwhile, in a large bowl, combine diced watermelon, avocado and arugula, season with a squeeze of lemon juice, extra virgin olive oil, salt and pepper and crumble the feta cheese on top.

❼ Serve shrimp with rice and a generous portion of watermelon avocado salad.

Zucchini
one of the easiest vegetables to home-grow

Although the zucchini is treated as a vegetable, like tomatoes it is technically a fruit. Pick and choose the smaller ones under 8" long: as zucchini grows its sweetness diminishes.

Low in calories, and high in folate, potassium, and vitamin A, zucchini is one of the easiest vegetables to home-grow in temperate climates. As a popular delicacy zucchini flowers are edible. These golden flowers are far too fragile to mass produce, but you'll find them in season at farmers' markets. The most popular way to prepare these lovely blossoms is fast frying.

Flounder with Beets and Zucchini

1 pound baby beets.

3 medium zucchini.

2 cups chicken stock.

1 teaspoon of butter.

1 cup long grain wild rice, thoroughly rinsed.

1 tablespoon olive oil.

2-2 ½ pounds flounder (you may also use cod, tilapia, flounder, tile or bass).
Juice of 1 lemon.

To serve

2 medium ripe tomatoes, seeded and diced.

¼ cup capers.

½ bunch fresh chives, thinly sliced.
Sea salt and freshly ground black pepper, to taste.

COOK
1 hour 20 minutes
SERVES
4-6

> **Preparation**

❶ Preheat oven to 375 °F.

❷ Slice zucchini lengthwise into wide strips; place in a container and refrigerate until needed.

❸ Wash thoroughly, but don't peel beets, season with sea salt and pepper and cover with aluminum foil.

❹ Place on a flat cookie tray or a heavy aluminum foil sheet and roast for 1 hour.

❺ Meanwhile, after beets have cooked for 45 minutes, start preparing the rice. Heat chicken stock in a sautoir pan, add butter and a pinch of sea salt; bring to a boil, and stir in rice. Cover, reduce heat to low and simmer for 20-25 minutes.

❻ Season zucchini with salt and pepper, drizzle with olive oil and lemon juice and lay flat on a roasting pan.

❼ Season fish with olive oil and a pinch of salt and pepper and place on top of the zucchini.

❽ Turn the heat up to 400°F and cook in the oven until fish is flaky, about 10-20 minutes.

❾ Remove beets from the oven and remove the tin foil, let cool then use a paper towel to push skins off with your thumb, slice and set aside.

❶❶ Serve fish over zucchini and beets, topped with diced tomatoes, capers and chives with a side of wild rice.

Beef and Lamb Meatballs with Roasted Squash and Pomegranate

COOK
60 minutes
SERVES
4-6

1   large butternut squash, peeled, seeded and diced into 1-inch cubes.
4   tablespoons olive oil.
3   garlic cloves, sliced.
½   pound spinach.
1   pound ground beef.
1   pound ground lamb.
2   eggs, lightly beaten.
1   cup panko or bread crumbs.
1   onion, minced.

For the pomegranate salsa

1   cup raw almonds, coarsely ground.
2   cups mint, shredded.
    Seeds from 1 pomegranate
    Juice of 1 lemon
    Sea salt and freshly ground black pepper to taste.

Preparation

❶ Preheat oven to 375°F.

❷ Place squash in a roasting pan, season with 1 tablespoon olive oil, a pinch of kosher salt and black pepper and mix; cook for 45 minutes.

❸ As the squash cooks, heat 1 tablespoon olive oil in a sautoir pan, add garlic and cook for 10 seconds, then add spinach and wilt for about 20 seconds; transfer to a plate and place in the refrigerator to cool.

❹ In a large bowl, place ground beef, lamb, eggs, panko, and onions. Roughly chop the wilted spinach and add to the mixture; combine thoroughly and then form into small balls.

❺ After the squash has cooked for 45 minutes, add meatballs to the same pan and return to the oven. Cook for 20 minutes longer, until meatballs are golden brown and butternut squash begins to caramelize.

❻ In a bowl, combine almonds, mint and pomegranate seeds with the lemon juice, remaining olive oil and season with salt and pepper.

❼ Serve meatballs and squash with the minted pomegranate.

Coriander Sirloin with Shallots, Sunchokes and Asparagus

1   pound sunchokes (option: substitute with artichoke hearts, water chestnuts, jicama, parsnips, or potatoes).

3   shallots.

2   tablespoons olive oil.

2   tablespoons butter, melted.

1   tablespoon minced thyme.

1   cup picked cilantro.

2   tablespoons whole coriander seeds.

2   pounds boneless sirloin steak (grass fed preferred).

2   cups beef broth.

1   bunch asparagus, trimmed.

2   tablespoons rice flour.

     Juice of 2 limes.

     Sea salt and freshly ground black pepper.

COOK
50 minutes
SERVES
4 -6

Preparation

❶ Preheat oven to 350°F.

❷ Slice sunchokes and shallots, place in a roasting pan, season with salt and pepper and coat with 1 tablespoon olive oil and the butter. Sprinkle with minced thyme, place pan in the oven and cook for 20-25 minutes.

❸ In a food processor, combine cilantro, lime juice, coriander seeds and remaining 1 tablespoon olive oil and pulse to a smooth puree. Coat the steak with the mixture and set aside.

❹ Once sunchokes have cooked for 20 minutes, turn the heat up to 500°F and place the steak in the same roasting pan; cook 12-15 minutes for seared medium.

❺ After 6 minutes, remove sunchokes and add asparagus to the roasting pan; cook asparagus with the steak for 8-9 minutes.

❻ Remove pan from oven and transfer the steak and cooked asparagus to a plate; leaving the juices in the pan.

❼ Place the roasting pan on the stovetop over a medium heat. Add beef broth and rice flour and whisk and cook for 10 -15, until gravy has thickened.

❽ Slice the steak and serve with the vegetables and gravy.

Louisiana Roast Beef with Pan Gravy and Mustard Brussels sprouts

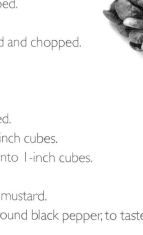

COOK
2 hours 30 minutes
SERVES
6

4-5 pounds beef tenderloin or top round.
1 small sweet onion, chopped.
2 celery stalks, chopped.
½ green bell pepper, seeded and chopped.
4 cloves garlic, minced.
½ teaspoon dry mustard.
½ teaspoon cayenne.
2 tablespoons butter, melted.
2 Yukon potatoes cut in 1-inch cubes.
2 large turnips, peeled cut into 1-inch cubes.
1 pound Brussels sprouts.
3 tablespoons whole grain mustard.
Kosher salt and freshly ground black pepper, to taste.

> **Preparation**

1 Preheat oven to 350°F. Place meat in a large roasting pan, fat side up.

2 Combine onions, celery, green pepper, garlic, dry mustard, cayenne pepper, kosher salt, black pepper, and melted butter in a bowl and mix together.

3 Cut slits in the meat, making 1-inch diamond pattern, and rub with the mixture. Add ½ cup water to the pan and cook, uncovered in the oven for about 1 hour and 30 minutes.

4 Remove pan from the oven, add potatoes and turnips, coat Brussels sprouts with whole grain mustard and spread evenly. Season with salt and pepper and cook for another hour. Meat thermometer should read about 160°F for medium doneness.

5 Remove from oven and let the meat rest for about 10 minutes, before slicing.

Stuffed Roasted Sweet Potato

4   sweet potatoes, scrubbed.

3   tablespoons extra virgin olive oil.

1   bunch Swiss chard, (preferably rainbow), stemmed and sliced.

4   cloves garlic, sliced.

1   pounds soft goat cheese.

1   cup crushed pumpkin seeds, chopped (preferably raw or roasted unsalted).

1   lemon, quartered.

    Sea salt and freshly ground black pepper, to taste.

COOK
1 hour 30 minutes
SERVES
4-6

Preparation

❶ Heat oven to 375°F.

❷ Brush sweet potatoes with olive oil, season with salt and pepper and place on a roasting pan. Cook in the oven for approximately 1 -1 ½ hours.

❸ After the sweet potatoes have cooked for 45 minutes, heat 1 tablespoon olive oil in a sautoir pan and lightly brown garlic. Add Swiss chard and season with salt and pepper. Cook for a few minutes, until tender.

❹ Remove the potatoes from the oven and slice down the center lengthwise; mash lightly with a fork and fill potatoes with Swiss chard, crumbled goat cheese and pumpkin seeds.

❺ Drizzle the remaining olive oil on top of the stuffing and serve with lemon wedges.

Roasted Vegetables

For the roasted vegetables

½ butternut squash, peeled cut into small chunks.

2 parsnips cut into chunks.

⅓ cup olive oil.

2 red onions, quartered.

I red bell pepper, seeded and sliced.

8 ounces shitake or crimini mushrooms, halved.

I medium eggplant, peeled and cut into large chunks or whole Brussels sprouts.

2 zucchini, skins on, sliced thick.

3 cloves garlic, minced.

4 sprigs fresh rosemary, stemmed and chopped. Sea salt and freshly ground black pepper, to taste.

For the watercress salad

I pound fresh watercress.

⅓ cup walnuts, chopped.

I honeycrisp apple, peeled, cored and thinly sliced.

For the dressing

¼ cup red wine vinegar.

1-2 teaspoons Dijon mustard.

½ cup extra virgin olive oil.

COOK
1 hour
SERVES
4-6

Preparation

1 Preheat oven to 400°F.

2 Place squash and parsnips in a roasting pan; drizzle with olive oil and season with salt and pepper. Place in the oven and cook for 30 minutes.

3 Meanwhile combine all the other vegetables in a large bowl. Add olive oil, rosemary and garlic and season with sea salt and freshly ground black pepper; toss to coat. Transfer to the roasting pan and place in the oven. Roast for 30-40 minutes or until tender and nicely browned (option: sprinkle a little goat cheese on top).

4 In a large bowl, combine watercress, apples and walnuts.

5 Whisk together red wine vinegar with mustard, add olive oil, whisk, and drizzle over watercress; season with a dash of sea salt and fresh black pepper and toss.

6 Serve salad with the roasted vegetables.

Stuffed Delicata Squash

2   large delicata squash
      (or butternut squash).
1   teaspoon nutmeg.
1   tablespoon cinnamon.
2   tablespoons olive oil, divided.
1   yellow onion, diced.
3   carrots, diced.
2   sprigs rosemary.
1   cup farro (or use quinoa
      or pearled barley, following
      cook times on package).
2   cups parmesan.
1   bunch watercress.
1   cup walnuts, rough chopped.
      Juice of 1 lemon.
      Kosher salt and freshly ground black pepper, to taste.

COOK
2 hours
SERVES
4

....

> **Preparation**

❶ Preheat the oven to 375° F.

❷ Slice the squash in half; carve out the seeds, season with salt, pepper, nutmeg and cinnamon, then place in the oven and cook for 1 ½ - 2 hours.

❸ Heat a sautoir pan with 1 tablespoon olive oil; add onions and carrots and sauté until softened, 3-5 minutes.

❹ Bring 3 cups water to a boil in a large saucepan and add rosemary and farro. Reduce heat to very low and cook covered for 45 minutes.

❺ Transfer cooked farro to a bowl and let cool for 15 minutes.

❻ Once cooled, combine farro with carrot and onion mixture. Fill roasted squash halves with the mixture and sprinkle with parmesan cheese.

❼ Dress watercress and walnuts with lemon juice, olive oil and black pepper.

❽ Serve stuffed squash with the watercress walnut salad.

Zucchini, Fennel and Tomato Tian

COOK
55 minutes
SERVES
4

2 fennel bulbs, green tops trimmed.
1 tablespoon olive oil.
¼ cup balsamic vinegar.
2 pounds zucchini.
2 large ripe tomatoes.
1 cup dill.
1 cup feta cheese.
½ cup panko or breadcrumbs.

> **Preparation**

❶ Preheat oven to 375°F.

❷ Dice fennel and coat with olive oil and balsamic vinegar. Place on a roasting tray and cook for 15 minutes.

❸ As the fennel cooks, slice zucchini and tomatoes into equal-sized slices. Pick dill and crumble feta cheese.

❹ Remove fennel from the oven and let it cool for 5 minutes. Layer zucchini and tomatoes slices on top, alternating with feta and dill in between.

❺ Cook in the oven for 40 minutes.

❻ With 15 minutes of cooking left, sprinkle panko or breadcrumbs on top of the vegetables and drizzle with olive oil.

❼ Raise the oven temperature to 400°F and cook until the breadcrumbs are golden brown.

Pilaf & Grain Bowls

Grains are among the most versatile food staples. In a short period of time, with minimal effort, the pilaf technique allows for a transfer of flavor from the cooking liquid to the grains themselves.

Moreover, grains are among the most affordable and nutrient-dense ingredients.

Grains

The Healthiest Budget Stretcher on the Market Today

A common misconception places white rice in the same category as other white foods such as white flour, pasta, and sugar. Rice, however, is not entirely made of carbohydrates. After carbohydrate, protein constitutes the second most abundant component in rice.[129] In fact, compared to other grains' protein, rice protein is considered one of the highest quality proteins. It has all eight of the essential amino acids, the building blocks of strong bodies. No wonder rice milk has become so popular as a milk substitute. Rice requires very little storage space and leaves no waste since it is completely edible. In terms of cost, there is no food on the planet that can approach to its nutritional value.

When professional chefs cook grains, they use specific methods to achieve the most appealing flavor and appearance. One of the most well known is rice pilaf. In America when most people hear rice pilaf, they most likely envision a side dish of seasoned rice and vegetables like carrots and peas. But pilaf can offer so much more than this. For the pilaf section we will explore both the traditional rice pilaf concept and an expanded pilaf array that includes other grains like quinoa, barley, and couscous. We are about to discover the extraordinary culinary possibilities of cooking with grains.

A Biography of Rice

Who would have ever thought this small, ancient grain called rice would become a staple food that sustains two-thirds of the world's population? Rice grows in a wide spectrum of climates: from the deserts of Saudi Arabia to the wetlands of Southeast Asia. This versatility has enabled rice to be become one of the most widely eaten foods in the world. Rice has been produced commercially in the USA for more than 300 years. Almost all the rice grown in the USA comes from six states: Arkansas, California, Louisiana, Mississippi, Missouri, and Texas.

Rice plays a vital role in providing fuel and nutrients to people across the globe, providing one fifth of the world's dietary energy supply.[127] Rice has fed more people over a longer period of time than any other crop in history.[128] Rice supplies carbohydrates to energize brain performance, enable bodily functions, and provide everyday growth and repair.

Rice is also healthy for what it doesn't contain. Rice is free of cholesterol and low in fat. The small amount of fat found in rice is mostly unsaturated. Rice contains practically no sodium, so if anyone in your family needs to watch their salt intake, rice is practically a super food.

Like braising and roasting both rice and pilaf have historic origins in the development of civilizations around the world over thousands of years. Chinese records of rice cultivation go back 4,000 years.[130] In classical Chinese the words for agriculture and for rice culture are synonymous. In several Asian languages the words for rice and food are identical. The custom of throwing rice at weddings derives from the ancient Chinese religious belief that rice is the symbol of fertility.

From China the cultivation of rice spread throughout India and then passed on to Greece and areas of the Mediterranean, Southern Europe, and parts of North Africa. From Europe rice was brought to the New World.

Portugal introduced it to Brazil, and it traveled from Spain to Central and South America.

Food historians date pilaf as far back as the fifth century BCE, possibly first appearing in the Middle East.[131] Many credit the Persian Empire with the dish's creation. During this period trading with Persia was widespread. Pilaf became particularly popular in Mediterranean dishes, especially in Greece, the Middle East, Israel, and parts of Eastern Europe.

One of the earliest literary references to pilaf can be found in the histories of Alexander the Great. According to legend, Alexander was served pilaf for the first time following his capture of the Sogdian capital of Marakanda (modern day Samarkand, Uzbekistan), and brought the dish back to Macedonia.[132]

There are hundreds of different types of rice. For our purposes, we'll mostly focus on long-grain basmati and jasmine rice. I find these varieties to be the tastiest and cook with them the most. And they contain less starch than other varieties, so the cooked grains are drier and more separate. Brown rice, which is also available in long-grain, is a lot chewier and heartier than white rice and takes about twice the amount of time and water to cook.

What is the difference between brown and white rice, exactly? When rice is harvested, it must be processed before being sent to the market to be sold. In the case of both white and brown rice, the inedible outer hull of the rice is removed to make the grain of the rice accessible. For white rice, the individual grains are further stripped of both the bran and germ. The grains are then polished to a smooth, white appearance.

What are the nutritional differences between white and brown rice? Because of the milling process in white rice, brown rice is higher in magnesium and other minerals. It also has more fiber. For example, a cup of white long-grain rice contains just one gram of fiber, whereas a cup of brown rice contains four.[133] As a point of reference, you're shooting for 19-30 grams of fiber per day for your kids depending on their age and gender.[134] As for adults, women need 25 grams per day and men need 38 grams per day.[135]

So if brown rice is more nutritional, then why is white rice so much more popular? In most parts of the world white rice is preferred because many people prefer the taste and texture. White rice cooks faster and tends to be fluffier. White rice can also be stored longer and in more unfavorable conditions than brown rice. Brown rice should ideally be refrigerated, and should be eaten within six months.

Whole Grains: Nature's Wealth of Nutrition

The popularity of ancient grains has exploded in recent years. Demand for foods containing quinoa, chia, millet, buckwheat, and amaranth has skyrocketed. Although this new fare is trendy to many of us, these grains have been main staples for populations around the globe for thousands of years. In some ancient societies grains were considered sacred and held their place as food for the gods.

Grains have surged in popularity due to consumers' desire to look for healthy options. Fortunately, the current push is to get back to basics by cooking foods that are clean and as close to their natural state as possible. More consumers today are trying to eliminate processed foods and put real food on the table. And that is exactly the philosophy of Two Pans and a Pot: buy fresh, cook fresh, and eat fresh along with engaging in regular physical activity.

Whole grains are seeds that nature intended to grow into new plants. Just like eggs contain all the necessary vitamins, minerals, and proteins to create life so do grains.[147] All grains start life as whole grains in their natural state growing in the fields. Whole grains are the entire seed of a plant. This seed is made up of three key edible parts—the bran, the germ, and the endosperm.

What about organic rice? This one is a no brainer. Go organic. Sure, it's more expensive, but if you buy it in 10lb bags, the cost difference per meal will be pennies, making it one of the more cost-effective ways to support sustainable agriculture and to ingest the richer array of micronutrients contained in plants grown organically.

The Germ

The germ is the embryo, which has the potential to sprout into a new plant. It contains many B vitamins and some protein, minerals, and healthy fats.

The Endosperm

The endosperm is the germ's food supply, which provides essential energy to the young plant so it can send forth roots retrieve water and sprout leaves to capture the sunlight's photosynthesizing power. The endosperm is by far the largest portion of the kernel. It contains starchy carbohydrates, proteins and small amounts of vitamins and minerals.

Whole Grains and Refined Grains

Grains are divided into two groups: whole and refined. Whole grains contain the entire grain kernel, whereas refined grains have been milled to remove the bran and germ. Refined grains are the flours used in most food products. In recent years, whole grains have grown in popularity over refined grains due to the loss of iron, fiber, and B vitamins in refined grains.

The good news is different types of grains are not difficult to cook. In staying true to our cooking technique philosophy throughout *Two Pans and a Pot*, if you learn to cook one grain, you can cook any grain. The main difference between cooking rice grains and other grains is the liquid ratio and cooking time; that's it. In the pilaf section we include a chart that gives you the grain-to-liquid ration of prevalent grains along with their cooking times.

Grains are high in fiber, protein and are inexpensive. Compared to any other food priced per pound no other food can come close to the nutritional and monetary value of grains, especially when you are feeding a family.

The Grain Controversy

Simultaneous to the current popularity surge in grains, there is also a growing movement of people who believe that humans should not eat grains. Similar to the vegan vs. omnivore debate people are advocating the elimination of grains from the diet, especially due to the gluten found within them. For someone with celiac disease, a gluten free diet is absolutely essential. Gluten is a general name for the proteins found in wheat, barley and rye. For more information on gluten see the "Are the Foods in Your Refrigerator and Cupboards Trying to Kill You?" section.

One of the most popular and influential diets in the last decade is the grain free Paleo diet. The Paleo diet or as some like to call it, the caveman diet is derived from a pre-historical diet based on evidence that we did not eat grains. [149] The Paleo diet is based upon the fundamental concept that the optimal diet is the one to which we genetically adapted; meat, vegetables, fruits, nuts and fats.

There is a real perception today that a gluten free diet is healthier, so why do people eat grains and why do we have a grain section in *Two Pans and a Pot*.

Grains are high in fiber, protein and are inexpensive. Compared to any other food priced per pound no other food can come close to the nutritional and monetary value of grains, especially when you are feeding a family.

Grains also contain important vitamins and minerals like magnesium and B vitamins, which are hard to get from other sources. Most importantly, by cutting out an entire food group, it's extremely difficult to maintain a balanced diet for you and your family.

In *Two Pans and a Pot* we advocate for an omnivorous diet, not cutting out major food groups or over indulging in one major food group over another. Unless you have food allergies or medical dietary restrictions a well balanced diet is key to a healthy mind, body and spirit.

Everyone should nonetheless pay close attention to the amount of refined grains your family consumes on a daily basis. So many kids and adults hardly eat a single meal without some type of refined grain. Common breakfast foods include cereal, toast, oatmeal, granola, donuts, pancakes and waffles. For lunch and snacks: sandwiches, heroes, subs, panini, crackers, wraps, burgers, and pizza. Then for dinner, breaded chicken, pasta, croutons in salad, and buttered bread on the side. Refined grains are so engrained in our culture that it seems we don't know how to eat a meal without them.

The bottom line: Eat everything in moderation, and eat a variety of different foods, whether it's grains, fruits, vegetables or protein. Eat whole grains rather than refined grains. Nutrition is going to be different for each individual, and sweeping generalizations like "Don't eat grains" or "No one should eat ever eat meat" should be taken with a grain of salt. What truly and sincerely matters is that you and your family eat real food and not processed packaged pseudo-foods.

Timetable and Measurement Ratio

For the Most Popular and Healthy Grains

GRAIN	CUPS GRAIN TO LIQUID	COOKING TIME	YIELD (CUPS)
Amaranth	1 to 3	15 minutes	2 2/3
Barley pearl	1 to 3	45 to 55 minutes	4
Basmati Rice	1 to 2	16 to 20 minutes	4
Brown rice	1 to 2 1/2	35 to 40 minutes	4
Buckwheat unroasted	1 to 2	15 minutes	3 1/2
Buckwheat roasted (kasha)	1 to 2	15 minutes	3
Bulgur	1 to 2	15 minutes	3
Couscous	1 to 1/2	5 to 10 minutes	3 1/2
Farro	1 to 3	45 minutes	3
Grits	1 to 5	40-50 minutes	3
Jasmine Rice	1 to 2	15 to 20 minutes	3
Millet	1 to 3	25 to 30, 10 minutes rest	5
Oats steel cut	1 to 4	20 minutes	2
Quinoa	1 to 2	10 to 12 minutes	3 1/2
White rice	1 to 2	18 to 20 minutes	3
Wild Rice	1 to 3	30 to 45 minutes	4

Dominate One Pilaf

You Can Dominate Any Pilaf

1

Slice and Dice

Dice all your vegetables and onions to roughly ¼ in. pieces. The more uniform your pieces, the more evenly they will cook. Mince garlic and/or shallot.

2

Sweat the Vegetables

Heat the sautoir over medium-low heat until hot, then add 1-2 Tbsp. olive oil. Add the vegetables then salt, pepper and dried spices and spice. Sweat the vegetables. Cook a 5-10 minutes stir frequently—remember, you don't want to brown the food, so keep it moving until vegetables are soft and onions are translucent. Add the meat or fish cook a few minutes to brown on both sides.
(Follow the recipe as to whether the meat stays in the pilaf to cook with the grain or it is removed and added later.)

3

Add the Grains

Add your rice or grain to the pan and stir so the grains are coated with oil.

4

Add the Broth

For great flavor add chicken, beef or vegetable broth; you can use water. How much liquid you add depends on the type of rice or grain you are cooking, different types of grains absorb different amounts of liquid.
For accurate measurements see the grain chart.
Cook covered. Bring the broth to a boil, reduce heat to low and cover. Do not stir the rice or grain for the rest of the cooking time. (Put meat or fish back in the pan if the recipe calls for it.)

Creole Andouille Chicken Rice Pilaf with Red Beans

2   tablespoons extra virgin olive oil.

1   medium sweet onion, chopped.

2   celery stalks, diced.

1   large green pepper, seeded and diced.

3   cloves garlic, minced.

⅛   teaspoon cayenne pepper.

2   links smoked andouille sausage, cut lengthwise into quarters
     then crosswise into ¼-inch wedges.

1   pound boneless chicken thighs cut into 1-inch cubes.

1   cup basmati rice, rinsed in cold water.

3   cups chicken broth.

1   bay leaf.

3   heads broccoli florets.

1   (15-ounce) can red beans drained and rinsed
     (option: use black beans or black eyed peas).
     Kosher salt and freshly ground black pepper, to taste.

COOK
50 minutes
SERVES
4-6

Preparation

❶ Preheat oven to 350°F.

❷ Preheat a sautoir pan over a medium-high heat; add oil, onion, celery and pepper. Stir to coat, reduce the heat to medium and sauté for 3- 4 minutes; add garlic and cayenne pepper and cook for 2 more minutes.

❸ Add sausage, increase the heat to medium-high and cook for 3 -4 minutes, until the sausage starts to brown.

❹ Add the chicken and cook 3-4 minutes, until browned. Turn over chicken and sausage and cook for another 3 minutes.

❺ Add rice, season with kosher salt and freshly ground pepper and toss to coat the rice.

❻ Add chicken broth, bay leaf and broccoli; bring to a boil, cover the pan and transfer it to the oven; cook for 30 minutes.

❼ Check for doneness with a fork, without stirring. If the broth hasn't evaporated, cover and put back in the oven for a few more minutes.

❽ Add beans on top 4 minutes before end of cooking time; cover and return to the oven.

Fresh Warm Barley Salad

4 tablespoons olive oil.

1 medium yellow onion, roughly chopped.

2 cups barley.

4 cups chicken stock (or water).

½ pound button mushrooms, halved.

1 pound carrots, sliced diagonally
into large ovals.

2 sprigs fresh rosemary.

1 cup frozen peas.

1 cup walnuts, roughly chopped.

1 cup ricotta.

2 cups arugula (½ box or bag).

½ cup fresh dill, picked.

1 tablespoon balsamic vinegar.
Juice of ½ lemon.
Sea salt and freshly cracked black pepper.

COOK
45 minutes
SERVES
4-6

```
Preparation
```

❶ Heat 1 tablespoon olive oil in a large sautoir pan, add onion and sweat over low heat for 1 minute.

❷ Add barley and toast for about 2 minutes.

❸ Pour chicken stock or water into the pan and heat over a medium heat until the mixture begins to simmer.

❹ Reduce heat to low, add mushrooms, carrots and rosemary, place lid on the pan and cook for 30 minutes, until barley is tender. Add frozen peas with 2-3 minutes left of cooking time.

❺ In a bowl, combine walnuts, ricotta and 1 tablespoon olive oil; season with salt and freshly cracked pepper.

❻ Remove cooked barley from the heat and let it cool for 5 minutes.

❼ In a large bowl, toss together barley, arugula, dill, lemon juice and remaining 2 tablespoons olive oil.

❽ Divide walnut and ricotta mixture between 4 serving plates, drizzle with balsamic vinegar and serve aside warm barley.

Umami Peanut Pilaf Chicken

1½ pounds chicken breast, cut into 1-inch cubes.
3   tablespoons soy sauce.
3   tablespoons white miso.
4   tablespoons sesame oil.
5   cloves garlic, chopped.
½   cup rice flour.
2   dried chilli peppers, chopped (including seeds).
¼   cup roasted peanuts, unsalted
    (optional: cashews or almonds).
1   bunch scallions, trimmed and chopped.
1   tablespoon rice wine vinegar.
1   tablespoon fresh ginger, peeled and minced.
2   medium shallots, chopped.
1   cup jasmine rice, rinsed.
2   cups chicken stock.
½   pound fresh snow peas.
    Sea salt and freshly ground black pepper, to taste.

COOK
45 minutes
SERVES
4-6

Preparation

1 Preheat oven to 375°F.

2 Place chicken in a large bowl and set aside.

3 In a small bowl or a cup, whisk soy sauce with 2 tablespoons miso and 1 tablespoon sesame oil; pour over the chicken and turn to coat.

4 Place rice flour on a plate and dredge chicken pieces to coat lightly; shake off excess flour.

5 Heat 2 tablespoons sesame oil in a sautoir pan over medium heat, place chicken pieces in the pan, turning to brown on all sides. Stir in chilli, peanuts, and half the scallions.

6 Mix remaining 1 tablespoon miso with ¼ cup water and rice wine vinegar, pour into the pan and turn heat off. Deglaze, removing all pieces stuck to the pan; transfer chicken and all other ingredients to a plate and set aside.

7 Add remaining 1 tablespoon sesame oil to the pan and stir in ginger, garlic and remaining scallions. Sauté for a few minutes, add rice and a dash of sea salt and sauté for 2 more minutes.

8 Add chicken stock, cover and cook for 10 minutes.

9 Remove cover and layer chicken and peanut mixture on top of the rice, (do not stir the rice). Add a layer of snow peas on top of chicken, cover and cook 10 -15 more minutes in the oven.

10 Remove cover, let cool for a few minutes and serve.

Umami
a pleasant
savory
taste

Taking its name from Japan, umami is a pleasant savory taste, passed on by glutamate, a type of amino acid, which occurs naturally in many foods, including meat, fish, vegetables, and dairy products.

Traditionally, it has been thought that our sense of taste is comprised of four basic tastes that cannot be replicated by mixing any of the other primary tastes together: sweet, sour, salty, and bitter.

In the 1980's various studies proved that umami, found in glutamate, actually constituted a legitimate fifth basic taste. Since then, umami's status as "the fifth taste" has been recognized internationally.

Mexican Lime Chicken with Avocado and Tomato Salsa

For the chicken

2 tablespoons grape seed oil (or canola oil).

1½ pounds chicken thighs.

6 cloves garlic, sliced.

1 green pepper, seeded and large diced.

½ tablespoon ground cumin.

1 large yellow onion, diced.

1 cup white rice.

2 cups chicken broth (organic preferred).

1 can black beans, drained and rinsed.

2 cups frozen corn.

⅛ tablespoon chilli pepper.

½ large bunch cilantro, stemmed and chopped.
Sea salt and freshly ground black pepper, to taste.

For the salsa

¼ large bunch cilantro, stemmed and chopped.

2 large tomatoes, diced small or ½ small box of cherry tomatoes, sliced in half.

1 large jalapeno, seeded and diced small.

1 avocado, diced small.

1 tablespoon olive oil.
Juice of 2 limes.

COOK
50 minutes
SERVES
4-6

> **Preparation**

❶ Preheat the oven to 400°F.

❷ In a sautoir pan, heat oil over a medium-high heat until very hot. Season chicken thighs, place in the pan and sear until golden brown. Do not flip or move the chicken until it is completely golden on one side - this should take about 6 minutes.

❸ Add garlic, jalapeno, green pepper, cumin and onion and caramelize lightly, about 5 minutes, then add rice and brown lightly, about 2 minutes.

❹ Pour in broth; add black beans and corn. Place pan in the oven and cook for about 30 minutes.

❺ For the salsa, in a medium bowl combine cilantro, diced tomato, jalapeno, avocado, olive oil, chilli pepper and half of the lime juice. Toss lightly and refrigerate until needed.

❻ Remove cooked chicken and rice from the oven, let it sit for 5 minutes, then mix in chopped cilantro, chilli pepper and remaining lime juice.

❼ Serve topped with a large spoonful of the tomato-avocado salsa.

Middle Eastern Lamb Pilaf

2   tablespoons olive oil.
3   large shallot, chopped.
4   cloves garlic, chopped.
2   pounds ground lamb.
1½ tablespoons ground cumin.
1   teaspoon ground cinnamon.
2   tablespoons tomato paste.
3   medium parsnips, peeled and cut into a medium dice.
2   cups chicken stock.
1   cup basmati rice.
1   pound fresh spinach, thoroughly washed.
1   cup raisins.
     Sea salt and freshly ground black pepper, to taste.

COOK
45 minutes
SERVES
4-6

> **Preparation**

1 Preheat oven to 375°F.

2 Heat oil in sautoir pan; add shallot and garlic and sauté for a few minutes, until soft.

3 Add ground lamb and cook for about 5 minutes, until nicely browned; drain any excess fat.

4 Add cumin, cinnamon and tomato paste to the pan and cook for 2 minutes.

5 Add chicken stock, rice and parsnips, bring to a boil and then place in the oven for 25-30 minutes.

6 With 5 minutes left of cooking time, add the spinach and raisins on top of the rice, without stirring; return to the oven.

7 Remove cooked rice from the oven and let it rest for a few minutes (option: cook on the stovetop over low heat for 25 minutes).

Brown Rice with Lentils

I	large yellow onion, diced.
2	cups brown rice.
/4	cup green lentils.
5 /4	cups vegetable stock (chicken stock works as well).
2	medium (about 6-ounces each) Yukon gold potatoes.
½	bunch parsley.
½	bunch celery, diced.
I	large red pepper, seeded and diced.
2	large shallots, thinly sliced.
½	cup sherry vinegar or red wine vinegar.
I	tablespoon olive oil.
I	cup chopped hazelnuts, lightly roasted.
	Sea salt and freshly ground black pepper, to taste.

COOK
50 minutes
SERVES
4-6

Preparation

1 In a sautoir pan, combine onion, brown rice, lentils and vegetable stock. Set to low heat, place a lid on the pan and cook for 40 minutes.

2 As rice and lentils cook, peel and cut potatoes into 8 chunks each. Add to the rice mixture with 15 minutes left of cooking time.

3 In a bowl, combine parsley, celery, red pepper and shallots; toss with sherry vinegar, olive oil, and hazelnuts; season with salt and pepper and set aside.

4 Once the rice and lentils have cooked, turn the heat off and the let rest for about 5 minutes.

5 Serve with the celery and red pepper salad.

Pickling

I never pickled anything until I started creating grain bowls and was looking for new ways to spice it up. Turns out you can pickle anything and in no time at all. Previously I was under the impression that pickling was a long, complicated process that required wooden barrels and lots of storage; however, all you need is a glass jar with a screw top and some vinegar, salt, and water.

Food by nature begins to spoil as soon as it is harvested. To survive long winters and famine ancient civilizations used pickling to preserve food, which enabled them to establish roots and live in one place for an extended period of time.

Pickling is a technique where foods are soaked in a strong acid such as vinegar that prevents the spoiling process. Spices, salt and sugars are added to the vinegar to create flavorful and spicy brines. Pickling not only preserves foods; it also enhances the taste and texture in refreshing and delicious ways.

Our ancestors from around the globe pickled fruits, vegetables, meat, and fish. There's the famous kosher dill pickle in New York City, chutneys in India, kimchi in Korea, pickled herring in Scandinavia, salsas in Mexico, tangy pickled peppers in Italy, and don't forget Japanese pickled ginger as an essential part of sushi.

In addition to pickling, we can also preserve foods by drying, curing, canning and freezing.

The pickling process is anything but complicated, so it's very difficult to mess up. You name it, you can pickle it, and here are the few key ingredients to pickling your favorite fruits and vegetables:

Vinegars
- White wine vinegar
- Distilled, white vinegar
- Bragg's apple cider vinegar
- Rice wine vinegar

Spices
- Dried bay leaves
- Black peppercorns
- Coriander seed
- Whole allspice
- Red pepper flakes
- Dill seeds
- Mustard seeds

Other Essentials
- Garlic
- Fresh Dill
- Chiles
- Sea Salt, fine
  (not iodized
  —it makes
  the liquid cloudy)
- Sugar, fine

Shrimp Couscous
with Sugar Snap Peas

1   cup couscous.
1 /4 cups vegetable or chicken stock.
1   small apple, peeled, cored and cubed.
1   pound sugar snaps peas, cleaned
     and stemmed.
1-1 ½ pounds shrimp, shelled
     and deveined (you can also use
     flounder, bass or cod).
1   large piece of ginger, 2 ½ -3 -inch
     long, peeled and sliced thin.
1   teaspoon ground cumin.
1   bunch scallions, thinly sliced.
1   cup sliced almonds, toasted.
     Juice of 1 lemon.

Pickled carrots (optional)
     Jar with lid, mason jars work well
1   pound carrots, peeled and cut
     into 5-inch long sticks.
1¼ cups water.
1   cup cider vinegar.
¼   cup sugar.
2   garlic cloves, lightly crushed.
1½ teaspoon fennel, dill,
     or anise seeds.
1½ tablespoon salt,
     coarse preferred.
2   bay leaves.

COOK
40 minutes
SERVES
4-6

*To make the pickled
carrots*

*To make the shrimp
couscous*

❶ In a saucepan, bring
1 ½ cups chicken stock
to a boil.

❶ In a small pot, bring
all pickling ingredients
to a boil. Reduce the
heat and simmer for
two minutes, until sugar
dissolves; remove from
heat and let cool.

❷ Place couscous into
a pot, mix in the apple
then place sugar snap
on top of the couscous.
Pour boiling stock over
the dry couscous and
sugar snap peas; cover
and let it stand for 5
minutes.

❸ Toast the almonds

❹ Season shrimp with
salt and pepper.

❷ Place carrots in a jar,
add the liquid and close.
Refrigerate for at least
45 minutes. The carrots
will pickle over the next
24 hours and will last for
one month in the fridge.

❺ Heat oil in a sautoir
pan over a medium-high
heat; add ginger, cook
until tender, about 5
minutes. Add shrimp,
¼-cup stock, the juice of
½ lemon and cumin and
cook for 5 minutes; add
sliced scallions and turn
off the heat.

❻ Serve the shrimp
over the couscous
sprinled with almonds

Korean Beef Pilaf with Pickled Cabbage

For the pilaf

1-1½ pounds ground beef.

2   tablespoons hot pepper paste or chilli sauce.

2   tablespoons sesame oil, divided.

2   leeks, thoroughly washed and diced.

1   large yellow onion.

6   large cloves garlic, sliced.

2   tablespoons ginger, diced small.

2   large carrots, diced small.

¼   pound shiitake mushrooms, or crimini, sliced.

2   cups white jasmine rice.

4   tablespoons sesame seeds.

3½ cups water or chicken stock.

2   tablespoons soy sauce.

10   eggs.
     Sea salt and freshly ground black pepper,
     to taste.

For the pickled cabbage: (optional)

1   head Napa cabbage.

2   cups water.

1   cup rice wine vinegar.

5   tablespoons raw sugar.

4   teaspoons salt.

COOK
40-50 minutes
SERVES
4

Preparation

1 To pickle the cabbage, combine water, rice wine vinegar, sugar and salt in a pot and bring to a boil. Stir to dissolve salt and sugar.

2 Cut off and discard the lower white part of the cabbage, slice thinly (chiffonade) and place in a large bowl or container; pour the hot liquid over it, cover and refrigerate.

3 Preheat oven to 375°F.

4 In a large bowl, mix together ground beef, hot pepper paste, 1 tablespoon sesame oil and 2 eggs. Season with salt and pepper to taste and form into small balls.

5 Heat 1 tablespoon sesame oil in a sautoir pan, add meatballs, leeks, onions, garlic, and ginger and cook until meatballs are browned and the vegetables are slightly caramelized.

6 Add chopped carrots, mushrooms, rice and sesame seeds, then pour in chicken stock and soy sauce and bring to a boil.

7 Place lid on the sautoir and put in the oven for about 30-40 minutes.

8 Hard or soft boil the eight eggs, cool, shell and cut in half.

9 Plate rice and meatballs, top with pickled cabbage and two hardboiled egg halves and serve.

Kale and Quinoa Sauté

2 cups quinoa.
3½ cups chicken stock (or water).
½ bunch scallions (or green onions).
2 tablespoons olive oil.
2 whole carrots, peeled and sliced thin.
5 cloves garlic, chopped.
2 large portabella mushrooms, diced small.
1 bunch kale, stemmed and cut into large strips.
¼ cup cilantro, chopped.
1 Serrano or jalapeño pepper, seeded and chopped.
3 tablespoons olive oil.
Juice of 1 lemon.
Kosher salt and freshly ground black pepper, to taste.

COOK
30 minutes
SERVES
4-6

> **Preparation**

1 In a pot, combine quinoa and chicken stock and bring to a boil over a medium-high heat. Reduce heat to low, place lid on pot and cook quinoa for about 20 minutes, until liquid is absorbed.

2 Thinly slice scallions, keeping green and white parts separate; set aside.

3 Heat oil in a sautoir pan; add carrots and cook for 3 minutes, then add garlic and the white part of the scallions.

4 Stir in portabella mushrooms and cook for approximately 5 minutes on low heat.

5 Add kale and scallion greens to pan; place the lid on and cook for approximately 3 minutes, until wilted; season with kosher salt and pepper.

6 Add cooked quinoa to the mushroom-kale mixture and stir and cook for another 2 minutes.

7 Add chopped cilantro, lemon juice, serrano or jalapeño pepper and olive oil and lemon juice and serve.

Super Food or Super Hype?

On the forefront of American pop culture, there is a new phenomenon. With claims like ancient nutritional health properties, instant energy, weight loss, and a cure for what ails you, consumer curiosity has been piqued in recent years by a new category: "Superfood."

Add social media buzz, talk show and cooking show appearances, new recipes, and product line extensions of health bars, power drinks, yogurts, and chips, food manufacturers have built the social credibility for its resounding claims. The campaign is converting non-believers into product adopters. A seed, leaf, berry, root, bark, or ocean product can very easily become the next "Superfood."

Jumping on the bandwagon commonly leads to disregarding other nutritious foods out of deference to the new "Superfood" ingredient. The real danger can be nutritional negligence because the "Superfood" replaced other foods you fed your family.

But were these "Superfoods" truly super to begin with?

Last year kale was all the rage. There is no doubt that kale is healthy and an excellent source of vitamins; however, let's compare kale to other greens like mustard, collard, and Swiss chard to see how it stacks up. Does Kale really hold so much more nutritional value than the other greens?

Take a look at the chart below. Mustard greens are a little higher in calcium and slightly lower in iron than kale. Collard greens are higher in fiber, protein, vitamin A, and calcium and double in iron. Swiss chard is higher in fiber, protein, and calcium and more than three times higher in iron.

All four of these greens are also rich in many other nutrients. At the end of the day, kale is extremely healthy and nutritious, but so are mustard greens, collard greens and Swiss chard.

The truth is, humans need a varied diet, and not one vegetable or seed is the replacement and miracle cure for what ails you. As I was writing this piece, guess what just popped into my inbox? "Breaking Email – New SUPERFOOD Makes Your Body Young Again"

OH REALLY?

Greens	Calories	Fiber	Protein	Vit A	Vit C	Calcium	Iron
Kale	36	3g	2g	345%	80%	9%	6%
Mustard Green	21	3g	3g	177%	59%	10%	5%
Collard Green	49	5g	4g	308%	58%	27%	12%
Swiss Chard	35	4g	3g	214%	43%	10%	22%

World News
http://nutritiondata.self.com

Grain Bowls

The grain bowl is a creative way to easily assemble nutritional powerhouse meals for your family. With a plethora of options, this ancient technique is the newest soul-satisfying dish to enter the family kitchen in a long time. Renewed from the ancient Japanese rice bowl called donburi, today's version consists of grains, proteins, and vegetables. The combinations are endless and fun to make. Even the pickiest of eaters can build bowls to satisfy their tastes, and it's a great way to reawaken leftovers.

These bowls are about taste, texture, and creativity: anything goes. Like an abstract expressionist artist exploring techniques for new results, experiment with different grains like quinoa, farro, wheat berries, barley, kamut, or grits. Build your grain bowl with small piles of greens, vegetables, or fruit. Add your proteins: fish, meat, chicken, nuts, seeds, or tofu. Intensify the tastes: add Kim chi, powder the top with cayenne, or roll in something pickled like carrots or red cabbage. Want more protein? Top it off with a hard-boiled, soft-boiled, or fried egg. Then hit it with a shot of hot sauce.

The grain bowl invites ingenuity. Try using almond or coconut milk to make your grits, add steamed shredded kale, poached eggs, and sausage and then top it off with pickled onions.

For pre- and post-workout (or sports) meals, grain bowls are a fantastic resource to modify your carb/protein ratio as needed. Working out in the mornings? Higher-carb grain bowls are the supreme breakfast meal to deliver energy. For post-workout meals, boost up the protein and reduce the carbs to help rebuild muscle tissue.

What I love most about grain bowls is you do not need a recipe—this is ingredient based cooking where you cannot make a mistake. All you need is a batch of cooked grains on hand. Use as many or as few ingredients as you have in your refrigerator or your pantry. It's so easy you can practically do it with your eyes closed.

Asian Beef Grain Bowl

Grain
1 ½	cups farro.
3	cups chicken, vegetable broth or water.

Protein
1	pound sirloin steak, sliced thin (grass fed preferred).
1	tablespoon grape seed or canola oil.
1	tablespoon butter.
2	tablespoons rice wine vinegar. Sea salt and freshly ground black pepper, to taste.

COOK
40 minutes
SERVES
4-6

Vegetables
2	tablespoons olive oil.
1	red onion, chopped.
2	clove garlic, minced.
2	teaspoons soy sauce.
½	tablespoon Chinese five spice powder.
2	tablespoons hoisin sauce.
½	cup water.
3	heads broccoli florets.
1	cup (8 ounce) fresh spinach, roughly chopped, uncooked.
⅓	cup sliced almonds, toasted.
1	red bell pepper, sliced thin, uncooked.
3	carrots, use the peeler to make paper thin strips, uncooked.

Dressing
¼	cup rice vinegar.
2	tablespoons soy sauce.
¾	cup olive oil.
2	tablespoons sesame oil.
½	tablespoon fresh ginger, finely grated.
½	clove garlic, minced.
1	scallion, green part only, finely sliced. Dash of Sriracha chilli sauce, optional.

To serve
Sour pickles, sliced.

> Preparation

❶ In a pot cook farro in broth or water, according to package instructions.

❷ Season the steak with salt and pepper and rub in oil and mixed spices. (option: let sit up to half hour to marinate)

❸ Preheat a sautoir pan over medium-high heat and add oil and butter; sear beef until brown-crusted, about 6-8 minutes, turn and sear for about 4 more minutes; remove beef and deglaze pan with rice wine vinegar.

❹ In another pan (or rinse out the sautoir pan), heat olive oil, add chopped onion and sauté a few minutes, add garlic, soy sauce, five spice powder, hoisin and water. Bring to a boil, reduce heat to very low, add the broccoli cover and cook 5 - 8 minutes.

❺ Toast almonds in the oven or toaster oven for 1-2 minutes.

❻ In a small bowl, whisk together dressing ingredients and set aside.

Create the Grain Bowl

❶ Spoon farro in bowls, layer beef on top, broccoli, spinach, almonds, peppers, and carrots.

❷ Drizzle with dressing and top with sliced pickles before serving.

Breakfast Grain Bowl

COOK
40 minutes
SERVES
4-6

Grain
1 cup amaranth (or grits).
3 cups almond milk, unsweetened.
½ tablespoon butter per bowl, melted.

Protein
1 pound bacon, nitrate free preferred.
8 eggs, soft boiled.
1 small log of goat cheese, crumbled.

Vegetables
8 ounce arugula, shredded.
1 cup watercress, roughly stemmed.
1 tablespoon olive oil.
   Handful of cherry tomatoes, halved.
   Juice of ¼ lemon.
   Kosher salt and freshly ground
   black pepper, to taste.

To serve
   Hot sauce, to taste.

> **Preparation**

1 Combine almond milk and amaranth in a medium pot, bring to a boil over a medium-high heat, then reduce heat to very low, cover and cook for 25 minutes or until all the liquid is absorbed. Check periodically and stir.

2 Preheat oven to 475°F.

3 Separate the bacon and lie down in a sautoir pan; place pan in the oven and cook for 15-20 minutes, until bacon is crisp. Transfer bacon to a plate lined with paper towels, let cool; then crumble and set aside.

4 In a bowl, mix together arugula, watercress and cherry tomatoes, drizzle with olive oil and the lemon juice. Season with kosher salt and pepper and mix.

5 Fill a stockpot with water, about ½-inch deep, add eggs and bring to a boil; reduce heat to low, cover and cook for 6 minutes. Remove eggs and cool off in cold water and peel shells.

Create the Grain Bowl

1 Spoon amaranth into a bowl, add melted butter and a little kosher salt, top with bacon, arugula salad and crumbled goat cheese.

2 Carefully cut eggs in half and place on top of the cheese.

3 Finish off with your favorite hot sauce.

Burpees
a fat burning machine

Doing burpees for exercise has become quite trendy, but burpees are not just a fad, and they are no joke. After a few rounds you'll know what I mean. Burpees will turn your body into a fat-burning machine while adding strength, all in one full-body exercise. Like pushups, do burpees anywhere anytime. Take it slowly your first few days and pick up speed as you go. The goal is go as fast as you can.

Here's how to do a burpee:
- Start in a squat position with your hands on the floor in front of you.
- Kick your feet back into a pushup position.
- Immediately return your feet to the squat position as fast as you can.
- Immediately jump up as high as possible from the squat position.
- Psyche yourself up— add a clap over your head when you jump up.

Spanish Grain Bowl

Grain

½ tablespoon olive oil.
2 shallots, chopped.
2 garlic cloves, chopped.
1½ cups long grain rice.
½ teaspoon turmeric powder.
2¼ cups chicken broth,
    organic preferred.
    Sea salt and freshly ground
    black pepper, to taste.

Protein

1 tablespoon olive oil.
1 jalapeno pepper, chopped.
1 green pepper, thin sliced.
2 cloves garlic, chopped.
1 small yellow onion, chopped.
1 pound ground pork, beef or veal.
1 (15-ounce) can red kidney beans,
    drained and rinsed (can also use
    black or white kidney beans).
    Cheddar cheese, shredded.

Vegetables

1 romaine lettuce, shredded.
1 large avocado, diced.
2 large ripe tomato, sliced thin.
1 small red onion, sliced thin.

To serve

⅛ teaspoon cayenne per bowl.
    Juice of 1 lime.
    Sour cream.

COOK
1 hour -
1 hour 50 minutes
SERVES
4-6

Preparation

1 In a stock pot, heat oil over a medium heat, add shallots and garlic and sauté until softened.

2 Add rice, turmeric and a pinch of salt and toss to coat the rice. Pour in broth, cover, reduce heat to low and cook for 15-20 minutes, until liquid is absorbed.

3 In the sautoir pan, heat oil over a medium-high heat, add onions, peppers and garlic and cook for 5 minutes, until soft; add ground meat and brown, stirring occasionally, about 5 minutes. Drain the fat and add kidney beans; reduce heat, cover and cook 3-5 minutes.

Create the Grain Bowl

1 Spoon rice into a bowl, sprinkle with shredded cheese, then layer meat and beans, lettuce, tomatoes, avocado and onion slices on top.

2 Add a dollop of sour cream, drizzle with lime juice and top with a dusting of cayenne.

Quinoa Bowl with Yogurt Sauce

Pickled cabbage: (optional)

I	small red cabbage, shredded.
I	cup red-wine vinegar.
½	cup warm water.
I	tablespoon sugar.
2	teaspoon kosher salt.
2	tablespoons olive oil.
2	bay leaves.

Grain

2	cups quinoa.
3½	cups chicken stock (or water).

COOK
30 minutes
SERVES
4-6

Protein

½	cup hummus.
I	(15-ounce) can chickpeas, drained and rinsed.

Vegetables

3	turnips (or I medium butternut squash), peeled and diced into 1–inch cubes.
2	tablespoons olive oil.
I	pound fresh spinach, washed thoroughly, roughly chopped.
2	avocados, peeled and sliced thin. Sea salt and freshly ground black pepper, to taste.

Sauce

1½	cups plain Greek yogurt.
I	cucumber, peeled, seeded and chopped.
4	tablespoons fresh herbs (dill, mint, cilantro, or basil), chopped.
I	tablespoon olive oil, extra virgin preferred.
I	clove garlic, minced.
I	teaspoon freshly ground cumin. Juice of ½ lemon Pinch of kosher salt.

To serve

Hot sauce, to taste.

> ### Preparation

1 To make pickled cabbage, quarter cabbage and discard the core. Using a sharp knife, shred cabbage as finely as possible and transfer to a large bowl.

2 In a medium bowl, combine red-wine vinegar, warm water, sugar, kosher salt, olive oil, and bay leaves and whisk until sugar is dissolved.

3 Drizzle the mixture over the cabbage and toss to combine. Loosely cover and let stand at room temperature for at least 45 minutes, tossing occasionally. Store in refrigerator, tightly covered.

4 In the sutoir pan set a steamer over boiling water add turnips or squash, cover and steam for 6-8 minutes, until soft.

5 In the stock pot or a medium pot, combine quinoa with stock, bring to a boil, turn heat to low, and cook for 20 minutes, until liquid has evaporated.

Create the Grain Bowl

1 Spoon quinoa into a bowl, add 2 tablespoons hummus and layer chickpeas, turnips or squash, spinach, avocado and red cabbage.

2 Dress with the yogurt sauce and finish off with your favorite hot sauce.

Vegetable Curried Brown Rice with Roasted Grapes Bowl

Grain
1   small yellow onion, chopped.
1   cup brown rice.
1   tablespoon curry powder.

Protein
¾   cup green lentils.
3½ cups vegetable broth.

Vegetables
1   medium sweet potato, cut into 1- inch cubes.
1   large turnip, cut into 1- inch cubes.
1   bunch Swiss chard, remove the thick spine and chop.
2   carrots, use the peeler to make paper thin slices.
¼   red cabbage, finely shredded. Juice of 1 lemon.

To serve
½   pound red seedless grapes, halved.
2   ripe avocados, peeled and diced.

Yogurt dressing
½   teaspoon ground cumin.
2   cups plain yogurt.
3   tablespoon cider vinegar
3   tablespoons honey.
    Pinch of cayenne pepper.
    Juice of 1 lemon.

COOK
45 minutes
SERVES
4-6

Preparation

❶ Preheat the oven to 350°F.

❷ Place grapes on a roasting pan or a rimmed cookie sheet, add a little water to the bottom and roast for 45 minutes.

❸ Preheat a sautoir pan, add olive oil and sauté onion until soft; add rice, lentils, broth, curry powder and a pinch of salt and bring to a boil. Cover and reduce to a simmer. Cook for about 35-45 minutes until liquid is absorbed.

❹ Place Swiss chard on top of the rice 10 minutes before end of cooking time and cover. Do not stir the rice.

❺ While rice is cooking, place sweet potato and turnip in a steamer basket and cook for 10-15 minutes; set aside.

❻ Place shredded cabbage and carrots into a large bowl and toss with half of the lemon juice, olive oil and a few pinches of salt.

❼ In a bowl, combine all yogurt dressing ingredients and mix well.

Create the Grain Bowl

❶ Spoon rice and lentils into a bowl, top with Swiss chard, and layer with steamed sweet potato, turnip, cabbage and carrot.

❷ Top with avocado and roasted grapes and drizzle with yogurt dressing.

Squash and Coconut Rice Grain Bowl

Grain

2	cups jasmine rice.
1	tablespoon olive oil.
2	large shallots, chopped.
1 ½	teaspoon ground coriander.
1 ½	teaspoon ground cumin.
1 ½	cups water.
1	cup canned unsweetened good quality coconut milk.
1	teaspoon kosher salt.
1	cup shredded coconut. Kosher salt and freshly ground black pepper, to taste.

Protein

2	avocados, peeled, pitted and mashed.
¼	cup fresh cilantro, chopped.
1	jalapeno, seeded and chopped.
1	small red onion, chopped.
1	lime, juiced.
¾	teaspoon curry powder.
½	teaspoon ginger powder.
1	teaspoon honey.

Vegetables

1	pound green beans, trimmed.
1	large kabocha squash, peeled, seeded and diced into 1-inch cubes (pumpkin also works). A pinch of cayenne pepper (optional).

To serve

1	cup basil or cilantro, roughly chopped.
½	cup pecans, roughly chopped. Thai chilli sauce, to taste.

COOK
50 minutes
SERVES
4-6

> **Preparation**

❶ Rinse rice in cold water and drain; set aside.

❷ Preheat sautoir pan over a medium heat, add oil and sauté shallots until softened; add coriander and cumin. Stir in rice, water, coconut milk, and kosher salt.

❸ Place pan over high heat and bring to a boil. Stir; reduce the heat to the lowest possible setting and cover. Simmer for 15 minutes.

❹ Five minutes before the end of cooking time, gently lay the string beans on top of the rice. Do not stir or disturb the rice and simmer 5-10 more minutes.

❺ Remove pan from the heat and let stand 10 minutes, covered.

❻ While the rice is cooking, place squash in a stock pot and steam over medium heat until soft, 10-15 minutes.

❼ Transfer to a large bowl drizzle with olive oil, season with kosher salt and black pepper. Add a pinch of cayenne if you wish.

❽ Mix all guacamole (protein ingredients) together in a medium bowl.

Create the Grain Bowl

❶ Spoon rice and string beans into a bowl, add guacamole and squash.

❷ Top with basil and pecans, a few coconut shreds and drizzle chilli sauce on top.

Quick Meals

You're more likely to make unhealthy food choices when you're pressed for time. Dinner is a hassle, so you don't feel like cooking.

In this section you'll discover how to overcome those obstacles and make nutritious meals in 30 minutes or less.

On The Fly Modus Operandi

The health and wellbeing of your children may be your highest priority, but it's easy to rationalize serving processed food when you're pressed for time. The reality is that the occasional processed meal or snack isn't harmful, but it sends a mixed message to your children. Is fast food okay once in a while? Or twice a week? Or once on Monday? Or once on Thursday and twice on Saturday? You are your child's dietary role model. If you are eating more fruits, nuts, and vegetables instead of fat, sugar, and salt, so will your kids.

Consider your state of mind. Is a healthy and delicious dinner imaginable only when someone else prepares it? Can you make what seems impossible happen? What if your family's health was in danger and a strict diet was required—or else? Would that open your mind to finding a way to cook fresh foods?

The idea of trying to lose weight renders many folks helpless because they've tried it before and failed. In their minds it has become an impossible task. Have you ever convinced yourself that something important was

"Everything is theoretically impossible, until it is done."
~ Robert A. Heinlein

impossible before you even tried it? Regularly making dinner using fresh ingredients can often feel like such an impossible task.

Today we tweet, read, and watch on TV amazing stories of people who, against their own mental, emotional, environmental, and physical challenges, have made the unthinkable achievable. They remind us that we cannot continuously control the events in our lives, but we can control how we respond to them.

For many kids today, attaining the American dream feels impossible. This is especially true for boys and girls in the American foster care system. Recently there was a movie about such a boy, growing up with a crack-addicted mother, moving from foster home- to- foster home, and from school- to- school. This particular boy grew up to become a football star. Maybe you saw the movie? It's called *The Blind Side*, and it starred Sandra Bullock, who won an Academy Award for her performance. The teenager was Michael Oher, offensive tackle for the NFL's Baltimore Ravens and the inspiration for the film.

After *The Blind Side* was released, Oher received thousands of letters from former foster children. He realized that in order to inspire children in the foster care system he needed to go beyond playing football. In his book, I Beat the Odds: From Homelessness, to *The Blind Side*, and Beyond, Oher says, "People used to say that my ability to forget was what allowed me to move on."[137] He states that failure was never an option for him. His story is about how a family helped him reach his full potential. His story is a true testament to human survival and success under the most difficult circumstances.

Most of our obstacles cannot compare to Oher's story. But the reality is that your life is in overdrive when you are raising a family, juggling work, and managing everything else that comes your way. Eating on the run becomes routine, expensive and unhealthy for your family's physical wellbeing as well as the household environment.

There's nothing simple about making meals for your family. It doesn't matter how much cooking experience you have, how well you cook, or even how much you love to cook. At the end of the day, who doesn't sometimes just want to order in or swing through a drive-thru? The impossible home-cooked meal only means that you haven't found solutions for your family's lifestyle yet. Cooking at home is not only the healthiest option for your children; it adds long-term stability to your children's life.

How to Make the Impossible Home-cooked Meal Possible

Uh oh! It's 6 p.m. again! Now what? There's a ton of laundry waiting to be washed, homework that needs to be done, the twins want Chipotle, Junior wants pizza, and your spouse is about to platz. You keep opening the refrigerator looking at the same shelves thinking each time that magically dinner will appear. Now your imagination starts to run wild. You wonder, "Can I make dinner with half a container of organic Greek yogurt, two cans of tuna, mozzarella cheese, and six slices of whole grain bread?"

Making home-cooked meals can happen. It is not impossible. Cooking large batches on the weekend for weekday meals is a sure-fire way to get and stay ahead. Late Sunday afternoon is a good time to braise or roast large batches of lean proteins and veggies. Leverage weekend kitchen time to also prep ingredients for during the week. Wash, chop, cut, and store vegetables, salads, and fruits so they are ready to use during the week for lunch, snacks, or dinners on the fly. Turn this into valuable time spent with your children by giving them small tasks to contribute and by teaching them about fresh, healthy foods. Tell them where the fresh foods they're preparing come from and why it's so essential to eat them.

Farmer's Markets and Frozen Vegetables

If you are fortunate enough to have a farmers' market in your neighborhood, take advantage of it. There is nothing better than buying seasonal, fresh, organic fruits and vegetables direct from the farm. For out-of-season vegetables, opt for frozen ones—organic whenever possible. It's the next best choice after farm fresh produce. Whole Foods has a great selection of frozen organic fruits and vegetables. The price is right, too. There are some clear advantages

to frozen fruits and vegetables: they are cleaned, chopped, ready to use, and can stay in your freezer for a long time.

Canned Foods

For quick meals, you can also take advantage of a select sampling of canned foods. I say select because of the properties of canning. Canning involves a high heat process, which depending on the food, can rob it of its vital nutrients like vitamin-C and folic acid.[138] In canned beans on the other hand, heat does not damage their high protein and fiber content in the same way that heat can damage vitamins and phytonutrients in canned fruits and vegetables. You can expect the same full protein and fiber benefits from quick and easy canned beans as you would from the many hours it takes to cook dry beans on your stovetop.

By all means, incorporate canned beans into your under-30 minute meals, although look for cans that do not feature Bisphenol A, a chemical compound that is used in the composition of plastics and resins. Also, try to stay away from additives, and look for minimal added salt (150-300 milligrams per cup). If possible, organically-grown beans are a better choice.

"The positive thinker sees the invisible, feels the intangible and achieves the impossible."
~Anonymous

"It is either easy or impossible."
~ Salvador Dali

Another pertinent benefit: canned salmon is usually wild caught, not farmed, which means that it is lower in mercury than fresh farmed salmon. Plus, it's much less expensive than fresh wild salmon.

Disadvantages of Canned Salmon
Because fat is removed during the canning process, fresh salmon contains twice as much omega-3 fatty acids than canned. Don't get me wrong—canned salmon still provides a healthy supply. As with canned beans, look for labels that do not feature Bisphenol A. Also, stay away from additives and look for minimal added salt.

Canned salmon is great in a pinch when you are tasked to feed the kids healthy meals with little time. When you have more time, fresh wild-caught filets are wonderful for throwing on the grill with a summer salad and fresh fruit. The bottom line is that each type has advantages and disadvantages. Overall, wild caught salmon—not farm-raised—is the healthiest choice, fresh or canned.

The Invention of Canning
As a way to nourish his constantly traveling army, in 1795 Napoleon Bonaparte offered a reward for whoever could develop a safe, reliable method to preserve food for his troops. Nicholas Appert took on the challenge, and developed a method that utilized heat to process food in glass jars.[139]

By 1810, Englishman Peter Durand invented a method for sealing food in tin cans. And in 1858, John Mason invented a glass jar with a screw-on thread on top, and a rubber seal lid.[139]

Batch Cooking
In the pilaf section you found meals to make in batches and store or freeze for the week or months ahead. Make large batches of rice, barley, and other grains so that you have them at a moment's notice. These foods are also great sources of fiber and protein. Easily mix the grains with kidney or black beans for complete proteins, steam a few vegetables, add an avocado on the

"We would accomplish many more things if we did not think of them as impossible."
~Vince Lombardi

Today families are recognizing the importance of including omega-3 fatty acids as a staple in their diets. Salmon, an excellent source of omega-3s, is a high-power, quick-meal food. But as parents you don't always have the time or budget to put a fresh piece of salmon on the dinner table. Fortunately, canned salmon is easily found at the supermarket, easy to store in your cupboard, and it's cooked and ready to eat. What about the nutritional value? Is canned salmon as healthy as fresh? Let's compare the two.

Advantages of Canned Salmon
Canned salmon actually has a nutritional advantage over fresh salmon. Both fresh and canned are high in omega-3 fatty acids, but canned salmon includes the bones, which supplies a hefty dose of calcium, giving canned salmon a nutritional edge over fresh. In fact, four ounces of canned salmon contain as much calcium as a glass of milk. Canned salmon is extremely versatile: salmon croquettes are fast and delicious, and canned salmon is fabulous on sandwiches and in salads and pasta dishes.

side drizzled with olive oil, and Voila! a power-packed, nutritious meal in minutes.

For breakfast, you can easily do the same thing by making large batches of oatmeal. Please do not use instant oatmeal. The processing required to make it "instant" degrades most of the nutrients. It doesn't take that much longer to cook regular oatmeal unless it's the steel cut style. But even steel cut oats are worth the extra time it takes to make them. Add fruits, berries, nuts, maple syrup, or honey for an energizing breakfast.

Sautéing

Sautéing is another technique for under-30-minute meals. You're going to incorporate the searing technique from braising along with the knife skills you've picked up along the way to bring the sauté technique into your repertoire. Sautéing is so fast and easy that it allows you to prepare meals or sides on a moment's notice.

To sauté you'll use a very hot sautoir pan and a small amount of oil to cook the food very quickly. Sautéing browns the food's surface as it cooks and effortlessly develops complex flavors and wonderful aromas. The technique is named after the French word sauter, which means "to jump." It earned its name from the technique of tossing or flipping the food in the pan.

Once you've added these culinary techniques to your repertoire, you can easily be creative and invent your own recipes with whatever ingredients, herbs, and spices you have around. That's the beauty of learning basic techniques: learn one sauté, and you can make any sauté. It's like learning how to read a financial statement. At first it can feel scarier than running into a vampire in a dark alley, but once you know what you're looking for, it's an easy process that gives you power to read any business's profitability reports.

A simple technique to cook these dishes under 30 minutes is to cut vegetables into small pieces. Dice the tomatoes, mince the onions, chop the garlic, and cut meat and fish into small, even cubes. You want to have fairly thin pieces because thick chunks will take longer to cook. All this can be accomplished ahead of time by taking advantage of the Sunday night prep plan. If that prep is done, mise en place can truly come alive in your kitchen, making you the family rock star.

The modus operandi for quick sauté 6 p.m. meals is to brown the outside of the food while the inside cooks just enough to remain juicy and tender. The real trick is to let the ingredients brown; don't mess with the food in the pan! You'll want to stir and turn food as it cooks, but here is where self-discipline comes into play. You must resist the urge to flip. The ingredients must lie undisturbed for a few minutes to brown.

When you brown cubed food quickly, the surface moisture evaporates, which allows the ingredient's proteins, carbohydrates, and fats to caramelize. That is what forms the crusty surface and golden color in your foods and enhances the innate delicious flavors of the ingredients.

The recipes in this section are designed with cooking on the fly in mind. You'll find dinners that can be made in under 30 minutes. What I love about these dishes is that Royal and I incorporated ingredients from the brain food section in each recipe to ensure your children's bones, muscles, and thinking caps are nourished. They include avocado, blueberries, dark greens, eggs, kidney beans, lean beef, nuts and seeds, salmon and tuna, and whole grains. Use these ingredients as your building blocks for fast, easy, and healthy meals.

"It's kind of fun to do the impossible."
~Walt Disney

Learn One Sauté
You Can Make Any Sauté

1
▶ Prepare the Food ▶

You can sauté meat, fish, vegetables, and even fruits. Cut the food in uniform-size pieces so it will cook quickly and evenly.

2
▶ Get ready ▶

Preheat the sautoir pan using medium-high heat. Lightly coat the pan with 1 Tbsp. of olive oil, canola, grape seed, sesame or butter. Butter adds a rich flavor, but it burns more quickly than oil at higher temperatures. If you use butter, watch it carefully and lower the heat if needed. It's nice to combine a little butter with olive oil for a thicker sauce. This allows you to sauté with butter at a higher heat.

3
▶ Sauté It ▶

Carefully add the food and reduce the heat to medium high. Do not cover the pan and do not add liquid. Stir the food with a spatula or wooden spoon, making sure the ingredients are coated with the fat and cook evenly without burning. You can shake the pan back and forth over the burner to sauté without using utensils. For chicken, meat or fish, cook one side until golden brown, then flip over to brown the other side. The quick sear helps the food retain its natural flavor and juices.

Optional
▶ Make a Pan Sauce ▶
(When sautéing meats)

Once the meat is cooked, remove from the pan and keep warm. Turn the heat to medium-high. Add your liquid to deglaze, such as chicken or beef broth, wine, or a combination of the two, scraping the pan with a spoon to dissolve all the flavorful fond stuck to the bottom. Bring to a boil and cook until the sauce is reduced by at 1/3 and syrupy. Remove from the heat. Add salt and pepper. For some added body stir in a couple of tablespoons of butter or cream to finish the sauce and flavor. Very French!

Shrimp Citrus Wrap

1	pound large shrimp, de-shelled and de-veined.
1	tablespoon olive oil.
1	head Bibb lettuce.
1	pink grapefruit.
1	tablespoon mayonnaise.
½	bunch (2 tablespoons) chives, chopped.
2	avocados.
10	sprigs dill, picked.
1	tablespoon mayo.
	Generous handful of cherry tomatoes, halved.
	Juice of ½ lemon.
	Sea salt and freshly ground pepper, to taste.

COOK
5 minutes
SERVES
4-6

> **Preparation**

1 Season shrimp with salt and pepper. Preheat a sautoir pan, add 1 teaspoon olive oil and quickly sear the shrimp on high heat.

2 Cut cooked shrimp into pieces, put in a bowl and refrigerate.

3 Wash lettuce leaves, being careful to not rip or tear; dry with kitchen paper towels and set aside.

4 Supreme the grapefruit, by completely removing the grapefruit skin and white membrane, to get only the sweet flesh.

5 Add mayonnaise, chives and lemon juice to the cooled shrimp, mix thoroughly and place back in the fridge.

6 Peel and slice avocado into thin strips.

7 Place 2-3 avocado strips onto each lettuce leaf, then layer with two pieces grapefruit, one tablespoon shrimp salad, a few tomato halves and finish with picked dill. Roll lettuce into wraps and serve.

Raw Collard Wraps

1 ½ pounds carrots.
2   tablespoons Moroccan seasoning.
4   tablespoons olive oil, divided.
½   cups raisins.
1   cup picked parsley.
1   cup cilantro with stems.
2   cups raw cashews.
4   tablespoons olive oil.
½   red cabbage.
1   bunch collard greens, leaves only.
     Juice of 1 lemon.
     Sea salt and freshly grated black pepper, to taste.

COOK
None
SERVES
4-6

> **Preparation**

❶ Grate carrots into a bowl; add lemon juice, Moroccan seasoning, 2 tablespoons olive oil and raisins. Mix together thoroughly and let macerate in the refrigerator while preparing the rest of the ingredients.

❷ Pick and clean parsley and cilantro.

❸ Place raw cashews, parsley, cilantro, remaining 2 tablespoons of olive oil, salt and pepper into a food processor and blend to a fine paste.

❹ Slice or shred red cabbage and wash with cold water.

❺ Wash and trim collard leaves so they are uniform, as flat as possible, and ready to be rolled. Carefully slice the thick spine thinner.

❻ Prepare wraps by layering cashew-herb paste, carrots and raw cabbage over the collard leaves; roll tightly and serve.

Shakshuka

2 tablespoons olive oil.
1 medium onion, chopped.
6 cloves garlic, roughly diced.
⅛ teaspoon chilli flakes.
1 teaspoon sweet paprika.
½ teaspoon cumin.
1 (28-ounces) can whole tomatoes.
¼ cup honey.
1 teaspoon red or apple cider vinegar.
8 eggs.
½ teaspoon cumin.
2 teaspoons sea salt.
½ cup crumbled feta, optional.
1 cup fresh spinach.
¼ cup fresh parsley, chopped.
   Toasted pita bread, to serve.

COOK
25-30 minutes
SERVES
4-6

> **Preparation**

❶ Preheat a sautoir pan, add olive oil and onions and cook for a few minutes until soft. Add garlic, chilli, paprika, and cumin and season with salt and pepper; cook a few more minutes.

❷ Add tomatoes, quickly cut tomatoes into quarters in the pan. Stir in honey and vinegar, reduce the heat to medium, and cook for 12 to 15 minutes.

❸ When the mixture starts to boil, crack the eggs in, keeping the yolks whole. Spoon the sauce over the eggs and cook until the egg whites are firm, 5-8 minutes.

❹ Sprinkle feta cheese on top, then spinach; turn heat off, cover and let rest for 1 minute.

❺ Sprinkle with parsley and serve immediately with toasted pita bread for dipping.

Color
can set your mood
and persuade
your thoughts

Color influences your choices and is used in products to encourage you to take action.

When you are shopping in the super market the color of foods and packaging are often the first elements you notice. The color entices you and engages your appetite to make you feel hungry.

When choosing fresh fruits and vegetables, you often rely on color to determine how ripe or fresh items are. If the color doesn't match your perception of quality you will perceive its taste differently.

This psychological effect is why many companies and growers use genetic modification to enhance the appearance of fruits and vegetables. If the apple is redder with no visible flaws, the consumer feels it will taste sweeter, and therefore the apple will sell faster.

Manufacturers add food coloring or dyes to processed and packaged foods in order to enhance the food's natural color and give the impression of better taste, flavor, and quality. Farm-raised salmon, for instance, can have a dull or gray color, so pink dye may be added to give the impression of quality and freshness.

People tend to think that all green foods are healthy, regardless of whether the food is nutritious or not. This pattern may be traced back to our ancestors' eating habits. Green foods were often viewed as being safe to eat and most likely not poisonous.

Food companies have long understood consumer behavior and how color impacts the perception of their products. [152] So next time you visit the supermarket, keep the persuasive power of color in your mind, and don't get tricked by food manufacturers' attempts to influence your choices.

Brie and Blueberry Lime Curd Baguette

1	pound blueberries.
2	teaspoons lime juice.
1/4	cup butter.
2	tablespoons water.
1	tablespoon honey.
2	eggs, well beaten.
1	large French baguette.
2	cups arugula.
2	teaspoon olive oil.
1	pound brie cheese, sliced.
	Zest of 1 lime.
	Sea salt and freshly ground black pepper, to taste.

COOK
15 minutes
SERVES
4-6

Preparation

❶ To make the curd, in a pot combine blueberries, lime juice, butter, water and honey. Cook over a low heat for approximately 10 minutes.

❷ Whisk eggs into the hot blueberry mixture, turn the heat to low and continue whisking for 1 minute, until smooth. Transfer to the fridge and let cool.

❸ Slice baguette lengthwise in half and toast.

❹ In a bowl, toss arugula with lime juice and olive oil and season with salt and pepper.

❺ Lay brie slices over the bottom half of the baguette and top with arugula. Spread the top half of baguette with the blueberry-lime curd, sprinkle with lime zest and place on top of the arugula. Cut and serve.

Center-cut Pork Chops with Cranberry Bulgur and Apple Confit

COOK
45 minutes
SERVES
4

4 medium center-cut pork chops, bone in preferred (great with turkey or chicken breast too).
Juice of 1 lemon.
2 tablespoons olive oil.
2 tablespoons fresh rosemary, chopped.
1 cup bulgur.
1 medium onion, chopped.
1 bay leaf.

$\frac{1}{4}$ cup cranberries, dried.
$\frac{1}{4}$ cup roasted sunflower seeds.
1 apple, peeled cored, diced.
2 medium shallots, roughly chopped.
1 tablespoon sherry vinegar.
2 large tomatoes, sliced.
2 cucumbers, peeled and sliced.
Sea salt and freshly ground black pepper, to taste.

Preparation

1 Preheat oven on broil.

2 Place pork chops in a roasting pan and season with lemon juice, 1 tablespoon olive oil, rosemary, salt and black pepper; flip and repeat. Set aside.

3 Pour 2¼ cups water into a pot, add bulgur, onion, and bay leaf, season with salt and black pepper and bring to a boil; reduce heat to low, cover and cook, without stirring, for 15 minutes, until most of the liquid is absorbed.

4 Place cooked bulgur in a bowl, drizzle with olive oil; add cranberries and sunflower seeds; mix and cover to keep warm.

5 For the apple confit, heat a sautoir pan with 1 tablespoon olive oil; add apple and shallot and sauté until caramelized, about 10 minutes. Deglaze pot with sherry vinegar and ½ cup water. Add a teaspoon of salt and cook for 8 more minutes over a low heat.

6 As the confit cooks, place pork chops in the oven and broil for 8-10 minutes, until crisp around the edges, flip and broil for 3 more minutes. Keep your eye on the chops so they don't burn.

7 Drizzle cucumbers and tomatoes with olive oil and season to taste.

8 Top the pork chops with apple confit and serve with sliced cucumber and tomatoes on the side.

Chimichurri Chicken Sandwiches

4 large boneless chicken thighs or breasts.
½ bunch parsley.
½ bunch cilantro.
3 cloves garlic1 teaspoon ground cumin.
½ teaspoon crushed red pepper flakes.
5 tablespoons olive oil.
⅓ cup apple cider vinegar.
4 eggs.
4 multigrain rolls.
½ head red leaf lettuce, shredded.
1 large ripe tomato, sliced.
Sea salt and freshly ground black pepper, to taste.

COOK
20 minutes
SERVES
4

Preparation

❶ Preheat a sautoir pan over a medium heat, add 1 tablespoon olive oil and heat for 1 minute. Season chicken with salt and pepper, place in the hot pan and sear, without moving the chicken, until golden brown, about 10 minutes. Flip the chicken, reduce heat to low and cook for another 3 minutes.

❷ Chimichurri. Clean parsley and cilantro, remove skin from garlic and place in a food processor, along with the cumin, red pepper flakes, 4 tablespoons olive oil and apple cider vinegar. Pulse until roughly chopped and set aside.

❸ In a large pan, heat 1 tablespoon butter over a medium heat. Crack 4 eggs into the pan and cook over easy.

❹ Toast the rolls and assemble the sandwiches by layering chimichurri, chicken, egg, and topping with more chimichurri.

❺ Garnish with shredded lettuce and tomato slices and serve.

Pumpkin Seed Crusted Flounder with Greek Zucchini

For the zucchini

3   zucchini.

I   tablespoon extra-virgin olive oil.

¼   cup feta cheese.

3   sprigs fresh dill, stemmed and picked.

I   lemon quartered.
    Kosher salt and black pepper, to taste.

COOK
20 - 25 minutes
SERVES
4-6

For the fish

⅓   cup pumpkin seeds (raw preferred).

⅓   cup sunflower seeds (raw preferred)

I   tablespoon fennel seeds.

⅓   cup panko or breadcrumbs.

I   tablespoon dried dill.

⅛   teaspoon cayenne pepper.

3   tablespoons olive oil, more as needed.

2-2 ½ pounds flounder filets (optional: sole, tilapia, cod, or halibut).

2   eggs.

Optional
Curry-lemon Sauce
for the Fish Filets

Mix together 1/3 cup mayonnaise, I teaspoon curry powder, juice of ¼ lemon, ½ finely chopped celery stick and ½ tablespoon white horseradish.

Preparation

❶ Bring a pot of salted water to a boil.

❷ Wash and cut zucchini into 1 ½ - 2–inch slices, skins on; put in the pot and cover. Cook 8-10 minutes, until tender.

❸ Drain in a colander, let cool and transfer to a large bowl; drizzle with olive oil, crumble in the feta cheese, sprinkle with fresh dill, squeeze juice of ¼ lemon and toss lightly.

❹ Meanwhile, chop coarsely pumpkin, sunflower and fennel seeds in a food processor; transfer to a large plate and mix seeds with panko, dried dill and cayenne; season with kosher salt and black pepper.

❺ In a bowl, whisk 1 whole egg and 1 yolk.

❻ Preheat a sautoir pan with olive oil over a medium heat.

❼ Lightly dip flounder fillets in eggs, then in seed mixture and sear until golden brown, adding more oil as needed. Cook fish in two batches and drain on paper towels.

❽ Serve fish and zucchini garnished with lemon wedges.

Fast French Salmon

1 medium leek.
2 tablespoons unsalted butter.
2 large shallots, thinly sliced.
1 cup chicken or vegetable broth.
4 garlic cloves, pressed.
1 tablespoon fresh tarragon, chopped.
1 ½ pounds salmon filet.
1 tablespoon chopped fresh dill.
 Juice of ½ lemon.

COOK
20 minutes
SERVES
4-6

> **Preparation**

❶ Cut off and discard green part and root of the leek, wash thoroughly, and cut lengthwise into thin strips; set aside.

❷ In a sautoir pan, melt butter over medium heat, add shallots and cook until softened, 3-5 minutes.

❸ Add 1 tablespoon broth and leeks and sauté for 3-5 minutes; add garlic and sauté for another minute.

❹ Pour in broth, add lemon juice, tarragon, sea salt and black pepper and bring to a boil.

❺ Meanwhile, rub salmon with a little olive oil and lemon, season with salt and pepper and place on top of leeks. Cover with a lid and cook for 6-9 minutes, until fork-tender.

❻ Serve sprinkled with chopped dill. Great with rice.

How important is good Posture?

How important is good posture? When you are talking about health for kids and adults, good posture is up there with eating right, exercising, and getting a good night's sleep.

Good posture means your spine and bones are properly aligned. It means your muscles, joints, ligaments, and vital organs can work as nature intended.

Children, teenagers, and adults with good posture look successful, confident, and alert to the world.

Exercises that encourage good posture are Thai Chi, Yoga, and Martial arts. [153]

Arepas de Queso
(Masa Cakes with Cheese)

For the cakes

3   cups masa harina.
1   cup all purpose flour.
1   tablespoon baking powder.
¼   cup canola oil.
1   tablespoon salt.
2¼ cups warm water.
1   tablespoon butter, to fry the cakes, more as needed.
1   pound cheddar or Mexican blend cheese, shredded.
    Kosher salt and freshly ground black pepper, to taste.

To serve

1   ripe avocado.
1   Serrano pepper, seeded and thinly sliced.
1   green pepper, seeded and thinly sliced.
¼   cup fresh cilantro, roughly chopped.
1   tablespoon olive oil.
1   cup sour cream.
⅛   teaspoon chilli pepper.
    Juice of 1 lime.

COOK
30 minutes
SERVES
4-6

Preparation

1 In a mixing bowl, combine all dry ingredients and mix thoroughly. Slowly add the oil and knead with your hands. After the oil is fully incorporated, mix in water; let rest for 15 minutes and form into ¼ -inch thick, 3-inch in diameter, patties. When making the patties, keep your hands wet so the dough doesn't stick to your hands.

2 Melt butter in a sauté pan, add patties and cook over low-medium heat until golden on each side, 6-8 minutes. Cook in batches of 3 or 4, adding more butter as needed.

3 Transfer patties to a plate and add 2-3 tablespoons shredded cheese on top of half of them, then place the remaining patties on top.;

4 Place cakes back in the pan and heat for a few minutes, until the cheese melts.

5 Dice avocado and mix together with limes juice, Serrano, green peppers, cilantro and olive oil; season with salt and pepper.

6 Serve cakes with the avocado-pepper mixture on top and finish with a dollop of sour cream and a dusting of chilli powder.

Steamed Cod with Zucchini and Tomato

2	cloves garlic, thinly sliced.
1	pound cherry tomatoes.
1	pound zucchini.
1	pound fresh green beans.
1½	pounds wild caught cod.
1	tablespoon olive oil.
2	tablespoons fresh oregano, chopped.
4	tablespoons olive oil.
	Zest of 1 lime.
	Sea salt and freshly ground black pepper, to taste.

COOK
30 minutes
SERVES
4-6

> **Preparation**

1 In a small pot, place garlic with the cherry tomatoes. Set the heat to low, place a lid on the pot and cook for 15 minutes; season with salt and pepper.

2 Trim and slice green beans and zucchini.

3 Place a steamer base in a sautoir pan, add water and bring to a boil.

4 Season cod with salt, pepper and olive oil, place in the pan cover and steam until tender, approximately 7-10 minutes, depending on the size.

5 Heat olive oil in a pan, add zucchini and cook over a medium heat until golden on one side; flip and add the string beans. Place a lid on the pan, season with salt and pepper and cook for another 3 minutes, until vegetables are tender. Add cherry tomatoes and turn off the heat.

6 Serve steamed fish on a bed of tomatoes and zucchini and sprinkle with oregano and lime zest.

Spanish Bean Stew with Rice

COOK
30 minutes
SERVES
4-6

For the stew

1	tablespoon olive oil.
1	medium sweet onion, chopped.
¾	pounds ground beef (for vegeatarian style leave out).
1	carrot, finely diced.
1	jalapeno pepper, seeded and finely chopped.
2	celery stick, finely diced.
3	ounces (5 tablespoons) tomato paste.
1	tablespoon dried thyme.
2	bay leaves.
2	garlic cloves, finely chopped.
½	teaspoon cinnamon.
1	teaspoon smoked paprika.
¼	teaspoon cayenne.
1	tablespoon red vinegar.
1¼	cup vegetable broth.
1 12	ounce can pinto or black beans, drained and rinsed.
1	bunch fresh mustard greens, remove spine, roughly chopped.

For the rice

2	cups jasmine rice (organic preferred).
4	cups chicken broth or water.

Preparation

❶ Bring chicken broth to a boil; add jasmine rice, stir, cover, and cook, without stirring, 20-25 minutes or until broth is absorbed.

❷ Preheat a sautoir pan over a medium heat; add olive oil and sauté onion for about 4 minutes, until softened.

❸ Add beef saute until browned, remove jucie.

❹ Add carrot, jalapeno, celery, tomatoes paste, thyme and bay leaves and cook, stirring, for 3 minutes.

❺ Stir in garlic, cinnamon, smoked paprika and deglaze with the red vinegar, then pour in broth and cover. Reduce heat to low and cook 4-5 minutes.

❻ Add mustard greens cover and cook for 5 minute; add beans and cook on medium heat for another 10 minutes. Serve bean stew with the rice.

Jalapeño packs a nutritional punch

The usage of the Jalapeno pepper dates as far back as the Aztecs. Still as popular today as then, the Jalapeno is one of the most commonly used and grown Chiles in Mexico and the USA.

Small in size, coming in under four inches long, the jalapeno packs a nutritional punch while adding wonderful hot and pungent flavors to the dish.

Jalapenos obtain their heat from a natural compound called capsaicin, which also delivers powerful health benefits. Jalapenos are low in carbs and a rich source of vitamin C and vitamin A, which supports skin and eye health.

Potato Goat Cheese Kale and Red Pepper Frittata

1	tablespoon olive oil.
1	large yellow onion, thinly sliced.
1	red bell pepper, seeded and diced.
2	medium size Yukon potatoes, skins on, diced.
2	cups kale, shredded.
10	eggs, lightly beaten.
3	tablespoons dill, stemmed and chopped.
½	pound soft plain goat cheese.
1	tablespoon extra virgin olive oil.
1	box spring salad mix.
2	tablespoons balsamic vinegar.
1	tablespoon olive oil.
	Kosher salt and freshly ground black pepper, to taste.

COOK
30-45 minutes
SERVES
4-6

....

Preparation

❶ Preheat oven to 375°.

❷ Preheat a sautoir pan over medium heat, add olive oil and onion and cook until partially caramelized, about 4 minutes.

❸ Add red pepper, turn heat to low and add diced potato. Season with salt and pepper, place a lid on the pan and cook on medium heat until the potato is fully cooked, about 15 minutes. Stir in kale and cook until wilted, 2-3 minutes.

❹ Season eggs with salt and pepper and stir in dill. Pour egg mixture over the vegetables, crumble goat cheese on top and place the pan in the oven. Cook for 10-15 minutes, until set.

❺ In a large bowl, dress the spring mix with balsamic vinegar and olive oil and season to taste.

❻ Cut frittata into wedges and serve with the salad.

Sunflower Seeds and Swiss chard Fettuccine

1 packet fettuccine.
½ cup raw sunflower seeds.
¼ stick butter unsalted.
½ cup extra virgin olive oil.
1 bunch Swiss chard, stemmed and chopped.
1 teaspoon nutmeg powder.
1 cup freshly grated parmesan cheese.
2 tablespoons fresh parsley.
  Zest of 1 lemon.
  Kosher salt and freshly ground black pepper,
  to taste.

COOK
20 minutes
SERVES
5-6

▶ **Preparation**

❶ Cook fettuccine in a large pot of salted water for about 8-10 minutes, drain well and return to the pot.

❷ Meanwhile, in a sautoir pan, toast sunflower seeds over medium-low heat for a few minutes and set aside.

❸ Heat olive oil and butter in a sautoir pan over a medium-low heat, add Swiss chard, and cook for 2-3 minutes, until wilted; add nutmeg and chilli flakes, season with kosher salt and black pepper and remove from heat.

❹ Gradually stir in parmesan cheese, until well blended and smooth.

❺ Pour mixture over the fettuccine, add sunflower seeds and parsley and toss together, using 2 forks.

❻ Place pot back on stove over low heat, tossing fettuccine so they are evenly coated, about 2 minutes; stir in the lemon zest and serve immediately.

Soba Noodles with Sesame Seeds

1	packet (½ pound) soba noodles.
2	tablespoons white miso paste.
3	tablespoons tahini (sesame paste).
½	teaspoon red chilli pepper flakes.
1½	cups water.
2	tablespoons sesame seeds, lightly toasted.
1	ripe avocado, diced.
1	large carrot, shredded.
1	cup green onions, thinly sliced.
	Sea salt and freshly ground black pepper, to taste.

COOK
10 minutes
SERVES
4

Preparation

1 Bring water to a boil, add noodles and cook until al dente, approximately 5 minutes (check package instructions). Drain and transfer to a serving plate.

2 In a bowl, whisk together miso, tahini, red chilli pepper flakes and water in a bowl. Mix in 1 tablespoon sesame seeds.

3 Pour the miso mixture over the noodles, add avocado and shredded carrot and toss lightly to combine.

4 Garnish with green onions and remaining sesame seeds and serve.

Turkey Burgers over Sautéed Spinach

1 ½ pounds ground turkey.
2   eggs, lightly beaten.
5-6 sprigs fresh tarragon, stemmed and chopped.
5-6 sprigs fresh rosemary, stemmed and chopped.
3   tablespoons olive oil, divided.
2   cloves garlic, chopped.
1   pound fresh spinach
4   cups mixed green salad.
2   ripe tomatoes, sliced.
2   tablespoons balsamic vinegar.
     Juice of ½ lemon.
     Kosher salt and freshly ground
     black pepper.

COOK
20 minutes
SERVES
4-6

❶ In a large bowl, mix ground turkey, eggs, tarragon, dill and rosemary; season with salt and pepper and form mixture into 1 ½ -inch thick patties.

❷ Preheat a sautoir pan with 1 tablespoon olive oil over a medium-high heat and sear the patties for 5-7 minutes, turn over and sear until nicely browned and thoroughly cooked; transfer to a plate and tent with aluminium foil to keep warm.

❸ Rinse out the pan and preheat with 1 tablespoon olive oil over a medium-high heat. Add garlic and sauté lightly, 1-2 minutes; add spinach and cook until wilted, about 3 minutes. Stir in lemon juice and season with salt and pepper.

❹ In a large bowl, combine mixed green salad with tomatoes and drizzle with the remaining 1 tablespoon olive oil and the balsamic vinegar; season and toss lightly.

❺ Serve burgers over the spinach and the salad and the side.

Meatballs with Zucchini Pasta

For the meatballs

1   pound ground beef.

½   pound ground turkey, veal or pork.

2   eggs, lightly beaten.

4   large cloves garlic, minced.

1   medium yellow onion, finely chopped.

1½ tablespoon (5-6 sprigs) fresh rosemary, finely chopped.

2   tablespoon olive oil, divided.

1   large jar of your favorite tomato sauce.
      Sea salt and freshly ground black pepper.

For the zucchini pasta

2   pounds zucchini.

2   tablespoons butter.

1   cup fresh picked basil, shredded.
      Juice of 1 lemon.

COOK
30 minutes
SERVES
4-6

> **Preparation**

❶ In a large bowl combine all meatballs ingredients, season with salt and pepper and mix well. Form into ¾-inch diameter balls.

❷ Heat olive oil in a large sautoir pan; add meatballs and cook for about 7 minutes, until browned. Add tomato sauce, reduce heat and simmer for 20 minutes.

❸ Slice zucchini with a spiral slicer or grate coarsely with a cheese grater and squeeze excess moisture.

❹ Melt butter in a stock pot, add remaining 1 tablespoon olive oil, and heat lightly. Add zucchini and cook, covered, over a low heat, for about 3-5 minutes, until tender. Mix in the lemon juice and shredded basil.

❺ Serve meatballs over zucchini pasta.

Sides Make Dinner a Meal

Just like famous music bands on stage, the main course is in the spotlight but what about the oh-so-important back up dishes outside the limelight just six inches from stardom? In this section you'll learn how to create side dishes from our brain food section that will certainly take center stage. I can hear the claps and standing ovations coming your way.

"In the massively entertaining and heartfelt documentary '20 Feet from Stardom,' audiences meet the most memorable voices in the world of backup singers. They perform with world-famous musical acts, but theirs are not household names. Their stories, however, are inspiring, heartbreaking and enthralling."

-Entertainment News

To create these outstanding sides you'll combine nuts, herbs, and vegetables that are rich in fiber and protein, that are ideal for a hungry crowd. With these tasty, nutritious sides harmonizing with your main courses, you'll have them coming back for more.

Let's paint a picture: fall has arrived with its changing leaves and bursts of color. Above the spectacular foliage, clouds scuttle across the sky, the sun breaking out in bursts. The game just ended. Imagine roasted butternut squash crispy on the edges, its rich, nutty flavor tasting a little like sweet potato; add toasted almonds, dates, and a twist of Israeli Tahini sauce. Hungry yet?

Two Bean Salad
with Feta and Avocado

3 tablespoons extra virgin olive oil, divided.
1 medium red onion, chopped.
½ teaspoon ground cumin.
½ teaspoon ground cinnamon.
1 medium red chilli, seeded, chopped.
2 cloves garlic, chopped.
1 15 ounce can black beans, drained and rinsed.
1 15 ounce can kidney beans, drained and rinsed.
  (optional: white beans or black-eyed peas).
¼ pound feta cheese (Bavarian sheep milk feta preferred).
¼ cup fresh cilantro, stemmed and picked.
1 avocado, cubed.
1 lime, cut into wedges.
  Juice of 2 limes.

COOK
15 minutes
SERVES
4-6

> **Preparation**

❶ Heat 2 tablespoons olive oil in a sautoir pan over a medium heat; add onions and sauté for a few minutes, until softened.

❷ Add cumin, cinnamon, chilli and garlic and sauté 2-3 minutes, then add beans, cover and cook for 5-8 minutes, adding a splash of water if too thick.

❸ Transfer beans to a large bowl and let cool, then drizzle with remaining tablespoon olive oil and toss together.

❹ Crumble feta cheese on top, sprinkle with cilantro, scatter avocado and drizzle with lime juice.

❺ Garnish with lime wedges and serve.

Acorn Squash with Dates, Almonds and Tahini

3   medium acorn squash, seeded and halved
1   tablespoon olive oil
5   sprigs fresh rosemary, twigs removed and roughly chopped
⅓   cup dates, pitted and roughly chopped
½   cup sliced almond
     Juice of ½ lemon
     Sea salt and freshly ground black pepper, to taste

For the dressing
½   cup tahini (sesame paste)
½   cup water
1   teaspoon rice vinegar
1   tablespoon soy sauce
½   lemons
1   cloves garlic, finely grated or pressed
¼   cup olive oil

COOK
1 hour 45 minutes
SERVES
4-6

> **Preparation**

❶ Preheat oven to 375°F and line a baking sheet or roasting pan with heavy aluminium foil.

❷ Place squash on the prepared baking sheet, drizzle with olive oil and sprinkle generously with chopped rosemary, kosher salt and black pepper.

❸ Roast for 1 hour, add dates on top of each squash half, and roast for another 30-45 minutes.

❹ Toast the almonds in a pan over low heat for a few minutes; sprinkle with a little salt as they begin to brown.

❺ For the dressing, whisk all ingredients, except olive oil, for 1-2 minutes in a bowl, or pulse in a food processor for 15-20 seconds, until smooth. The dressing will be thick, so if you prefer a thinner consistency, add slowly a bit more water. Transfer to a bowl and whisk in the olive oil.

❻ Remove squash and dates from the oven, arrange on a large plate, sprinkle toasted almonds on top and with drizzle tahini dressing and lemon juice.

Roasted Carrots with Avocado and Chives

1	pound carrots, peeled, leave whole.
¼	cup extra virgin olive oil.
1	teaspoon fresh thyme.
1	cup chives, chopped.
1	avocado.
¼	cup balsamic vinegar.
1	tablespoon honey.
¼	cup pumpkin seeds, roasted.
	Juice of ½ lemon.
	Kosher salt and freshly ground black pepper, to taste.

COOK
25 minutes
SERVES
4

> **Preparation**

❶ Preheat oven to 350°F.

❷ Boil water in a large pot, add ½ teaspoon salt and blanch carrots for 3-5 minutes; drain and place in a single layer in a large roasting pan.

❸ Lightly drizzle olive oil over carrots, season with thyme, kosher salt, and black pepper, and roast for 25 minutes. Remove from oven; let cool for a few minutes, then lay carrots in rows on a plate.

❹ Scatter chives over carrots.

❺ Pit and thinly slice avocado, drizzle with lemon juice and arrange on top of chives.

❻ In a small bowl, whisk until smooth vinegar, olive oil and honey and drizzle over carrots.

❼ Sprinkle with pumpkin seeds before serving.

Roasted Kabocha Squash and Broccoli Salad with Ginger Vinaigrette

1   Kabocha or butternut squash peeled, seeded and cut into ½-inch cubes.
1   tablespoon olive oil.
2   large heads broccoli.
    Sea salt and freshly ground black pepper, to taste.

For the vinaigrette
½   bunch cilantro.
1   tablespoon fresh ginger, grated.
1   teaspoon honey.
¼   cup olive oil.
    Juice of three limes.

COOK
1 hour 10 minutes
SERVES
4-6

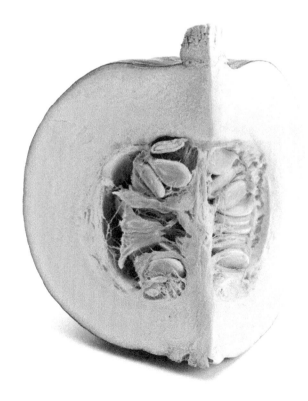

Preparation

❶ Preheat oven to 375°F.

❷ Place the squash in a roasting pan; drizzle olive oil, season with salt and pepper and roast for 1 hour.

❸ Increase oven temperature to 400°F.

❹ Cut broccoli into medium florets and toss with olive oil, salt and pepper. Add to the roasting pan and cook with the squash for 10 minutes.

❺ Chop cilantro, place in a small bowl and mix with lime juice, ginger, honey and olive oil.

❻ Pour vinaigrette on top of squash and broccoli before serving.

Baby Bok Choy
with Cashews

2 tablespoons olive oil.

1 cup scallions, chopped.

3 cloves garlic, chopped.

1 pound baby bok choy, trimmed, leaves separated and thoroughly washed.

½ teaspoon sesame oil.

½ teaspoon Chinese five spice powder.

½ cup raw cashews.

  Sea salt and freshly ground black pepper, to taste.

COOK
10 minutes
SERVES
4-6

> **Preparation**

❶ Heat olive oil in a large pan on medium high heat; add scallions and sauté until soft then add garlic and bok choy. Sprinkle with sesame oil, five spice powder and salt.

❷ Cover and cook for 3 minutes; remove cover, reduce heat to low, stir and cook for 1-2 minutes.

❸ Meanwhile, chop cashews, salt and toast a few minutes in a toaster oven.

❹ Mix in cashews and serve.

Broccoli with Sesame Vinaigrette and Toasted Almonds

6 cups broccoli florets.

¼ cup sliced almond.

For the vinaigrette

½ tablespoon rice vinegar.

2 tablespoon sesame oil.

1 tablespoon soy sauce.

1 tablespoon fresh ginger, finely chopped.

2 garlic cloves, chopped.

1 tablespoon sesame seeds.

1 tablespoon honey.

3 tablespoons orange juice, freshly squeezed.

COOK
15 minutes
SERVES
4-6

Preparation

❶ Place sesame seeds in a dry sautoir pan or skillet, and toast over low heat for about 2 minutes. Transfer to a plate and set aside.

❷ Add a dash of sesame oil to the pan, add almonds and toast over low heat until golden, a couple of minutes. Set aside.

❸ Set a steamer over boiling water and steam broccoli for 6-8 minutes, until crisp-tender.

❹ Meanwhile combine toasted sesame seeds and the rest of vinaigrette ingredients in a saucepan and bring to a simmer; cook for 5 minutes.

❺ Place broccoli in a serving bowl, add vinaigrette and almonds and toss together.

Beets with Radish, Watercress and Blue Cheese

4   beets, skins on.
2   tablespoons olive oil.
½   pound blue cheese, crumbled.
1   cup sour cream.
1   bunch red radishes, trimmed
    and thinly sliced.
1   bunch watercress, stemmed.
    Juice of 1 lemon.
    Sea salt and freshly ground
    black pepper.

COOK
1 – 1 ½ hours
SERVES
4

Preparation

❶ Preheat oven to 400° F.

❷ Place beets in a sautoir pan, season with salt, pepper and 1 tablespoon olive oil, cover and cook in the oven for 1 - 1 ½ hours.

❸ Remove beets from the oven and let cool for 5 minutes; rub the skins off using paper towel and cut into wedges.

❹ In a bowl, whisk together blue cheese and sour cream and set aside.

❺ In a bowl, combine watercress and radishes with lemon juice and remaining 1 tablespoon olive oil and season with salt and pepper.

❻ To serve, add a dollop of blue cheese dressing to the plate, lay beets on top and add watercress and radish salad.

Zucchini Pea Pancakes with Yogurt Mint Sauce

2-3   pound zucchini, grated.

1   medium onion, diced.

2   eggs, lightly beaten.

½   cup rice flour.

2   tablespoons olive oil.

1   teaspoon ground cumin.

½   teaspoon sandia chilli pepper powder.

½   cup grape seed or canola oil,
       for frying, more as needed.
       Sea salt and freshly ground
       black pepper, to taste.

For the yogurt sauce

1½   cup cucumber, diced.

½   bunch mint, roughly chopped.

1   cup Greek yogurt.

1   cup frozen peas.
     Juice of 1 limes.

> **Preparation**

COOK
30 minutes
SERVES
4-6

❶ In a large bowl, mix together zucchini, onions, eggs, rice flour, olive oil, cumin and chilli pepper; season with salt and pepper.

❷ Heat a large pan over a medium-high heat and add enough grape seed oil to generously cover the pan surface. Drop 2 tablespoons of the batter to make small round pancakes.

❸ Cook until browned, flip and cook on the other side. Transfer to a paper-lined plate and repeat until all the batter is used.

❹ Blanche frozen peas for 2 minutes in boiling water drain and put in the fridge for a few minutes.

❺ In a small bowl, whisk together cucumber, mint, Greek yogurt, lime juice and add cooled peas.

❻ Serve pancakes with a dollop of pea yogurt sauce.

Kale, Avocado and Apple Salad

2   avocados, halved, pitted and flesh scooped out.

2   tablespoons olive oil.

2   apples, peeled, seeded and grated.

2   bunches kale, stemmed and finely chopped.

½   cup sunflower seeds.

     Juice of 1 lemon.

     Sea salt and freshly ground black pepper, to taste.

COOK
None
SERVES
4

> **Preparation**

❶ In a large bowl, combine avocado, lemon juice and olive oil. Using a fork, mash the avocado to a smooth paste, season with salt and pepper and set aside.

❷ Grate apples into a large bowl, add the kale and sunflower seeds and mix thoroughly.

❸ Drizzle salad with the avocado dressing and serve.

From My Family to Yours

It brings me great joy to have inspired you to enjoy your cooking journey, embrace fresh ingredients, and relish the bonds healthy meals add to your family's table. The days of fretting over missing a single step or ingredient in a recipe are behind you. Involving the whole family is the best way to promote family mealtime and physical activity for your kids.

Letting your meal inspiration come directly from your ingredients at hand allows you to move away from recipes, freeing you to create fast, healthy, delicious meals. If at any time you feel your confidence diminish, come back to this book. I'm here to help you unlock your culinary kingdom.

When I was little, my family went every Sunday afternoon for dinner to my grandmother's house in Williamsburg, Brooklyn. Grandma spoke very little English and lots of Yiddish. She loved to cook up a storm for us, and everything was fresh and handmade. Blintzes, chopped liver, chicken noodle soup, fresh vegetables —everything was always amazing. Grandma cooked old school; a meat grinder was bolted to the counter. Rumor had it that grandma bought live chickens and plucked off their heads and feathers. Rumor also had it that she stomped grapes in the bathtub to make wine for Grandpa. She was, in every way, a living legend in the neighborhood.

There was a family joke about me as a toddler, that the only toy I had was a pot and a wooden spoon. At two years old I loved to be in Grandma's kitchen to watch her cook, to smell the aromas, and to listen to her speak to me in Yiddish (even though I had no idea what she was saying), while she chopped, minced, seared, and rolled. As soon as we got to her house, I'd run for the cabinet under the counter to the left of the sink, open the door, crawl halfway in, and take out a huge pot. Then I'd sit down on my diaper and plop that pot upside down in front me. Grandma would give me a wooden spoon to bang the pot with. She'd cook, and I'd watch and bang the pot like a drum.

That is what gave me the idea for the title of this book, *Two Pans and a Pot*. I was a minimalist from the diaper days on. That early love of food, cooking, and family is what started me on the path to where I am today. This book is a labor of that love, and I want to thank you for taking the time to read it.

Cooking satisfying and healthy meals need not cost a fortune nor take excessive amounts of time away from your already hectic schedule to create. I wrote *Two Pans and a Pot* to chronicle my own journey and highlight the benefits of feeding children healthy and home cooked meals, to inspire the chef within each of you and to ignite the skills that are already innately buried inside of you (no matter how disastrous past cooking attempts may have been). My hope is that this book will give you what cooking has given me—the ability to take good care of yourself and your family as you move through this incredible food-filled journey called life.

My hope for you as you finish these last pages is that you'll get into the kitchen more. I hope you come out of reading this book a more confident chef and parent. And I hope that the knowledge that you can control your fitness and food choices inspires you to tap into your creativity.

From my family to yours—I wish you health and happiness!

Basic Cooking Terms Defined

Like so many areas of interest there's a lingo that comes with the culinary territory. Basketball has it, social media has it, teenagers have it, and even five year olds have it. There were times when I honestly had no idea what my teenage son meant by the words leaving his lips. Good meant bad and bad meant good. It took a while but I caught on. Then it immediately changed again. When it came to cooking, at first I thought "blanche" was a woman's name. The good news about cooking is the terms rarely change so you only have to learn them once. Here are cooking terms that are good to know. You don't want to sear when the recipe says simmer.

Bake: Cooking in an oven.

Baste: Keeping foods moist during cooking either by pouring liquid over or brushing liquid over the food with a brush.

Batter: A mixture of liquid, flour and other ingredients that can vary in consistency.

Beat: Making a mixture smooth and creamy by whipping in a brisk motion, by hand or machine.

Blanch: Precooking food by briefly cooking it in boiling liquid. Great technique for vegetables.

Boil: Bring a liquid to it's is boiling point, 212° F of rapid bubbles.

Braise: Cooking large pieces of meat or poultry slowly over low heat in a small amount of hot liquid in a tightly covered pan.

Breading: Coating a raw food that has been dredged in a liquid such as eggs, buttermilk, then coated or dusted with bread crumbs or flour.

Broil: Cooking a food by placing it on a rack in the oven that is directly under the heat source.

Brown: Fry, broil or bake food to deepen it's natural surface color but not cooking it.

Caramelize: To cook until the sugar in the food has browned, as with onions or garlic. This process brings out the sweetness in the food and adds color.

Chiffonade: To shred or finely cut vegetables or herbs.

Chill: To refrigerate until cold.

Chop: To cut food into small, uneven pieces.

Cream: Mixing one or more foods together until soft and creamy.

Cube: To cut food into small, equal size squares about 1/4 to 1/8 inch in size.

Deglaze: To use vinegar, broth or wine to remove the flavor-packed brown bits stuck to the bottom of a pan.

Dice: Cutting food into small cubes of equal size and shape.

Drain: To strain away the liquid.

Flambé: To ignite warmed spirits in a pan of food, often a dessert, for effect, and to caramelize the dish.

Fricassee: Braising small pieces of meat in a small amount of liquid.

Fry: Cooking food in a hot fat (ie. vegetable oil, shortening).

Garnish: To decorate food with edible items like sliced fruit or herbs.

Grease: To rub the inside of baking pans with butter, margarine or baking sprays to prevent from sticking.

Julienne: To cut vegetables into thin strips similar to matchsticks.

Knead: to work dough into a smooth texture by pressing and folding with the heels of your hands.

Let Stand: To let food cool down.

Marinate: Making foods more flavorful and tender by soaking them in a liquid for several hours or overnight. Generally marinades are made of oils, spices, vinegars or some combination of citrus and spices.

Mince: To chop food into very fine pieces

Parboil: Cooking food in a boiling liquid until it is only partially cooked.

Pare: To remove the stem and the very thin layer of peel of a fruit or vegetable with a paring knife or peeler.

Poach: To slowly simmer in a hot liquid

Preheat: To turn on an appliance or oven to a desired temperature about 5-10 minutes before the food is to be placed in it.

Puree: Blending a cooked vegetable or fruit until it is smooth.

Sauté: To lightly brown or cook food in a small amount of hot fat over moderate heat.

Sear: Browning meat rapidly by using extremely high heat.

Simmer: Cooking a food in a hot liquid just below boiling point. Bubbles will form slowly but will not reach the surface.

Slice: To cut food into large, thick or thin flat pieces.

Stew: Simmering slowly in a small amount of liquid, usually for several hours.

Sweat: To slowly cook vegetables in a covered pan until they are soft, but still hold their shape. This is often done with onions or garlic.

Whip: Beating a food rapidly so as to add air to it.

Cook Fresh!

Sources

1 "Healthy Tips for Preventing Childhood Obesity - Article by Empowerher.com 21 Apr. 2014,
   http://www.empowher.com/obesity/content/healthy-tips-preventing-childhood-obesity.

2 http://www.restaurant.org/Pressroom/Press-Releases/What-s-Hot-Culinary-Forecast-Predicts-Locally-Sour

3 NY Times May 26th 2013, Breeding nutrition out of food.

4 What caused the obesity crisis in the West? http://www.bbc.com/news/health-18393391, June 2012

5 http://kidshealth.org/parent/nutrition_center/staying_fit/exercise.html and
   http://www.parents.com/fun/sports/exercise/10-benefits-of-physical-activity/

6 http://www.mayoclinic.org/healthy-living/fitness/in-depth/exercise/art-20048389

7 Choose MyPlate Replaces Food Pyramid. http://www.goldenrule.com/health-wellness/choosemyplate-replaces-food-pyramid/

8 Chick-Fil-A Removing Artificial Dye, High Fructose Corn Syrup. www.huffingtonpost.com/2013/12/03/chick-fil-a-artificial-dye_n_4379189.html

9 Choose Water as a Drink. http://www.healthykids.nsw.gov.au/kids-teens/choose-water-as-a-drink-kids.aspx

10 The Truth About White Foods. http://www.webmd.com/diet/features/truth-about-white-foods

11 Postprandial Energy Expenditure in Whole-Food and Processed-Food Meals: Implications for Daily Energy Expenditure.
    http://www.foodandnutritionresearch.net/index.php/fnr/article/view/5144/5755

12 The Human Body Is Designed to Move. http://www.bodyzone.com/site/posture-principles/the-human-body-is-designed-to-move.html

13 Pandora's Lunchbox, Melanie Warner, Scribner, A division of Simon & Shuster. Copyright 2013.

14 Food Processing and Obesity, Robert H Lustig, M.D., Professor of Clinical Pediatrics, Division of Endocrinology, Director, Weight, Obesity
    Prevention Special Edition Contributor. Updated on May 17, 2010.
    http://www.education.com/reference/article/food-processing-obesity-2/

15 Salt, Sugar, Fat, Michael Moss. 2014 Random House Trade Paperback Edition, copyright 2013 by Michael Moss

16 How Salt Works, by Shanna Freeman. http://science.howstuffworks.com/innovation/edible-innovations/salt.htm

17 It's not just a grownup problem: salt is bad for kids, too, September 2012, Dr. Claire McCarthy.
    http://www.boston.com/lifestyle/health/mdmama/2012/09/its_not_just_a_grownup_problem_salt_is_bad_for_kids_too.html

18 Artificial sweeteners: sugar-free, but at what cost? Holly Strawbridge. July 2012.
    http://www.health.harvard.edu/blog/artificial-sweeteners-sugar-free-but-at-what-cost-201207165030

19 List of Good Fat Foods | LIVESTRONG.COM, http://www.livestrong.com/article/27454-list-good-fat-foods/ (accessed June 26, 2014).

20 Salisbury High School Library, Organic Foods Production Act of 1990, Food, 2011.
    http://ic.galegroup.com/ic/scic/ReferenceDetailsPage/ReferenceDetailsWindow?query=&prodId=SCIC&contentModules=&displayGroup-
    Name=Reference&limiter=&disableHighlighting=false&displayGroups=&sortBy=&search_within_results=&p=SCIC&action=2&-
    catId=&activityType=&documentId=GALE%7CCX1918600187&source=Bookmark&u=pl2763&jsid=b9e9b4b646566d800a81d2f-
    6c660b532 (Accessed June 26th 2014)

21   Is it better to buy local or organic food?, How Stuff Works.
     http://recipes.howstuffworks.com/local-or-organic.htm (accessed June 26, 2014).

22   Organic Farming, Eden Memory Research Center Ltd. http://edenmemory.com/organic-farming/ (accessed June 26, 2014).

23   Stanford Scientists Cast Doubt on Advantages of Organic Meat and Produce. September 3, 2012, New York Times. http://www.nytimes.
     com/2012/09/04/science/earth/study-questions-advantages-of-organic-meat-and-produce.html?ref=health (accessed June 26, 2014).

24   Executive Summary, April 2014, Environmental Working Group. http://www.ewg.org/foodnews/summary.php (accessed June 26, 2014)

25   Economic History of Tractors in the United States, Economic history Association, eh.net.
     http://eh.net/encyclopedia/economic-history-of-tractors-in-the-united-states/, (accessed June 26, 2014)

26   The Chemical Age Dawns in Agriculture, livinghistoryarm.org.
     http://www.livinghistoryfarm.org/farminginthe40s/pests_01.html (accessed June 26, 2014)

27   Pesticides, Wikipedia. http://en.wikipedia.org/wiki/Pesticide#Economics, (accessed June 26, 2014)

28   Pesticides & Profit, Pesticide Action Network. http://www.panna.org/issues/pesticides-profit, (accessed June 26, 2014)

29   Rearing Cattle Produces More Greenhouse Gases than Driving Cars, UN Report Warns, November 29, 2006, UN News Centre.
     http://www.un.org/apps/news/story.asp?newsID=20772&#.U42jn8bfZuY

30   In Rooftop Farming, New York City Emerges as a Leader, July 11, 2012, New York Times.
     http://www.nytimes.com/2012/07/12/nyregion/in-rooftop-farming-new-york-city-emerges-as-a-leader.html (accessed June 27, 2014).

31   Food Channel Reveals 2014 Top 10 Food Trends, Food Product Design,
     http://www.foodproductdesign.com/news/2013/12/food-channel-reveals-2014-top-10-food-trends.aspx (accessed June 27, 2014).

32   What is a GMO, Non GMO Project, http://www.nongmoproject.org/learn-more/what-is-gmo/ (accessed July 18, 2014).

33   Food and Agriculture Organization of the United Nations | Biodiversity for Food and Agriculture.
     http://www.fao.org/sd/epdirect/epre0040.htm, (accessed June 27, 2014).

34   Anthocyanins and Human Health: An In Vitro Investigative Approach, The National Center for Biotechnology.
     http://www.ncbi.nlm.nih.gov/pmc/articles/PMC1082894/, (accessed June 27, 2014).

35   Corn Subsidies Make Unhealthy Food Choices the Rational Ones.
     http://grist.org/article/food-2010-09-21-op-ed-corn-subsidies-make-unhealthy-food-choices/ (accessed June 27, 2014).

36   Gluten: 5 things you need to know, CNN.com http://www.cnn.com/2013/04/05/health/gluten-5-things/ (accessed June 27, 2014).

37   Statistics, The National Chicken Council. http://www.nationalchickencouncil.org/about-the-industry/statistics/ (accessed June 27, 2014).

38   Should You Buy Organic? Study Complicates Decision, CNN.com.
     http://www.cnn.com/2012/09/03/health/organics-versus-conventional/ (accessed June 30, 2014).

39   Corporate Definitions of 'Natural' | How Consumers Are.
     http://www.cornucopia.org/2014/04/corporate-definitions-natural-consumers-deceived/ (accessed June 27, 2014).

40   Feast Food & Animal Welfare, Tufts University. http://www.tufts.edu/programs/feast/animalwelfare.htm (accessed June 27, 2014).

41   Meat and Poultry Labeling Terms | The United States Department of Agriculture.
     http://www.fsis.usda.gov/wps/portal/fsis/topics/food-safety-education/get-answers/food-safety-fact-sheets/food-labeling/meat-and-poultry-
     labeling-terms/meat-and-poultry-labeling-terms (accessed June 27, 2014).

42   Decoding Meat & Dairy Product Labels, Environmental Working Group.
     http://www.ewg.org/meateatersguide/decoding-meat-dairy-product-labels/ (accessed June 27, 2014).

43 What Do Chicken Labels Really Mean?, Salon.com.
    http://www.salon.com/2011/01/20/what_chicken_labels_really_mean/ (accessed June 27, 2014).

44 Kashrut Jewish Dietary Laws | Judaism 101. http://www.jewfaq.org/kashrut.htm
    (Accessed June 27, 2014).

45 All About The Egg, Iowa Egg Council. http://iowaegg.org/education/all-about-the-egg/a/#sthash.1Uu5brR1.dpbs (accessed July 18, 2014)

46 All About The Egg, Iowa Egg Council. http://iowaegg.org/education/all-about-the-egg/o/#sthash.qQKTv5ty.dpbs (accessed July 18, 2014)

47 How to Read Egg Carton Labels, The Humane Society of the United States.
    http://www.humanesociety.org/issues/confinement_farm/facts/guide_egg_labels.html (accessed July 18, 2014)

48 What's New and Beneficial About Eggs, The World's Healthiest Foods.
    http://www.whfoods.com/genpage.php?tname=foodspice&dbid=92 (accessed July 18, 2014)

49 Reading Between the Lines, EggIndustry.com. http://eggindustry.com/cfi/faq/ (accessed July 18, 2014)

50 The Difference Between Brown and White Eggs, Today I Found Out.
    http://www.todayifoundout.com/index.php/2014/02/difference-brown-white-eggs/, (accessed July 18, 2014)

51 Chicken Nuggets Recalled for Undeclared Milk, Food Safety News.
    http://www.foodsafetynews.com/2012/11/chicken-nuggets-recalled-for-undeclared-milk/ (accessed July 18, 2014).

52 Kroger Ice Cream May Contain Undeclared Allergen, Food Safety News.
    http://www.foodsafetynews.com/tag/ice-cream/#.U8mFVlbfZuY, (accessed July 18, 2014).

53 Vermont Gov. Signs Law to Require Labels on GMO Foods, USA Today.
    http://www.usatoday.com/story/news/politics/2014/05/08/genetically-modified-foods/8860423/ (accessed July 18, 2014).

54 A Body Sculpted by History, Cavemandoctor.com.
    http://www.cavemandoctor.com/2012/11/12/foods-that-sculpted-the-human-body/, (Accessed July 18, 2014)

55 BOLD Study | Mississippi Beef Council, http://www.msbeef.org/beefnutrition.aspx, (Accessed July 18, 2014)

56 Inspection & Grading of Meat and Poultry: What Are the Differences?, United States Department of Agriculture.
    http://www.fsis.usda.gov/wps/portal/fsis/topics/food-safety-education/get-answers/food-safety-fact-sheets/production-and-inspection/
    inspection-and-grading-of-meat-and-poultry-what-are-the-differences_/inspection-and-grading-differences, (Accessed July 18, 2014)

57 Fast Food is a Major Public Health Hazard | Organic Consumers Association.
    http://www.organicconsumers.org/foodsafety/fastfood032103.cfm, (Accessed July 18, 2014)

58 Animal Feed, Grace Communications Foundation. http://www.sustainabletable.org/260/animal-feed, (Accessed July 18, 2014).

59 The Grassfed Primer, Your Guide to the Benefits of Grass Fed Beef, animalwelfareapproved.org.
    http://animalwelfareapproved.org/wp-content/uploads/2012/07/The-Grassfed-Primer-online.pdf, (Accessed July 18, 2014).

60 King Corn. http://www.kingcorn.net (Accessed June 30, 2014).

61 Processed Meats Too Dangerous for Human Consumption, April 2012, Institute for Natural Healing.
    http://institutefornaturalhealing.com/2012/04/processed-meats-declared-too-dangerous-for-human-consumption/

62 Asthma | The World's Healthiest Foods, whfoods.org.
    http://www.whfoods.com/genpage.php?tname=disease&dbid=12 (Accessed June 30, 2014).

63 Are These Common Foods Causing Your Allergies? Dr. Susanne Bennett , Huffingtonpost.com.
    http://www.huffingtonpost.com/dr-susanne-bennett/allergies_b_1363995.html (Accessed June 30, 2014).

64 Hunter-Gatherers to Farmers, Historyworld.net. http://www.historyworld.net/wrldhis/PlainTextHistories.asp?historyid=ab63

65   Opposition to the Use of Hormone Growth Promoters in Beef and Dairy Cattle Production, American Public Health Association, apha.org. http://www.apha.org/advocacy/policy/policysearch/default.htm?id=1379 (Accessed June 30, 2014).

66   The Surprising Sources of your Favorite Seafoods, Fishwatch U.S. Seafood Facts, FishWatch.gov, http://www.fishwatch.gov/features/top10seafoods_and_sources_10_10_12.html (Accessed June 30, 2014).

67   The Origins of California's High-Seas Tuna Fleet, August Felando and Harold Medina, sandiegohistory.org. http://www.sandiegohistory.org/journal/v58-1/v58-1felando.pdf (Accessed June 30, 2014).

68   Clean Energy | Environmental Protection Agency, epa.gov. http://www.epa.gov/cleanenergy/energy-and-you/affect/air-emissions.html

69   Bluefin Tuna 101, Biology, Ecology, Economics, and Politics, National Geographic. http://channel.nationalgeographic.com/channel/wicked-tuna/articles/bluefin-tuna-101/(Accessed July 1st, 2014).

70   Tuna Lover's Dilemma: To Eat or Not to Eat? | National Geographic. http://news.nationalgeographic.com/news/2014/02/140220-tuna-guide-skipjack-yellowfin-albacore-bluefin-bigeye-sushi/ (Accessed July 1st, 2014).

71   Skipjack Tuna | World Wildlife Fund, worldwildlife.org. https://www.worldwildlife.org/species/skipjack-tuna (Accessed July 1st, 2014).

72   Albacore Tuna | World Wildlife Fund, worldwildlife.org. https://www.worldwildlife.org/species/albacore-tuna (Accessed July 1st, 2014).

73   Childhood Obesity Facts | Center for Disease Control CDC. http://www.cdc.gov/healthyyouth/obesity/facts.htm (Accessed July 1, 2014)

74   Americans Fighting Fat, but Odds are Stacked Against Them | National Collaborative on Childhood Obesity Research, NCCOR.org, http://nccor.org/e-newsletter/enewsletter_2012_december.php#news_3 (Accessed July 1, 2014)

75   Michelle Obama Announces New Fitness Initiative in Chicago. http://articles.chicagotribune.com/2013-03-01/health/ct-met-michelle-obama-visit-20130301_1_first-lady-childhood-obesity-lady-michelle-obama (accessed July 1, 2014).

76   Ancient Olympic Games, Olympic.org. http://www.olympic.org/ancient-olympic-games (accessed July 4, 2014).

77   Is Weight Training Safe For Today's Youth? | Total Human. http://www.totalhumanperformance.net/2010/10/is-weight-training-safe-for-todays-youth/ (accessed July 1, 2014).

78   Strength Training and Your Child, kidshealth.org. http://kidshealth.org/parent/nutrition_center/staying_fit/strength_training.html, (accessed July 1, 2014).79 This is a citation

79   Physical Activity Guidelines for Americans U.S Department of Health & Human Services http://www.health.gov/paguidelines/guidelines/, (accessed July 19, 2014).

80   Physical Activity and Strength Training in Children and Adolescents. http://www.uptodate.com/contents/physical-activity-and-strength-training-in-children-and-adolescents-an-overview (accessed July 1, 2014).

81   Overview of Physical Activity and Strength Training in Children and Adolescents, cursoenarm.net. http://cursoenarm.net/UPTODATE/contents/mobipreview.htm?25/5/25681?source=related_link (accessed July 1, 2014).

82   School Health Guidelines to Promote Healthy Eating and Physical Activity, September 16, 2011, Centers for Disease Control and Prevention, CDC.gov. http://www.cdc.gov/mmwr/preview/mmwrhtml/rr6005a1.htm, (accessed July 1, 2014).

83   Flexibility Activities for Kids, Livestrong.com. http://www.livestrong.com/article/525645-flexibility-activities-for-kids/ (accessed July 4, 2014).

84   Abdominal fat and what to do about it | Harvard Health Publications, health.harvard.edu. http://www.health.harvard.edu/newsweek/Abdominal-fat-and-what-to-do-about-it.htm (accessed July 4, 2014).

85   Healthy Eating During Adolescence, John Hopkins Medicine, http://www.hopkinsmedicine.org/healthlibrary/conditions/pediatrics/healthy_eating_during_adolescence_90,P01610/ (accessed July 4, 2014).

86   Anemia in Adolescents: The Teen Scene, January 14, 2009, Anemia.org http://www.anemia.org/patients/feature-articles/content.php?contentid=000348 (accessed July 4, 2014).

87   Brain-Boosting Foods To Fuel Concentration And Keep Your Mind Sharp, November 20, 2011, Awaken.com.
     http://www.awaken.com/2011/11/brain-boosting-foods-to-fuel-concentration-and-keep-your-mind-sharp/ (accessed July 4, 2014).

88   Power Up! Foods that Fuel the Brain | MightyNest.
     http://mightynest.com/blog/power-up-foods-that-fuel-the-brain (accessed July 4, 2014).

89   7 Foods to Boost Your Child's Brain Power, Jill Castle.
     http://jillcastle.com/2012/10/7-foods-boost-childs-brain-power/ (accessed July 4, 2014).

90   Antioxidants in Fruits | WebMD. http://www.webmd.com/diet/features/antioxidants-in-fruits (accessed July 4, 2014).

91   10 Brain Foods for Kids | WebMD. http://www.webmd.com/add-adhd/childhood-adhd/features/brain-foods-kids (accessed July 4, 2014)

92   8 Underrated Vegetables With Extraordinary Health Benefits,
     http://www.huffingtonpost.com/2014/04/01/best-vegetables-_n_5042989.html (accessed July 4, 2014).

93   Eggs: A Good Source of Choline | Patient Information. http://nurse-practitioners-and-physician-assistants.advanceweb.com/Sharedre-
     sources/advanceforNP/Resources/DownloadableResources/NP050108_p29PatHandout_PH.pdf (accessed July 4, 2014).

94   Iron, foodfix.com. http://foodfix.ca/health.php (accessed July 4, 2014).

95   Children's Health Pictures Slideshow: Top 10 Brain Foods for Children | Medicine Net.
     http://www.medicinenet.com/top_10ain_foods_for_children_pictures_slideshow/article.htm_br (accessed July 4, 2014).

96   10 Brain Foods for Kids | Lifestyle, http://recipeandlifestyle.com/10-brain-foods-for-kids/ (accessed July 4, 2014).

97   A Better Breakfast Can Boost a Child's Brainpower, September 04, 2006, NPR.
     http://www.npr.org/templates/story/story.php?storyId=5738848 (accessed July 4, 2014).

98   Health Benefits of Tuna and Salmon | Dairy Council of California.
     http://www.healthyeating.org/Healthy-Eating/All-Star-Foods/Meat-Beans/Article-Viewer/Article/89/health-benefits-of-tuna-and-salmon.
     aspx (accessed July 4, 2014).

99   What foods are good for a child's brain? | How Stuff Works.
     http://recipes.howstuffworks.com/menus/foods-are-good-for-childs-brain.htm (accessed July 4, 2014).

100 What Are Overweight and Obesity? | National Heart, Lung, And Blood Institute.
     http://www.nhlbi.nih.gov/health/health-topics/topics/obe/printall-index.html (accessed July 4, 2014).

101 Carbohydrates, Proteins, and Fats | The Merck Manual Home Health Handbook.
     http://www.merckmanuals.com/home/disorders_of_nutrition/overview_of_nutrition/carbohydrates_proteins_and_fats.html,
     (accessed July 19, 2014).

102 Good fats and bad fats: the basics | Raising Children Network. http://raisingchildren.net.au/articles/fat_basics.html (accessed July 4, 2014).

103 Fats and Cholesterol: Out with the Bad, In with the Good | Harvard School Of Public Health.
     http://www.hsph.harvard.edu/nutritionsource/fats-full-story/ (accessed July 4, 2014).

104 Olive Oil Nutrition Facts, December 9, 2013 | Oliva di Vita, Oil of Life.
     http://www.olivadivita.com/olive-oil-nutrition-facts/ (accessed July 4, 2014).

105 Health Benefits of Walnut Oil | Seeds of Sustainability.
     http://www.seedsofsustainability.org/uncategorized/health-benefits-of-walnut-oil/ (accessed July 4, 2014).

106 Richard Wrangham (2009) Catching Fire: How Cooking Made Us Human, Basic Books, ISBN 978-0-465-01362-3

107 No.1 The Knife, August 31, 2005 | Forbes Online.
     http://www.forbes.com/2005/08/31/technology-tools-knife_cx_de_0831knife.html (accessed July 4, 2014).

108 The Chef's Knife | New West Knife Works.
     http://www.newwestknifeworks.com/content/information/about-chef-knives/chefs-knife-history (accessed July 4, 2014).

109 Eat Smart, Play Hard | Together Magazine, 2009, North Dakota State University NDSU.
http://www.ag.ndsu.edu/eatsmart/eat-smart.-play-hard.-magazines-1/2009-eat-smart-play-hard-magazine/test-item (accessed July 4, 2014).

110 Family Nutrition: The Truth about Family Meals, University of Florida IFAS Extension.
http://edis.ifas.ufl.edu/fy1061 (accessed July 4, 2014).

111 Is Frequency of Shared Family Meals Related to the Nutritional Health of Children and Adolescents? | Pediatrics.
http://pediatrics.aappublications.org/content/127/6/e1565.full (accessed July 4, 2014).

112 The Importance of Spices in World History | The Spice House. http://www.thespicehouse.com/info/lore/ (accessed July 4, 2014).

113 Ferdinand Magellan Exploration | history.com. http://www.history.com/topics/exploration/ferdinand-magellan (accessed July 4, 2014).

114 What type of salt is best?, Mar. 2009 | The Ecologist.
http://www.theecologist.org/green_green_living/health_and_beauty/270993/what_type_of_salt_is_best.html (accessed July 4, 2014).

115 Herbs and Spices | naturalhealthbenefits.org.
http://www.naturalhealthbenefits.org/category/nutrition/herbs-and-spices/ (accessed July 4, 2014).

116 Eight Health Benefits of Cayenne Pepper | Three Fat Chicks on a Diet.
http://www.3fatchicks.com/8-health-benefits-of-cayenne-pepper/ (accessed July 4, 2014).

117 Health Benefits of Cinnamon, Cinnamon | Voque.com. http://cinnamonvogue.com/cinnamoncommonuses.html (accessed July 4, 2014).

118 Spices: Cumin Seed, Commodity Trading Corporation, http://www.ctcin.com/cumin.php (accessed July 4, 2014). (accessed July 4, 2014).

119 Herb Profile: Oregano - Uses and Benefits, Wellness Mama.
http://wellnessmama.com/8409/herb-profile-oregano/ (accessed July 4, 2014).

120 Amazing Health Benefits of Nutmeg, April 12, 2013, care2.com.
http://www.care2.com/greenliving/8-amazing-health-benefits-of-nutmeg.html (accessed July 4, 2014).

121 Top Ten Healthy Spices List | Complete Health Dallas.
http://completehealthdallas.com/Top10SpicesForHealth.html (accessed July 4, 2014).

122 The Top 10 Spices that Boost your Metabolism |
http://clickbankpocket.blogspot.com/2013/01/the-top-10-spices-that-boost-your.html (accessed July 4, 2014).

123 15 Health Benefits of Garlic | Underground Health.
http://www.undergroundhealth.com/15-health-benefits-of-garlic/ (accessed July 4, 2014).

124 Learn How To Make Ginger Ale | Healthy holistic living healthy,
http://www.healthy-holistic-living.com/how-to-make-ginger-ale.html (accessed July 4, 2014).

125 Richard Wrangham (2009) Catching Fire: How Cooking Made Us Human, Basic Books, ISBN 978-0-465-01362-3.

126 Meat and Poultry Roasting Chart | Foodsafety.gov. http://www.foodsafety.gov/keep/charts/meatchart.html (accessed July 4, 2014).

127 Ingredient Information Rice | Inrfoods.com. http://www.inrfood.com/ingredients/1663 (accessed July 5, 2014).

128 Rice, UCDavis University of California | http://www-plb.ucdavis.edu/labs/rost/Rice/ricehome.html (accessed July 5, 2014).

129 Nutritional Facts About Rice | Savitri Group. http://www.savitrigroup.com/?p=219 (accessed July 5, 2014).

130 Rice: History of Rice Cultivation | Infoplease.com.
http://www.infoplease.com/encyclopedia/science/rice-history-rice-cultivation.html (accessed July 5, 2014).

131 History of Pilaf | Smart kitchen.com. http://www.smartkitchen.com/resources/history-of-pilaf (accessed July 5, 2014).

132 Pilaf, | ifood.tv. http://www.ifood.tv/network/pilaf (accessed July 5, 2014).

133 Brown rice, the worlds healthiest foods | whfoods.org.
http://www.whfoods.com/genpage.php?tname=foodspice&dbid=128 (accessed July 5, 2014).

134 How Much Fiber Does My Child Need? | Super kids nutrition.com.
http://www.superkidsnutrition.com/nutrition-articles/nutrition_answers/meal_tips/meal-tips/mt_howmuchfiber/ (accessed July 5, 2014).

135 Fiber: How Much Do I Need? | WebMD.
http://www.webmd.com/food-recipes/features/fiber-how-much-do-you-need (accessed July 5, 2014).

136 Whole grains cooking chart cooking with whole grains | Idaho State Department of Education, Child Nutrition Programs.
http://healthymeals.nal.usda.gov/hsmrs/Idaho/Cooking_with_Whole_Grains/007_CookingChart.pdf (accessed July 5, 2014).

137 How The 'Blind Side' Kid 'Beat The Odds' | NPR,
http://www.npr.org/2011/02/09/133625802/How-The-Blind-Side-Inspiration-Beat-The-Odds (accessed July 5, 2014).

138 Optimizing your diet | Massachusetts Institute of Technology, MIT http://web.mit.edu/athletics/sportsmedicine/wcrvitamins.html

139 The history of canning food | reference.com. http://www.foodreference.com/html/artcanninghistory.html

140 A Healthier You | blogspot.com, http://normbryant.blogspot.com/ (accessed July 27, 2014).

141 Eight Benefits of High-Intensity Interval Training | American College Of Sports Medicine (ascm.org)
http://www.acsm.org/about-acsm/media-room/acsm-in-the-news/2012/02/13/eight-benefits-of-high-intensity-interval-training,(accessed July 23,2014)

142 8 Amazing Fat-Burning Intervals | Men's Fitness,
http://www.mensfitness.com/training/cardio/8-amazing-fat-burning-intervals (accessed July 27, 2014).

143 Interval Training, Original Interval Training, New Interval |
http://www.newintervaltraining.com/old-interval-training.php (accessed July 27, 2014).

144 Emil Zátopek Medals | Olympic.org, http://www.olympic.org/emil-zatopek (accessed July 27, 2014).

145 The Past, Present, and Future of Interval Training | STRETCH,
http://seeadamtrain.wordpress.com/2010/04/14/exercise-the-past-present-and-future-of-interval-training/ (accessed July 27, 2014).

146 Celiac disease foundation, sources of gluten, http://celiac.org/live-gluten-free/glutenfreediet/sources-of-gluten/., November 7th 2014

147 Whole grain council.org, What is a whole grain,
http://wholegrainscouncil.org/whole-grains-101/what-is-a-whole-grain, November 8th, 2014

148 Celiac disease foundation, what is gluten, http://digestive.niddk.nih.gov/DDISEASES/pubs/celiac/#what, November 8th 2014

149 The pale diet.com, Abouthttp://thepaleodiet.com/about-the-paleo-diet/, November 8th 2014

150 The healthiest foods in the world,Miso, http://www.whfoods.com/genpage.php?tname=foodspice&dbid=114, November 9th 2014

151 source: http://mission-blue.org, accessed November 20th, 2014

152 How color affects your perception of foods, http://sensing.konicaminolta.us/2013/01/how-color-affects-your-perception-of-food/

153 http://www.familiesonline.co.uk

154 Mark Schatzker, Raising the Steaks, Slate Magazine.
http://www.slate.com/articles/life/shopping/2006/11/raising_the_steaks.html. Accessed November 28th, 2014

*"We enjoyed cooking with you and look forward
to our next culinary adventure together.
Stay tuned for future hot topics at: www.twopansandapot.com."*

· · · Notes · · ·

Notes

CPSIA information can be obtained at www.ICGtesting.com
Printed in the USA
BVOW10*0114140815

412952BV00012B/62/P

9 780692 373774